WET FLIES

2ND EDITION

Tying and Fishing Soft-Hackles, Flymphs, Winged Wets, and All-Fur Wet Flies

---

Dave Hughes

Illustrations by Richard Bunse

STACKPOLE BOOKS

To the late Sylvester Nemes, author of *The Soft-Hackled Fly*, who wrote so beautifully about so beautiful a subject, who showed me how to tie his soft-hackled flies, and by taking me fishing, showed me how to fish them.

To the late Vernon S. "Pete" Hidy, co-author with James Leisenring of *The Art of Tying the Wet Fly & Fishing the Flymph*, who showed me how to tie and fish his magical and mysterious flymphs.

To the late Polly Rosborough, author of *Tying and Fishing the Fuzzy Nymphs*, who showed me the relationship between his fuzzy nymphs and all-fur wet flies, taught me how to fish them using wet-fly methods, and let me fool a 6-pound trout using a big wet fly he tied himself, fishing it on his own bamboo fly rod.

And to all those who appreciate the fun and magic inherent in tying and fishing wet flies and catching trout on them, often when no other types of flies will fool them.

Copyright © 2015 by Dave Hughes

Published by
STACKPOLE BOOKS
4501 Forbes Boulevard, Suite 200
Lanham, Maryland 20706
www.stackpolebooks.com

Printed in India

SECOND EDITION

Cover design by Caroline Stover
Cover images by the author
Photos by the author

Library of Congress Cataloging-in-Publication Data

Hughes, Dave, 1945–
    Wet flies : tying and fishing soft-hackles, flymphs, winged wets, and all-fur wet flies / Dave Hughes ; illustrations by Richard Bunse. — 2nd edition.
       pages cm
    Includes bibliographical references and index.
    ISBN 978-0-8117-1624-6
    1. Flies, Artificial. 2. Fly tying. 3. Fly fishing. I. Title.
    SH451.H785 2015
    688.7'9124—dc23
                                            2015015693

Contents

Foreword to the Second Edition

Since *Wet Flies* was first published nearly twenty years ago, some things have changed a little. Body furs, for example, are now often blended with snippets of Sparkle Yarn, adding a bit of twinkle that might make a fly look more lifelike. Trout like that, and we'd be foolish to neglect it.

A few things have changed a lot. Experiments have been made in the direction of incorporating beads—glass, brass, and horrors, even tungsten—into wet flies. In most cases it's again for that bit of lifelike flash, but when it's for weight, then we have to wonder: Are they wet flies or nymphs? That wonder can cut in two directions. The few plates in G. E. M. Skues's 1921 book *The Way of a Trout with a Fly* depict flies on their way to becoming nymphs from their sources as wet flies. These sorts of movements are made continually; the border between wet flies and nymphs can be difficult to pinpoint precisely.

It's certainly best that these experiments with materials and tying techniques continue. If they hadn't, Skues wouldn't have gotten into trouble with the dry-fly purists of his day, and we might not have nymphs in our day. It's fortunate that we have all these sorts of flies, and it's not sinful to combine aspects of one with those of another. If you're a wet-fly purist, it's also not sinful to simply call those experiments nymphs. Each of us should stick with what pleases us, and let others continue on with what pleases them, calling their flies what they will. The main goal in all of it is to improve ways to please the trout.

Many things have not changed at all. The history of wet-fly tying and fishing, for example, has not been rewritten, nor should it be. The traditions, and the fly styles that emerged from them, are still the same. A soft-hackle is still a fly tied with a pliable hackle, usually from a land bird. A flymph is still a wet fly tied with a rough, fibrous body. A winged wet is still a wet fly tied with a wing, usually of paired feather sections . . . simple enough.

The fuzzy nymphs that I wrote about in the first edition, with a passing mention of all-fur wet flies, have perhaps completed their transition from fuzzy nymphs to all-fur wets. Polly Rosborough's roughed-up nymphs are now the source; all-fur wet flies are the logical result. I sometimes add beads between the fur body and fur hackle of an all-fur wet. There are those who would call the result a nymph, and I wouldn't pursue the argument very far against them. But I fish them as I would wet flies, and I call them wets.

Part of the definition of wet flies might lie in the way the flies are fished. Not long ago, on Montana's famous Bighorn River, I fished two Pheasant Tail nymphs for an hour or so before a BWO (*Baetis*) hatch began. One was tied in the original Frank Sawyer manner, using pheasant tail fibers bound with copper wire rather than thread. It was clearly a nymph. The other had the same pheasant tail fiber body, but a pine squirrel fur thorax, along the lines of a sparse spun-hackle wet-fly collar. It was a nymph as well, though it approached being an all-fur wet.

The water was a long, broad run with slow and even flows, three to four feet deep, with enough upwellings of water down its length to tell of boulders along its bottom. A few trout rose, their takes subsurface, probably to restless BWO nymphs. They were so scattered that it was not wise to rush to each rise, try to cover it. Instead I rigged a 10-foot rod with a floating line, a leader the length of the rod, and that brace of size 18 Pheasant Tails separated by 2 feet of 5X tippet. I waded in, cast long at an angle about forty-five degrees down and across the current, held my rod high, mended a few times as the flies slowly swam down and around below me. It was wet-fly fishing, it was Atlantic salmon fishing, it was summer steelhead fishing, right out of all the traditional books.

Every few feet, as I fished downstream, step and cast, step and cast, I'd feel a pluck or a tug. I would do nothing until the down-sweeping curve of line from my lofted rod tip began to straighten out, until I felt the increasing weight of a trout out there. Then I would bring the tiny hook home and play the trout out, or lose it, in about equal portions. They were browns and rainbows, 14 to 18 inches long, mostly portly. They took the Sawyer nymph or the squirrel-hackled dropper in about equal proportions.

I might have been nymphing, because I was fishing with nymphs. But it felt like wet-fly fishing, and I think that's what I was doing.

I've fished wet flies, and wet-fly methods, extensively in the two decades since the first edition of *Wet Flies* was written. I've stuck with wet-fly traditions where they worked and experimented when they didn't. I've learned some new things on my own, fished with some new folks and learned more things from them, and read some new books and fiddled with their ideas when it seemed they might help. I've incorporated these explorations into this new edition of *Wet Flies*.

Acknowledgments

I would like to thank Cal Cole, curator of the Fly Fisher Foundation Library, part of the Fly Fisher's Club of Oregon, for trusting me with about fifteen old and valuable volumes loaned for the research for the first edition of this book.

I also deeply appreciate the gentleman on the Bighorn River who passed in a boat, called out, "Aren't you Old Whitehead?" and when I reluctantly admitted I was, said, "Thank you for writing *Wet Flies*."

Introduction

I've read, and also written, that a trout willing to strike a dry fly would be slightly wasted if taken any other way. I dropped that errant philosophy a long time ago, abruptly, on what I'd always considered a perfect dry-fly day.

The July sun struck down through conifers and alders to ignite the plunge pools of my favorite small stream. The air was hot above the forest canopy but pleasantly cool down in the canyon. Lots of insects danced around in the air above the stream, but none of them was so dominant as to be defined as a hatch. Caddisflies, alderflies, flying ants, and occasional mayflies were all in the air. A few Olive Sally stoneflies, no bigger than size 16, dropped from the heights on fixed wings, looking like odd green sparks lit by the sun. They settled slowly and were suddenly extinguished when they hit the water to lay their eggs, struggled, and soon subsided.

It seemed a perfect dry-fly day on perfect dry-fly water. The tiny stream bounded from rock to rock in its hurry to get out of the coastal hills, deliver itself up to the nearby Pacific Ocean. Almost all of the stream's pools were formed by miniature waterfalls. The flow dropped a foot or two, dove into darkened depths, leaped up in a froth of bubbles and foam. Then it sped through a short riffle or run, or spread into a slight pool, before collecting itself at the lip of the next plunge, diving down again.

Trout in those pools were what I'd always considered perfect dry-fly fish: coastal cutthroat, small to suit the size of the water in which they lived, so secretive they were almost never seen until they revealed themselves to strike a fly. A 12-incher was one to play cautiously but land swiftly, admire briefly, release at once in honor of all the heavy-water winters and low-water summers it had succeeded in surviving. Timid trout could never survive such a harsh environment, pass on their genes to next generations. Recklessness became a necessity during eons of cutthroat evolution. When we anglers arrived and offered dry flies to them, they took them in all eagerness, and we called them stupid for it: the perfect dry-fly fish. They'd have been truly stupid to pass up anything that resembled food, without giving it at least a look and perhaps a try, in the parsimonious conditions in which they lived.

The perfections gathered there for me that bright July day—the fine weather, the small water, the supposedly stupid trout—somehow failed to add up to good fishing. I didn't know then what I do now, that even the most reckless trout are bashful about dashing to take something afloat on the surface in the brightest midsummer sunshine. It's another survival mechanism, armor against osprey, heron, and kingfisher—all the most alarming predators if you're a trout in a tiny stream. I didn't know that bashfulness about exposure to predation in such bright sunlight was the reason dry-fly fishing was poor that day. I learned that a long time later. But the lack of success with dry flies didn't bother me a lot.

I'd gone to the stream with a specific purpose. It was my intention to fish soft-hackled wet flies upstream. The reason was somewhat vague. I'd read an article by Sylvester Nemes, author of *The Soft-Hackled Fly*, about a trip he'd taken to Scotland to fish the waters where soft-hackles originated. I wanted to make that same trip myself, but thought I ought to learn how to fish wet flies on my own small streams before I went—I still haven't gone— so that I wouldn't embarrass myself when I got there. All I wanted that bright day was a little practice fishing wet flies upstream.

What I got instead was an epiphany.

I carried an Altoids Peppermints tin eviscerated of its contents, converted into a fly box by glueing a sheet of foam into its bottom. I frisked my vest for this tin, found it, opened it, peered at row after row of Partridge & Yellows, Partridge & Greens, Partridge & Oranges, and March Brown Spiders: all soft-hackles, all from Sylvester Nemes's book. I'd tied them myself immediately after reading his book, but before coming across that article. I was quite proud of the sparse and speckled flies lined up so neatly; it was a long time later that Sylvester told me they were not nearly sparse enough. My fly boxes usually display such neatness only when they contain flies that are rarely used, which gives you a hint about the extent of my soft-hackle fishing at that ancient instant.

I selected a big and showy size 10 Partridge & Yellow from the little tin, hoping I'd be able to follow its drift in the clear, sunlit pools. I thought about selecting two flies, one bright and one drab, one as the point fly and the other as a dropper, because that's the way I'd always read that wet-fly fishing was done. But I gazed around for a moment at the restrictions of my small-stream surroundings, and decided that one fly would get me into enough trouble with drooping alder limbs and overhanging huckleberry bushes. I nipped off the dry fly I'd been using and tied the single Partridge & Yellow to the same tippet.

The first pool I stalked originated in a 2-foot plunge, narrowed nicely in a frothed current tongue, then put on its brakes in clear, green water 3 to 4 feet deep. It was no more than 6 feet wide and 10 feet long, and had little tailout. The current dropped directly between two mossy boulders into the next pool, a few feet downstream. I crept up behind one of those boulders at the foot of the pool. It was so big, and the drop behind it into the next pool so abrupt, that I was able to stand nearly straight up while keeping my body out of sight of the pool I was about to fish. I pressed against the soft moss that covered the boulder and lifted my head so that I could peer at the pool upstream. Rays of sunlight struck down through the water where it deepened suddenly at the lower end of the current tongue, enabling me to see not only onto the pool, but also into it. As usual, no trout were in sight.

It required no particular brilliance to make the perfect cast in this situation. I flicked the rod to propel just 15 feet of line and leader out and set the soft-hackle on the water with a slight splat, right at the trailing edge of the current tongue. It's difficult to make a gentle entry with a big wet fly, but it turned out not to matter. In fact, it might have been the forceful entry that attracted attention and caused a cloud of trout to dash out of nowhere and surround the sinking fly. I'd been fishing dry flies on the same pools for so long that day, with so little result, that I was startled by the sudden appearance of four or five trout milling around my sunk fly in such a tiny pool.

The sun clearly exposed the fly, and also the dark and swiftly moving forms of the trout, creating such a beautiful sight that I forgot to set the hook when one of those fish took the fly into its mouth and just as quickly ejected it back out. The fly drifted a couple feet farther downstream toward me, at the same time sinking a few inches deeper into the clear water of the pool. From my very near point of view, hidden behind the boulder, the soft-hackled fly drifting through the pool and slowly sinking, with its hackle spread above and its body dangling straight down from it, appeared almost precisely like Mary Poppins's umbrella might have looked descending over London had she not been suspended beneath it.

Another trout took the fly, turned, and fled out of sight with it.

I forgot to set the hook again, but this time the trout took so confidently, turned so quickly to get out of that revealing sunlight and back into whatever dark cover it had left in its excitement about the fly, that it hooked itself. I led it throbbing back into the sunlight of the pool, then thrashing across the surface, and finally squirming into my hand. I admired it briefly. It was one of the larger specimens of cutthroat that the tiny stream had ever offered, and I returned it quickly.

At that moment I did not take time to wonder why so many nice trout appeared out of nowhere in such a small pool, nor why they milled around and quarreled about which one got to take the soft-hackled wet, nor why they took the sunk fly but had earlier aimed only splashy and disdainful refusals at a dry fly, if they paid it any attention at all. Most of these questions got answered a long time later. One thing became clear to me at once: There had always been that many trout in the pools I had fished for so many years; I'd just never gotten so close to them that I noticed it.

I found this out by casting again to the same pool and having the same cloud of trout, minus one, come out to take turns inhaling the sunk fly. Three more trout, in descending sizes, surrendered themselves to my hand before the rest got scent of some frightful pheromones. Even then they continued to rush out and examine the fly each time I cast it, before refusing it and rushing in panic back to the crevices and ledges they'd left.

Pool after pool, as I fished my way up the old, familiar stream that day, revealed the same unfamiliar clouds of trout. Pool after pool gave up three or four fine fish before the rest caught on to the plot, left the fly alone. This was one of the largest satisfactions to me. With dry flies, I rarely take more than a trout or two from these small-stream plunge pools. I took several from each pool on the soft-hackle that first day I fished them on my home waters.

By the end of that day I'd taken more trout on soft-hackles than I'd ever taken on any similar day, on the same small stream, casting dry flies. Such success, in such a beautiful place, and in such a beautiful way, startled me. The sight of those dark, sleek forms darting visibly around my wet fly and so eager to take it was a revelation to me. When you fish dry flies, you see the strike: a splash out there at the end of your cast. That's all. Fishing the wet, creeping right up onto the pools so that I could see the fly during its drift, and then see the trout—the many trout—rush out to take it, let me observe the entire exciting sequence of a take, not just the final splash of it on the surface at some remote distance.

It has never subtracted from my pleasure in fishing dry flies, but that first day fishing soft-hackled wets on my favorite old trout stream was as startling to me as it was to the fish that got stung by my hooks. Things happened that I could not explain then, though I think I can explain some of them now. I've found that such success can be repeated with soft-hackles, flymphs, and wingless wet flies, and yes, even with lightly weighted nymphs, not only on small mountain streams, but also on typical freestone trout streams, large and small trout rivers, and even on tailwaters and spring creeks where the most selective trout swim around like snots, at times rejecting all dry flies.

Wet flies have a place on all sorts of trout water, and they work at times when other types of flies will not. At least a small box full of them should enter your possession, along with knowledge of a small set of tactics to fish them. That small box of flies and core set of tactics are what this book is about.

PART I

SUBSURFACE SUCCESS

Chapter One

The Wet Fly and the Natural Insect

I've had four bits of luck in my life (four that pertain here; I've had others). First was the opportunity to sit down at his kitchen table and tie flies with Pete Hidy, co-author of the 1941 book *The Art of Tying the Wet Fly* and its 1971 revised edition *The Art of Tying the Wet Fly & Fishing the Flymph*. Pete demonstrated how to tie flymphs, and explained how to fish them, in the way that his own mentor and co-author, James Leisenring, had done for him on Brodheads Creek in Pennsylvania.

Second was the chance to sit alongside Polly Rosborough's messy roll-top tying desk, in his home alongside Oregon's Williamson River, watching him tie his famous fuzzy nymphs. Later he took me fishing on that rich river, and showed me how he fished his slender nymphs almost exactly as you would fish wet flies.

Third was meeting and fishing with Sylvester Nemes, author of that 1975 classic *The Soft-Hackled Fly*, then *The Soft-Hackled Fly Addict*, and later *Soft-Hackled Fly Imitations*, for which I wrote the foreword.

Before any of those, my biggest bit of luck was signing up to audit an aquatic entomology course at Oregon State University, in 1974, while pursuing a degree in a separate subject. The professor was Dr. Norman Anderson, noted among anglers for his studies of aquatic insects, though he is wise enough not to be an angler himself. His lab assistant did happen to be a fly fisherman. Rick Hafele was in his twenties, tall, skinny, with a thick hat of hair. He had an enthusiasm for his subject that most of his students could not understand.

I had no trouble understanding it. I sat in on the class to discover what I could about the insects that trout eat. Rick was there teaching it, about to complete his master's degree in aquatic entomology, for the same reason. He'd chosen his profession because of his love for fly fishing.

While Rick and I peered through microscopes in that lab, surrounded by other students who had a strange variety of reasons to be interested in aquatic insects themselves, we talked about trout fishing. I would raise my hand and wonder what some insect was; Rick would glance at it and place it in the taxonomic universe in an instant. I wanted to go fishing with Rick because I thought he might part with some of that awesome information he held in his head if I could get him out on a stream, looking at bugs in the environment where trout ate them. I owned a new Leonard Duracane bamboo fly rod that I dangled as bait, said I'd let him fish it. Bamboo was a big ticket in those days.

It worked out perfectly. Rick fished with my rod and didn't break it. I picked his brain about bugs and didn't damage it, though we've often talked about how we both went astray in unplanned ways that probably wouldn't have happened if we had not met in Professor Anderson's aquatic entomology class.

At lunch that day, we sat in sunshine on a gravel bar, at the junction of a tiny feeder creek with the mountain stream we fished, discussing our luck, which had been no better than fair. A shallow and rocky riffle ran in front of us for a hundred feet. It was June; the sun was hot. I folded my felt-soled hip boots down to keep cool; Rick peeled his black latex Seal Dry waders to his knees because the sun pooled on them and nearly cooked him. He placed a long-handled insect collecting net on the gravel next to him, in easy reach. That same net had revealed mystery after mystery to me in the morning: scuttling mayfly nymphs, lumbering caddisfly larvae, the immature aquatic stages of stoneflies, alderflies, all sorts of other flies.

The two of us lay back in the sun and sipped beers kept cool in the stream, nibbled at cheeses melted to softness by the sun, and idly watched the water. We were in an ambling conversation about all the insects we'd seen, about what fly patterns might match them, when Rick spotted a big insect flying up near the leafed alder tops, lit by the sun and beginning a slow descent over the riffle, at about the same angle a helicopter might take to come in for a landing.

Rick shouted, "Holy *something*, a Salmonfly!" He jumped to his feet, grabbed his collecting net, and galloped off after the insect. I'll never forget that sight: Rick running straight down the riffle, in a shower of spray, waving his collecting net in one hand and holding up his waders with the other. The descending insect saw or sensed its danger, held itself at an altitude just beyond reach of the net. Every few feet Rick gathered himself, leaped into the air, flailed at the stonefly.

The struggling insect was not able to maintain its altitude as long as the leaping entomologist was able to sustain his antics. The insect wound up in the net, and later ended its days pickled in a vial of alcohol. It was indeed a Salmonfly, though it was the only one we saw that day, and it meant little to our fishing.

Rick and I fished together as often as possible after that, and we still do, though it's not just for Rick's entertainment value or because I own a bamboo fly rod and let him cast it once in awhile.

Our studies of insects and the fly patterns that match them grew over the years into a seminar that we called "Entomology and the Artificial Fly." We collected aquatic insects, studied entomology texts and fly-fishing books, tied flies recommended by experts, and cast them over waters with wary trout in them. We went fishing a lot, fished over many hatches. We taught seminars in most of the Western states, and while doing so met many knowledgeable anglers. Some knew of hatches we had not encountered, fly patterns we had not tied, books we had not read. A few even took us fishing.

Rick and I fished together and butted heads about insects and their life stages—what each might mean to the trout and whether they were important to trout fishermen or could be ignored. We collected insects and took photos of them, tied and tried flies to match them, and eventually wrote a forty-page booklet as a handout for the folks who took our seminar because many of them took notes so frantically that they rarely took time to look up and notice the slides of naturals we'd worked so hard to get. Don Roberts, then editor of the magazine *Flyfishing the West*, got a copy of that booklet, looked it over, and wrote to us, "This would make a book; get to work on it." It took years. In 1981 it became *Western Hatches*.

Rick's work and mine for those seminars, and later for the book, had four essential parts. First, we collected an insect that we found important to trout. Second, we identified the insect. Third, we made a literature search for patterns that were a suggestion, an impression, or an imitation of the insect. Fourth, and far from least, we watched the behavior of the insect: the way it crawled, danced, or swam in or on the water. Proper presentation is based on behavior, and presentation, it's well known, is at least half of imitation.

Many of the things that Rick and I discovered about the relationship between insects and trout, in those early years, led toward this book about wet flies and wet-fly fishing.

As an example, one of our first adventures took place in late winter on the Malheur River, an Oregon stream at the northern end of the Great Basin. The weather at that time of year out there is frigid, but there are no motels for 50 miles, so we camped. The first morning we woke up, went to boil water for coffee, found the water jug frozen solid. The sun arrived over the canyon rim at mid-morning, and by early afternoon the river warmed enough to coax a trickle of small Blue-Winged Olive mayflies (*Baetis*) into hatching. Trout fed in the slow, weedy currents, nipping at the duns, or so we thought.

We tried the traditional size 16 Adams. Trout refused it. Then we tried size 18 Little Olive Duns, out of Ed Koch's beautiful book *Fishing the Midge*. Trout looked at them but turned away without taking. We tried other dry flies. None worked. Rick set his rod aside, got out his collecting net, held it steady in the surface currents for a few minutes to seine out whatever

Young Rick Hafele on Oregon's high desert Malheur River, casting over the sort of long, slow pool that puts up hatches of small Blue-Winged Olive mayflies. Trout feed on subsurface nymphs during the hatch at least as often as they rise to take duns from the surface itself. It's wise to watch riseforms, and make sure you're fishing your fly at the same level trout are taking naturals. Sometimes a small wet fly will work wonders while a dry is ignored by the trout.

might be drifting on them or just beneath them. Often, we've discovered, when it seems obvious that trout are taking something visible on the surface, a few minutes spent collecting reveals something entirely different suspended just beneath it.

In this case, what Rick found was not radically different. It was merely a squirming of tiny nymphs that were just inches of water and moments in time from becoming the duns we could easily see, and just as easily match, on the surface. Our frustration with drys, coupled with the steady feeding of all the trout around us, showed the potential held in those nymphs.

That night, while the water jug was busy freezing again, Rick scattered his fly-tying gear over the tailgate of the pickup. I lit the lantern, then warmed my hands by wrapping them around a mug of hot chocolate laced with blackberry brandy, while Rick struggled to construct a scant few size 16 soft-hackles that he hoped trout might mistake for the nymphs he'd collected. His simple creation had wisps of blue dun hen hackle for tails, a dubbed body of gray muskrat fur, and a couple of turns of the same hen for a hackle collar.

Rick stopped tying when his fingers seized up, which was almost my misfortune. The next afternoon, when the same BWO hatch happened, I was stuck with the same dry flies that had failed so well the day before. Rick tied on one of his soft-hackles, fished it upstream exactly as if it were a dry fly,

The simple soft-hackled dressing that Rick Hafele tied to imitate BWO nymphs that trout sipped during a hatch on the Malheur River. The pattern might have the advantage of imitating a drowned dun as well as the rising, emerging nymph.

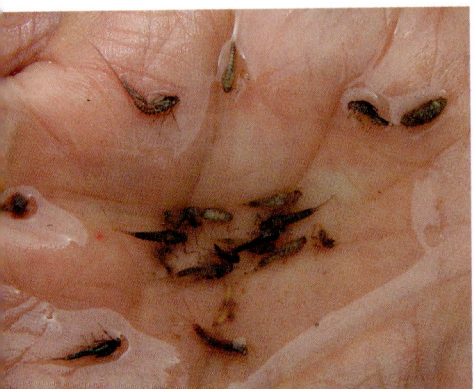

Whenever your collecting reveals a preponderance of BWO nymphs, suspect that trout are feeding on them rather than on the duns that will soon emerge from them. Winged insects on the surface are easier to see, and their presence makes it easy to believe you're in a dry-fly situation. If you try drys and don't do well with them, switch to a small soft-hackle the same size and color as the naturals, or use a standard Pheasant Tail nymph if that suits you.

and coaxed satisfied rises out of lots of trout. For a while he didn't consider himself to have enough extras to loan me one. After driving the point home with a few more fish, however, he gave in to my whining and let me have one of his flies. It worked wonders on those trout.

In our research for our seminar, and then for *Western Hatches*, we commonly ran into situations where the best match for a specific stage of a hatch was a wet fly. Incidents like the one with the BWO turned me toward a systematic look at all of the stages of insects that were best matched with wets.

It began with the mayflies, as most research about fly patterns for trout does. It didn't take long to add to the list that started with those drifting BWO nymphs. Though mayfly duns are best known for hatching in the surface film, right out in open water, a few secretive groups become duns beneath the surface and must struggle to the top with their wings beginning to unfold. Many *Heptagenia* mayflies are most noted for this. They include Quill Gordons in the

Pale Evening Dun mayflies hatch on moving waters, typically in soft edge currents not far from boisterous water, and almost always in late afternoon or evening right through until dark. Though you'll see duns on the surface, and trout rising to feed among them, those fish are often taking naturals rising toward the surface rather than right on top. The dun emerges from the nymphal shuck on the bottom, and it's the dun, not the nymph, that swims through the gauntlet of trout. When trout focus on those rising duns, a pale cream wet fly will serve you better than any dry.

East and Pale Evening Duns in both East and West. The nymph gets a grip on a rock surface at the bottom, usually near the edge of fast water but not in it. The nymphal skin then splits and the dun emerges at the bottom. A traditional winged wet fly is the perfect match for the dun as it drifts downstream and struggles toward the top. My favorite when this happens is the Light Cahill.

Other duns, such as *Rhithrogena morrisoni*, or Western March Browns, emerge in the surface film most of the time. But some jump the gun. The nymph skin splits early, and the dun is released to its own struggle within a few inches of the surface. Trout know about this, and Rick Hafele does, too. Early in our research he devised a March Brown Flymph, and he's caused me such embarrassment with it that I intend to leave the telling of it to a later chapter, when I can bear it better. His flymph imitates the dun as it nears the surface film.

During any mayfly hatch in somewhat rough water, for example a riffle or boisterous run, many individuals make it to the surface and escape the nymphal shuck there, but the duns suffer disaster soon thereafter. Their wings get wet, they are unable to fly and escape into the air, and instead they subside beneath the surface. Or they get knocked down by a wave and drown. A small proportion of duns gets shipwrecked in any hatch, even on smooth water. If the water is choppy, the percentage goes up, and trout find more and more of their bites beneath the surface during and after a hatch. When trout feed on a substantial number of such drowned duns, a wet fly

If you watch rises carefully, and learn to read them, you can usually tell if a trout—or a pod of them—feeds on the surface or just beneath it as this trout does. The telltale sign is usually a bubble or bunch of them left in the center of the rise after the trout has gone down. Bubbles are an indication the trout has broken the surface with its take, and this is an indication that you should fish dry flies or surface-film emergers—something afloat.

approximately the size and color of the natural dun that is emerging can be far more fruitful than a dry fly that matches the dun to perfection. Often a dry will float unmolested while trout feed with visible rises just inches deep and all around it, making it look like they're taking on top.

The absence of any bubbles, much more common than most folks notice, is a signal that the trout has not broken through the surface, though the rise might be so close to the top that it appears the trout is feeding on floating insects. When bubbles are missing, you'll always do better by switching to something sunk. The best bet is to choose a wet fly, whether soft-hackle, flymph, or winged wet, in the same size and color as the natural nymph or pupa that is about to emerge, or one that roughly resembles the adult insect itself. Fish it to the rises, the same as you would a dry fly, but a few inches deep rather than on top.

The trout in the above photo holds and feeds so near the surface that it's breaking the surface with its tail. But you can tell by the white flash of its mouth that it's feeding on either rising nymphs or drowned adults, even in the presence of the myriad of insects floating right over its head.

If you see a rise in the area where you take your sunk fly to reside, set the hook gently. Other signs of takes might be a slight jump in your line tip or in any visible part of your leader. If you're in luck, you'll see the flash of a turning flank as a trout takes your wet fly. No matter what prompts you, set the hook with a gentle stroke. If the trout is there, you'll hook it without breaking off. If it's not there, you'll pull your fly away without blowing the feeding trout out of the area.

Mayfly spinners, the final reproductive stage of the insect, mate in the air above the water. Most males, lucky fellows, return to streamside vegetation to live out their brief lives, though some fall to the water and drown. But females must lay their eggs on the water. At times trout feed on them at the surface, especially if they fall spent but continue to float. Just as often trout feed on female spinners that drown and are carried along in subsurface currents. Sparse wet flies usually work better than drys when this happens. Because it's often at dusk, it's easier to feel a take to a wet than it is to spot a rise to a dry.

Research into the caddisfly order of aquatic insects revealed the not-so-surprising fact that though we nearly always see adult caddis in the air, and therefore nearly always fish caddis hatches with dry flies, trout have more constant opportunities to take the pupae as they rise toward the surface for emergence. Trout gather most of their caddis groceries before the aerial adult ever gets launched. This was not common knowledge when Rick and I began studying aquatic insect hatches, but has since been written about in many magazine articles, and also in books such as Larry Solomon and Eric Leiser's *The Caddis and the Angler* and Gary LaFontaine's *Caddisflies*.

The transitional pupa is a stage that is only briefly exposed to predation by trout. The mature larva encloses itself in its case, on the bottom. Inside the safety of that case, it transforms through the pupal stage into a fully formed adult encapsulated inside a thin skin: the pupal shuck. At this point it's ready for emergence, and is technically called a *phaerate adult*. I'll bow to that technicality here, but will continue to call it a pupa until the winged adult emerges out of it.

At maturity the pupa tweezers its way out of the larval case on the bottom and heads for the surface. The pupa is buoyed toward the top by gases trapped beneath the outer pupal skin. Some species swim quite well and shoot toward the top in a rapid ascent. Others swim feebly. Most approach the surface at an angle, drifting downstream pushed by the current while they swim toward the top.

After reaching the surface, some caddis pupae drift along for a few feet before penetrating the surface film. Others are more vigorous, banging through that slight barrier in a hurry and bolting right off as winged adults. In either case trout get a more prolonged chance at caddis as they rise in the pupal stage than they do once the insect has transformed into an adult. Trout often take pupae so near the surface, and so hastily, that it appears a floating adult has gone down in the swirl. This is the reason a soft-hackled wet fly fished just below the surface can turn a day barren of trout into one that suddenly provides fish after fish. They're taking pupae, though they appear to be taking adults, and they're happy to accept your soft-hackle if it's a reasonable imitation of the natural and is fished the way the real insect might move.

The biggest surprise in researching the relationship between caddisflies and wet flies came in the adult stage itself. Rick and I got hints, in our

Caddis pupae are characterized by trailing wing cases, legs, and antennae. Trout eat far more caddis in this transitional stage than they do winged adults. An appropriate soft-hacked wet or all-fur wet will often interest far more trout than a dry fly that matches the adults you see in the air or even on the water. If nothing else, it's wise to dangle a pupal imitation off the hook bend of the dry, allowing trout a choice. They'll let you know whether they prefer a dry fly or wet.

research and our reading, of the news that some female caddis adults dive down to the bottom to deposit their eggs. At first we assumed this behavior took place in a few rare species, on remote and rarely fished waters. Over the years it slowly seeped into us that two major groups of trout-stream caddis shared this same behavioral trait. *Hydropsyche* caddis, the Spotted Sedges, are net-spinners in the larval stage. They are common on most streams, and their populations are often overwhelming on tailwaters. *Rhyacophila* caddis, Green Rock Worm larvae that turn into Gray Sedge adults, are predators as larvae. They crawl around among riffle rocks, prowling for tiny prey.

These are two of the most abundant and important groups of caddis on most trout streams and rivers. On many waters Spotted Sedges are the single most important insect to trout and therefore to trout fishermen. The gravid females of both groups fly into the water, pop beneath the surface film, and swim to the bottom encased in a bubble of air, to lay their eggs there rather than at the surface. The adult stage of the caddis, it turns out, is the perfect model for a short series of wet flies, not drys.

Stoneflies emerge by crawling out on protruding rocks or sticks as nymphs, or by hiking up the bank, becoming adults only after they've gotten to shore safely. Thus most stonefly fishing is done with nymphs during non-hatch periods, and with dry flies during egg-laying flights. But I made three small discoveries relating wet flies to stoneflies while fishing during stonefly activity.

The first was that when Little Brown Stones were out, in late winter and early spring, a Partridge & Orange soft-hackle took more fish than a Little

Brown Stone dry fly. The reasons are still not clear to me. I suspect a lot of the adults hang around the water and get forced into it by the whims of winter weather. When they drown, trout take them, and therefore the fish easily mistake an appropriate soft-hackle for the real thing. I have not often seen Little Brown Stone adults over the water or in it, laying their eggs, but that doesn't mean trout don't see them.

I do know that the wet fly works better than a floating imitation when Little Brown Stoneflies are out and about. The British have long had a soft-hackle called the February Red, with a red silk body and brown grouse hackle. It's listed as an early stonefly dressing, and is without much doubt tied for the same set of small brown stoneflies that I see on my own waters.

The second discovery was similar, though it happened far later in the season. Whenever the mid-summer sun stands straight over my tiny mountain streams, lots of Olive Sallies take flight over the water. They get up high, then parachute in on set wings. When one hits the surface, the water washes off a ball of eggs, which sinks to the bottom. The adult usually manages to lift off the water and launch itself for another flight. Sometimes I see a trout take one before it can escape from the surface. It seems like a perfect setup for a dry fly.

In the Introduction, I noted that trout are bashful about the surface when the light is bright. A rise to the top exposes them to kingfishers and other aerial predators. They prefer their food be delivered beneath the surface. A Partridge & Green or a Partridge & Yellow soft-hackle takes advantage of this. During flights of the smaller stonefly groups, whether green, yellow, or brown, it's nearly always wise to fish a small soft-hackled wet rather than toss a dry fly atop those bright waters.

The third discovery about stoneflies was most astonishing to me. Entomology texts declare that all stoneflies crawl out of the water to emerge. But one day while I fished Oregon's broad and placid Willamette River, the air got full of thunderheads, turned almost black, and then suddenly both the air and the water were speckled by winged Yellow Sally stonefly adults. Trout responded to the insects with splashy rises. I responded to the rises by searching my fly boxes and tying on the nearest dry fly I had on me: a size 14 Elk Hair Caddis. It failed to work. I tried other drys, but did not take any trout until desperation drove me to try a Light Cahill wet fly in the same size. I don't remember why I went to that wet fly, but the results were striking. Trout began taking the Cahill on a shallow swing with exactly the same splashy rises with which they were taking the natural adult stoneflies on the water.

A long time later, I re-read Ernest Schwiebert's *Nymphs* and came across a similar report in those fluent pages. One day, as a youth, Schwiebert caught trout after trout on a Light Cahill wet, without knowing quite why. When he lost this single wet fly, he could not fool the fish on any other. When he did stomach autopsies later, Little Yellow Stonefly nymphs by the hundreds were among the dead.

Both nymphs and adults of the Yellow Sallies, also called Little Yellow Stones, are taken by trout either on the swim or drowned. The nymphs are agile swimmers, rare among stoneflies, most of which are able to plod along clumsily at best when knocked loose into the currents. An appropriate wet fly—a Partridge & Yellow soft-hackle or a traditional Light Cahill wet—will often solve the situation better than an exact nymph imitation or a dry fly fished for the adult.

Rick Hafele began finding a few references in entomology journals to open-water emergence among some smaller stonefly species. That information seemed to tie what had happened out on the wide Willamette River to what we thought we knew about stonefly behavior. But most entomologists still disagree, calling what looks like emergence behavior an actual egg-lying flight. The adults subside beneath the surface, then manage to struggle back to the top and fly away. It looks like they're emerging. That is the standard answer, and it's probably correct. Only stomach or throat-pump samples would prove the point one way or the other. If both nymphs and adults turned up in them out in open water, it might indicate mid-water emergence. I haven't had the chance to take such samples since I've discovered the need for them.

When Yellow Sally adults are in the air, it might be an emergence, but it is more likely an egg-laying flight. The trout don't care. An appropriate wet fly fished just subsurface will often take far more trout than the most imitative dry fly when any small, pale stoneflies are in the air and on the water. It would be wise advice to try dry flies first; they might work. If they fail, don't waste a lot of time before you switch to a wet. Whatever is happening might not continue to happen for very long.

The list of specific occasions for the wet fly, during what seem like dry-fly moments, goes on and on through the insect orders. I fished with the late Sylvester Nemes once in April just downstream from the Bear Trap Canyon

The late Sylvester Nemes, guru of the soft-hackled fly, fishing his Syl's Midge during a hatch of the tiny dark insects on the edge currents of the Madison River, during an early spring snowstorm. It was difficult to fish a dry fly, but the small wet did wonders because takes could be felt, and it was not necessary to follow the drift of a dry fly in such poor light.

reach of Montana's Madison River. The weather was nasty, more like winter than spring. We sat in his car above the river, watching out over it, drinking coffee, shivering at the sight of a sudden snowstorm that descended and closed off sight of all but the edges of the river right in front of us. Syl, who knew exactly why he was sitting in that place at that time, was first to notice trout rising subtly in the water flowing quietly along the banks.

"There they are," he said. "Midges are starting to hatch now." He was able to point out a few soft rises to me through the snow-covered windshield, but I couldn't see the tiny midges until we wadered up and hiked the few feet down the sagebrush banks to the river. Then I saw them: tiny black specks, perhaps size 22 or 24, drifting in swirls down the edge currents. I tied on a cluster midge, a dry fly, and was able to take a few small trout. But it was nearly impossible to separate the dry fly from all the naturals in the poor light, beneath that dark sky.

Syl had no such problem. He waded out a few feet from the bank. Then he tied on a tiny Syl's Midge, no more than a peacock herl body and a turn of gray partridge hackle twisted onto a size 16 hook. He cast this fly

Midge adults can be tiny, making it difficult to imitate them with dry flies. When they hatch in fantastic numbers, and in low light, following the drift of a floating imitation can be almost impossible.

Syl's Midge, a tiny and sparse soft-hackle tied specifically to solve midge hatches, is much easier to fish than a dry fly during such activity because it's not necessary to follow the drift of the fly, and takes can be felt rather than seen. Even when the naturals are size 20 or smaller, the size 16 wet fly seems satisfactory to trout.

upstream from the rising trout, let it swing slowly downstream among them, got a sullen pull on nearly every cast. He did not have to see the fly or observe the rise. He felt each take, and by the time he was able to feel it, the sharp point of the tiny hook was already home. Every few minutes he would lift his rod, shout, "Here's another!" and cause me to lift my eyes and once again lose sight of my neglected dry fly.

Sylvester gave me one of his soft-hackled wets then, and I began catching more and bigger trout. They were browns and rainbows in the 12- to 15-inch class, very nice trout to be taking in such awful conditions. We did so well it almost made the day pleasant.

The alderfly adult is a blocky, dense insect, unable to float long when it lands on the surface of the water.

Charles Kingsley's wet Alder is ancient, past the midpoint of its second century. But it's still the best medicine when natural adult alderflies wing their way to the water and quickly subside beneath it.

Terrestrial insects often get into the subsurface diet of trout and into the wet-fly fishing puzzle. I've had days when black flying ants were busy bustling about in the summer sun on rocks sticking out of riffles. These seem perfect times to fish drys above and below the same boulders. But dry imitations rarely succeed in catching many trout. A winged Black Gnat wet fly in the right size will entice lots of trout in the same set of conditions.

Alderflies are aquatic, not terrestrial insects, though their larvae crawl out of the water and pupation takes place in damp soil near the shoreline. In the adult stage they look a lot like big, dark caddisflies, but they lack the hairs on their wings that define caddis. Adult alders begin showing up when the sun is bright and the air warm, starting as early as April and May, becoming most abundant in June and July. They fly awkwardly through the trees, bounce into your rod, land on your hat, crawl up your shirtsleeves.

Apparently their specific gravity is higher than that of water; when alder-fly adults land on it they soon sink. Their struggles seem to help escort them through the surface film. They go down with reluctance, but without means to prevent their sinking.

I've fished forested lakes and ponds all my life. Whenever alderflies were out, which was often, I tried dry flies, because it was obvious to me that the winged adults were being taken in surface swirls by feeding trout. Finally I took time to observe an awkward alderfly as it fell to the water. It hit with a slight splat, sank at once, and was instantly taken by a trout. The take was subsurface, not on top. When I got home I searched my fly pattern books and found a fly designed specifically for the alderfly. It was a winged wet, appropriately called the Alder, devised in the 1850s by Canon Charles Kingsley for his favorite beat on the River Itchen in England.

I tied a few. I cast them to rising trout the next time alders were out. They worked then, and they work to this day, one and a half centuries after they were invented.

That is true about lots of flies. The February Red soft-hackle that I use during a late-winter Little Brown Stonefly hatch is no more than the March Brown that Alfred Ronalds wrote about in his *Fly-Fisher's Entomology*, first published in 1836. We think of the March Brown as a mayfly hatch, famous East and West, but Ronald's tied his wet March Brown as an imitation for early season stonefly hatches.

All of these years of research into the relationship between natural insects and wet flies slowly led me to a couple of conclusions. The first was that nature treats her insects about the same way our fishing forefathers treated their wet flies: She just tosses them out there, lets the current have its will with them. A close look into entomology reveals lots of times when chuck-and-chance-it, the easiest but also often the most denigrated way to fish wet flies, is exactly what's needed to solve the situation. It works so often because it lets you show your wet flies to trout just about the same way nature shows her natural insects to them.

The second conclusion my research into naturals led me to was the need for a more thorough search of fly-fishing literature. I wanted to look into the historic development of wet flies and the tactics used to fish them.

Chapter Two

Looking into Literature

I'm not a historian, and you're going to be glad. The history of tying and fishing wet flies is quite a tangle. I'm merely going to dip into it now and then to pluck out some points of departure.

The first is Dame Juliana Berner's *Treatyse of Fysshynge wyth an Angle*, from 1496 in England. It's interesting that fly patterns, in what is considered the first fly-fishing book in written history, were already imitations of natural insects. W. H. Lawrie, in his 1967 *English Trout Flies*, analyzed the dozen flies listed by Berners. She included flies for the March Brown, Olive Dun, stonefly, Great Red Spinner, mayfly, sedge, alderfly, and Grannom. Her patterns unfolded through the fishing season, matching the hatches in order as they emerged.

It's also interesting that the listed dressings can be interpreted today into three styles of flies. Some have only bodies and hackles: soft-hackles. Others have tails, bodies, and primary feather section wings: winged wets without hackles. Many have tails, bodies, wings, and hackle: the same traditional wet-fly form we tie to this day.

I have a slender manuscript, a reprint and translation from a Spanish original dated 1624, titled *El Manuscrito de Astorga*, by Juan de Bergara. It was privately printed in Denmark and was presented to me by the famous Danish fly tier and author Preben Torp Jacobsen, after we'd fished together on one of my favorite streams along the coast of Oregon. This early Spanish book lists dressings for thirty flies. They were tied to imitate specific hatches, again marching through the seasons just as Berners had done. Treating the hatches month by month is a simple formula. It works well as long as hatches are few in number and clearly defined in order. Apparently they were in Spain, and still are in Britain. But like the literature of wet-fly fishing, American hatches are much more of a tangle on account of the vast

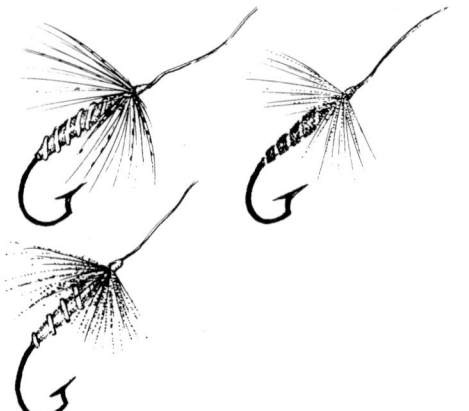

Juan de Bergara dressings for fishing swift Spanish streams. They might have fished dry for moments, but are much closer to current soft-hackled wet flies. They were fished on small- to medium-sized streams, upstream, in gangs.

geography to which our aquatic insects have adapted, though regionally they still can be given seasonal treatment.

Twenty-four of de Bergara's listed dressings have been interpreted by an artist in the manuscript I own. They all have the same form: no tails, ribbed bodies of yarn that vary from slender to rather rotund, and bushy hackle collars. The flies might have floated momentarily. They could be, and have been, considered dry flies. But it's not likely that any of them floated for long, especially after they'd been drowned by a fish or two. Likely they were tied and fished as wet flies.

Izaak Walton's *The Compleat Angler* was first published in 1653. It's a delightful read but contains little about fly fishing. Charles Cotton added twelve short chapters to the fifth edition, in 1676, under the subtitle *Being Instructions how to angle for a TROUT or GRAYLING in a clear Stream.* Cotton's addition is considered the seat of modern fly fishing: the first clear instruction. Some of its advice is still apt. For example, his note that "to fish fine and far off is the first and principal Rule for Trout Angling" doesn't miss by much what we often must do to this day. Since he fished with a long rod and line a little longer, but no reel, it's certain that his "far off" was somewhat nearer than ours.

Cotton fished with flies in fast water, with bait where the water slowed down. His rod was 15 to 18 feet long, his horsehair line just a little longer. The line tapered down to a single hair, sometimes two of them twisted, for the leader. He doesn't note it, but it's probable that he usually fished with casts of three flies: a *stretcher* at the point, and two droppers on the leader up above.

Cotton's list of flies, like that of Berners and de Bergara before him, follows the hatches through the fishing season. We can guess that they imitated the adult winged stages of some abundant stoneflies, the predominant caddis species, and of course mayfly duns. Other flies imitated midges, tied "as little

Ronalds's excellent color plates, published in 1836, included drawings of natural insects and their imitations, which were fished as wet flies.

as can possibly be made," and *palmers*, which we call caterpillars, or the famous Woolly Worms.

Cotton's method was what he called *daping*, and we would today call dapping, done downstream. The stretcher, or point fly, probably swam in the water while the droppers danced above and beneath the surface, fishing both dry and wet.

The next literary leap is into beauty and a certain thoroughness. Alfred Ronalds's *Fly-Fisher's Entomology* was published in 1836, 150 years after the Cotton addition to *The Compleat Angler*. Ronalds's book introduced color plates to depict the insects and the flies that matched them. But it did far more than that. It began with a chapter on the nature of trout and grayling, including notes on their senses: sight, hearing, smell, and taste. His observations were surprisingly accurate. Since the senses of trout are the basis for our approach to them, and our presentation of flies to entice them, Ronalds's observations were extremely important then and are still worth reading today.

Ronalds's book melded his knowledge about the senses of trout with notes on equipment and fly patterns, combining them into tactics to apply against the trout. This thoroughness is the first thing that sets his book apart from those before it, and many after it. The second is the beauty of its color plates. Each plate shows three natural insects, followed by drawings of the three imitations that fish for them. The facing page for each plate lists the order, family, genus, and species of each insect. The entomology is sophisticated. The full dressing for each fly is given. The tying instructions, together with the materials lists and the color plates, make it easy to for the reader and tier to replicate the fly.

The insects shown in Ronalds's plates are all adult, winged stages. They include mayflies, stoneflies, caddis, midges, alderflies, lacewings, and terrestrials such as ants and beetles. The fly patterns listed for the insects are all wet flies. They are divided into two categories: buzz flies with palmered hackles to represent insects in motion; and flies with wings set in the posture the naturals would have when at rest in streamside vegetation, not when drowned in the water, though when wet, of course, most of them would assume the more lifelike posture.

Ronalds recommended casting across and downstream, the current then acting against the line and causing the fly to drift slowly down and around, "as a natural fly when struggling might be supposed to do." It is the exact tactic used today and referred to, often with disdain, as *chuck-and-chance-it*: the down-and-around wet-fly swing. It's a mistake to neglect the old method. It works as well today, when conditions are right for it, as it did when Ronalds first recorded it.

W. C. Stewart was a Scottish lawyer. His book *The Practical Angler* was first published in 1857. He fished wet flies upstream in the choppy riffles, fast runs, and brief pools of small Scottish hill streams. It's possible that he brought wet-fly fishing on such water to a peak not surpassed to this day. My own home streams tumble through the coastal hills of Oregon in the same way, though they are forested, not open. I've fished small streams all over the world that are shaped in about the same way. I've studied Stewart's upstream methods, tied and fished his flies, and find that I sometimes take more trout when fishing his way than I catch fishing with what is today the most common way: casting dry flies to the same kind of small and fast water.

The standard fly-fishing method at the time Stewart wrote his book was captured in Ronalds's earlier formula: the cast slightly upstream and across, the drift natural but downstream and around. Standard flies at the time were bushy winged wets, tied as rough imitations of adult insects.

Stewart did not believe it was necessary to imitate natural insects, but he did feel that it was crucial to fish upstream, with a dead drift, to imitate their behavior. "It is singular inconsistency," he wrote, "that anglers, scrupulously exact about a shade of colour, draw their flies across and up stream in a way in which no natural insect was ever seen moving, as if a trout could not detect an alteration in the motion much more easily than a deviation in the colour of a fly."

Stewart is best known for his three spiders, which covered the colors of the most common stream insects both then and today. They are the Black

W. C. Stewart's three spiders as interpreted on modern hooks, tied with 8/0 threads and hen hackles. From left: Black Spider, Red Spider, and Dun Spider.

Spider, merely a starling hackle wound with brown silk; the Red Spider, a landrail hackle with yellow silk; and the Dun Spider, a dotterel or light starling hackle wrapped with silk of a color, probably yellow or gray, that Stewart neglected to mention. These three flies were alarmingly simple. They took most of Stewart's trout. He tied them on hooks that would be size 12 to 16 on the modern scale.

Stewart's spiders had no bodies, beyond the silk thread with which they were tied. They had sparse, soft hackles spread over the front half of the hook. That's it. You can tie the same three flies today with black hen, red-brown hen, and blue dun hen, then go out and fool a bunch of fish with them on your favorite small waters. Try it. You'll catch trout.

Stewart's tackle was light for his day. His rod was single-handed, 10 feet long, with a butt of ash, middle of hickory, and top of bamboo. It carried a brass reel. His line was a combination of horsehair woven with silk. His leader butt was 7 or 8 feet of gut, made of three strands twisted together. Four or five more 1-foot gut sections tapered down to the point, or tippet. He fished casts of three or more flies, the droppers 2 feet apart, hanging from the main leader about 3 inches.

Stewart claimed four advantages from fishing his spiders upstream on such "light" tackle. First, he remained out of sight of the trout. Second, he had a greater chance to set the hook by drawing his hook downstream into a trout, rather than upstream away from it. Third, his wading did not disturb water he intended to fish. Fourth, the upstream cast and downstream drift made the movement of his flies similar to those of a natural insect.

All of these advantages accrue on small streams. Stewart elevated the art of small-stream fishing to a new level with his insistence on fishing his flies with a free drift. But a note in his writings hints at a problem that would not

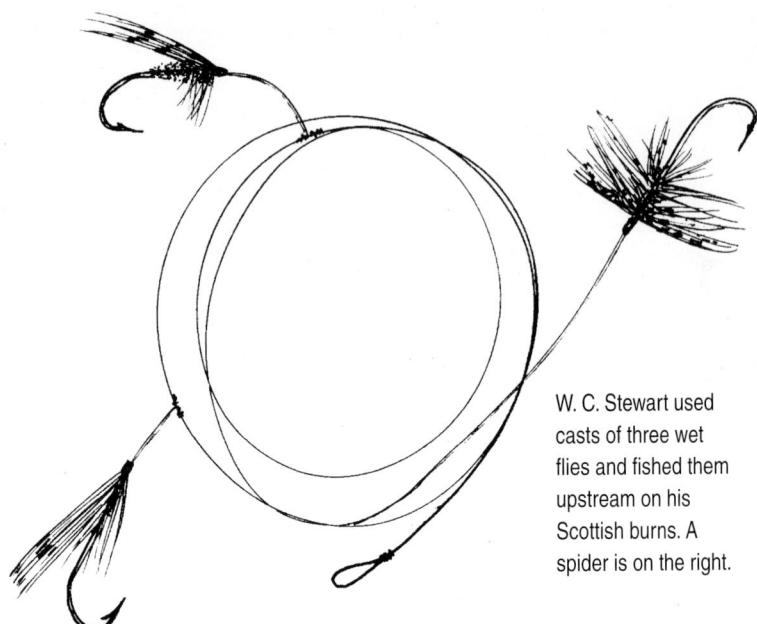

W. C. Stewart used casts of three wet flies and fished them upstream on his Scottish burns. A spider is on the right.

be solved for another fifty years, on the chalkstream rivers in the south of England. When speaking of fishing the smooth water of a small-stream pool, or the glassy water of a larger river, Stewart wrote, "if there is no wind, it is useless commencing till you come to where the water is agitated." In other words Stewart's upstream method, using the tackle of his day, was not effective on anything but rough water.

The new dry fly swept consideration of wet flies aside, though Stewart's upstream casts and free downstream drifts were necessary for success with the drys. The problem of fishing sunk flies on flat water, over fussy trout, was not studied until a London lawyer, G. E. M. Skues, turned his attention to feeding trout that couldn't be taken on drys, but would accept subsurface wets and what then became the new nymphs.

Skues recorded his first experiments, which had already been declared heretical by dry-fly purists, in his 1910 book *Minor Tactics of the Chalk Stream*. It was an "endeavor to put the wet fly in what I conceive to be its right place on the chalk stream," he wrote. The term "minor tactics" announced his belief that the sunk fly was subsidiary to the dry fly, although important to the angler who wanted to catch trout in all types of weather.

Skues's early experiments were with flies tied to imitate mayfly duns. They had upright wings but were designed to sink at once and take trout feeding beneath the surface. Every aspect of these early Skues imitations was calculated to absorb water rather than repel it. They sank, but they took with them beneath the water the posture of the perfect mayfly dun. He fished them during hatches, as imitations of shipwrecked and sunk duns.

Skues cast these flies only to visible, feeding fish. Because of the demands of his smooth chalkstreams, he realized that "if I were to succeed, it must be by a wet-fly modification of the dry-fly method of upstream casting to individual fish."

This marked a turning point in the history of subsurface fly fishing. Skues's wet-fly predecessors failed to catch trout during a rise without the assistance of wind to disturb the water. By setting his mind to taking trout when the water was calm, and when the fish refused drys, Skues began a set of experiments that led toward refined wet flies, and finally the earliest nymphs, fished with methods suited to the demanding trout of his chalkstreams.

Skues found that drag on a surface dry fly was fatal, but that drag on a subsurface fly did not put trout away. Some slight drag at the beginning of the drift, he supposed, might even be attractive to trout. This observation is reflected in James Leisenring's later work on wet-fly fishing in America. It was translated into the Leisenring Lift. Frank Sawyer, riverkeeper on the River Avon and author of the 1958 book *Nymphs and the Trout*, touched on the same thing when he fished nymphs with a coaxing movement to con chalkstream trout with his "induced take." Both methods are effective to this day. Both have their roots in Skues's minor notes on his chalkstreams.

In *Minor Tactics*, Skues imitated upright duns that subsided beneath the surface but kept their posture. In his 1921 book, *The Way of a Trout with a Fly*, Skues dropped his up-winged wets and evolved flies of a different style, which he named *nymphs*. These were unweighted and straddled the border between what we now separate into wets and nymphs. They were tied with hackle fibers for tails, slender abdomens of herl, quill, or dubbing, and thicker thoraxes of fur that served to prop up a turn or at most two of short and soft hen hackle for a collar. These flies were at the transitional point on the continuum between wet flies and nymphs.

Skues tied hackled subsurface dressings to match the prevailing mayfly nymphs of his chalkstreams. He did not venture out into imitations of any other aquatic insect orders, partly because it might have been considered unsporting in light of his time and place, but largely because mayfly hatches dominated his home waters.

In keeping with the rules of his day, on the waters he fished, Skues cast his unweighted nymphs only upstream, to single rising trout. The intent was to match the prevailing natural and present the fly in such a way as to deceive the trout into believing the artificial to be the exact natural on which it was feeding, at the moment it was feeding on it. By limiting himself in this manner, Skues was able to carry the prevailing imitative dry-fly ethic, if not the dry fly itself, beneath the water.

Skues's early nymphs were hackled, and show their place in the transition from wet flies to nymphs. They are remarkably like the imitations we tie for many insects to this day. They could easily be considered the earliest emergers. This is the author's interpretation of a dressing shown in one of the plates in Skues's book *The Way of a Trout with a Fly*. It was tied for the Olive nymph in southern England, and in size 16 would fish well for BWO nymphs all over our own continent.

Skues's last book, *Nymph Fishing for Chalk Stream Trout*, was published in 1939. It codified his upstream method with the sunk fly. It also set his imitations in their final form after his eyesight had faded to the point where he no longer was able to tie flies or fish them effectively. But he did not necessarily believe his patterns to be unalterable. He wrote, "an author became merely a suggester of experiment."

In the end, Skues declared that "A new Ronalds is called for to classify and illustrate the successive series of nymphs and larvae for the benefit of the anglers. Let him stand forth!" That man did not emerge until 1973, when American Ernest Schwiebert compiled his great work *Nymphs*.

Chapter Three

How Wet Flies Happened in America

Skues's advances in wet-fly fishing, and later nymph fishing, took place over bashful brown trout in southern British chalkstreams. Browns have been fished over for centuries, which adds up to a lot of generations if you're a trout. They gave their nod or refused. Tackle, tactics, and the surface and subsurface flies tied to match British hatches all got refined.

American anglers received no such lessons from their trout until the first browns were brought from Britain and Germany in the early 1800s. Even then, browns were a minor implanted population among the much more widespread native brook trout.

Brookies, like cutthroat of the American West, evolved without the selective pressure of angling. Waters where they hovered on quivering fins tended to be more like swift Scottish burns than placid English chalkstreams. Quick decisions about food became a tactic for survival. Brook trout took flies eagerly, and got a reputation for being stupid, when the truth is they'd have been stupid not to be hurried when it came to tipping up and back down with some bit of food delivered on a rushing current. They had to beat all their brethren to it.

The unhesitating hunger of brook trout gave direction to early American fly development for most of one hundred years. The result was a tradition of fancy wet flies, bright with reds and yellows and blues. They looked good to fishermen. They were showy in the water. They attracted trout. They were seen, and they were taken. Selective pressure for fancy wet flies turned our fly boxes gaudy.

Brook trout populations declined when lumbering, followed by industrialization, dirtied and warmed their waters. They were not tolerant of such early pollution, and retreated into chilly mountain headwaters. They were replaced by planted brown trout, which lacked their eagerness for those fancy wet flies. But browns survived in waters where brook trout could not. It was better to have reluctant trout than no trout at all.

The advent of the brown trout was concurrent with the swift rise of the dry fly. Fished over browns rather than brookies, flashy wet flies no longer took so many trout. When American anglers turned away from bright wets, they turned not to the subdued and submerged patterns that Skues was developing at that instant on his British chalkstreams, but to the suddenly remarkable dry fly.

Ray Bergman' s 1938 *Trout*, with its beautiful fly plates, codified the fancy wet fly, and also an age that had already ended. Of his sixteen plates, nine are of wet flies, four of dry flies. Of the four hundred or so wets shown, about half a dozen are palmers, another half dozen soft-hackles. The rest are traditional winged and hackled wet flies, most with leanings toward the fancy.

Though his plates are predominantly of wet flies, Bergman's chapters dwell on the dry fly, the streamer, and the new nymph. The nymphs shown in his plates are *plastic* patterns, stiff and unrealistic in appearance, nothing like those already being described in books by Skues. Bergman's nymphs would not be useful today, though the tactics he described for fishing them would be very useful indeed.

Bergman provided only one illustration of wet-fly tactics, and a short description of the method illustrated. It reflected back to Alfred Ronalds and his book *Fly-Fisher's Entomology*. The cast was made upstream and across at a 45-degree angle, then fished on the drift downstream until the line began to tug at the fly or flies, usually at a point about 45 degrees downstream from the angler. At that point the fly was either picked up for the next cast or fished down and around on the swing. In this part of the presentation, the fly was either allowed to swing freely or given some coaxing action. Bergman recommended trying both.

Bergman did little to relate wet flies to natural insects, either in the tying or in the fishing. This does not subtract from the importance of his classic *Trout*. It contained advice on dry-fly fishing that is excellent to this day, and it recorded wet-fly and nymph fishing as it was done in that day. It contained some of the most relevant information on fly fishing, and it was written with a rare, quiet grace that makes it one of the finest reads in any day.

James Leisenring and Pete Hidy co-authored *The Art of Tying the Wet Fly* in 1941. It got lost in the tides of World War II, which is a tragedy, because the book transported the lessons of Stewart and Skues across the Atlantic and applied them to American waters and hatches. Since our trout streams tend to average out the swift gradients of Stewart's hill streams and the gentle flows of Skues's chalkstreams, those lessons were and still are of enormous value.

Pete Hidy was a college student when he met Leisenring while fishing on Brodheads Creek in Pennsylvania. Hidy watched the master tie his flies. Then he watched while the older man fished them. Leisenring kept detailed notes at streamside. Hidy collected those notes and observations into the 1941 book.

Most of the small book is about materials and tying methods. Only one fishing tactic, the famous Leisenring Lift, was recorded. Before he passed away, Pete told me at his home in Boise, Idaho, that Leisenring had intended that they write another book on the art of fishing the wet fly. "The Lift," Pete said, "was just one of many techniques that Jim used. It's too bad that today everybody believes it was the only method he used."

Leisenring considered the body the most important part of a subsurface fly, the wing least important. He tied and fished a few wet flies with wings for adult caddis and stoneflies, but most of his ties were what he called *hackles*, lacking any wings at all. The bodies for many of his flies were of bronze peacock herl or blackish turkey, raven, or crow herl. But most of his bodies were made of natural furs spun on waxed silk threads. These bodies were prepared separately and stored on slotted cards, incorporated into the wet fly as it was tied later.

Leisenring used Pearsall's Gossamer Silk for tying thread. It is thicker than the synthetic threads we tend to tie with today. He wrote, "The color of tying silk should be chosen to harmonize with the body materials you intend to use in imitating a particular insect, keeping in mind the *undercolor* which you wish to show out through the dubbing."

Silk colors called for most often in Leisenring's fly patterns include primrose yellow, claret, green, and hot orange. It's easy to think of many natural insects that share those colors: Sulphurs, Pale Morning Duns, and Pale Evening Duns for the yellow silk; Little Brown Stones, March Browns, and mahogany mayflies for the claret; Olive Sally stones, Blue-Winged Olive mayflies, and an abundance of caddis pupae for the green; and myriads of caddisflies, both pupae and adults, for the orange. That is far from a complete list of insects that carries those four colors.

The furs that Leisenring spun over these silks were most commonly mole, muskrat, hare's mask and hare's poll (the area between the ears), and various shades of Australian opossum. The combinations created from these body colors and the four silk undercolors are superbly similar to the colors of the insects that nature offers to trout.

Once the bodies were spun and stored, Leisenring incorporated them into finished flies on demand. He tied in the hackle of a wet fly first, leaving it unwound while fixing the tail. Then he selected a pre-spun body from a card, tied it on ahead of the tail, wound it forward to the hackle, and tied it off. The hackle was usually wound back over the body in two to three spaced turns. This half-palmered effect is important because it causes the fibers to emanate from the front one-third of the fly, just as the legs and wings of a natural insect are attached to its three thoracic segments, not just to the back of its head, as a conventional wet-fly hackle is wound.

Leisenring used stiff rooster hackles on wet flies tied to be fished in swift riffles and pocket water, medium-stiff hackles on flies tied for slower runs and streamy pools, and soft rooster hackles on wets tied to fish pools, flats, and other types of idle water. He chose hackles with an iridescent sheen to reflect light. Today, high-grade hen capes can be found with this same sheen, and I've been substituting hen for rooster necks in nearly all of my own wet-fly tying.

Starling body and wing feathers, with the same iridescence, were Leisenring's favorite hackles for his gnats and small spiders. W. C. Stewart used starling for his earlier spiders as well. They are excellent to this day for tying soft-hackled flies to match midges and small caddis. Leisenring also used feathers from the wing shoulders of land birds such as grouse, woodcock, and snipe.

Leisenring tied his wet flies on light-wire hooks if he wanted to fish them just beneath the surface film, and also when he wanted to *paraffin* the fly and fish it floating in the film itself, which apparently he did often. I fish flymphs as floating emergers during a few hatches, especially the tiny BWOs, sometimes applying the same floatant I use on dry flies. Leisenring switched to heavy-wire hooks for wet flies that he wanted to sink quickly. Most often, he wanted this quality in what Pete Hidy later called Leisenring's *soft-hackled thorax nymphs.*

In Leisenring's list of twelve favorite wet flies, ten are *hackles*, tied without wings. Only two are winged. In a second list of twelve favorite nymphs, eleven have sparse and stubby hackles; only one lacks them. As with Skues's nymphs, these straddle the border between wet fly and nymph. We must classify them as nymphs, however, because Hidy and Leisenring, who authored the book about them, called them that.

Leisenring's notes about fishing his flies with the Lift were as sparse as the way he dressed his flies. His goal was to fish a wet fly "so that it becomes deadly at the point where the trout is most likely to take his food." Leisenring ideally spotted a feeding fish, or cased the likely lie of one, before making his presentation. He made his cast across stream, 10 to as much as 20 feet upstream from the trout or the lie. He allowed no slack in the line, but was careful not to let the line tug at the fly and hinder its sinking. Leisenring wrote, "The fly comes straight down to him bumpety-bump over the gravel and stones along the bottom with the current." When the fly reached the position of the trout, he stopped his rod, which caused the fly to lift, look alive, and incite a strike.

James Leisenring co-authored *The Art of Tying the Wet Fly*, with V. S. "Pete" Hidy. COURTESY OF LANCE HIDY

A few notes must be made about the Leisenring Lift. First, he did not weight his wet flies or soft-hackled nymphs. To make the fly sink, he tied a very sparse dressing on a heavy-wire hook. Second, he needed a lie at least 2 feet but no more than 4 feet deep, situated so that he could wade into position across from it without any conflicting currents between his position and the point where he expected to connect with the trout. Third, the lie had to be in water where it was feasible to cast several feet upstream and get a long drift while the fly sank. Fourth, the current had to be slow enough to allow a wet fly tied without weight to get down and go *bumpety-bump* along the bottom.

It's often overlooked that the Leisenring Lift was designed to fish the fly *lifting off the bottom.* Of course, the method can be applied against trout working in mid-depths or nearer to the top, but then it more likely might be called an Induced Take, after Sawyer, rather than the Lift, after Leisenring. Sawyer cast only to visible, feeding trout, presumably higher in the water column.

It's also often overlooked that the circumstances ideal for the Lift are rather restricted. You'll come across them once in a while in the average waters that you fish. It's likely they were common on the Brodheads, with its low gradient and long pools and glides, when Leisenring fished it, before hurricane floodwaters reshaped it. It's not so likely that you'll find more than a sprinkling of ideal situations for the Leisenring Lift on average American trout streams. Still, it's an excellent method to master. But as Pete Hidy told me, it's far from the only method that Leisenring used, and was actually one that he didn't use as much as he used others. That's why it's a tragedy they did not write that promised second book, on methods for fishing their wet flies and soft-hackled thorax nymphs.

I spoke about this at a meeting of a fly-fishing club in Philadelphia some years ago, describing the set of conditions necessary to fish the Lift: that visible trout or marked lie, 2 to 4 feet of depth, a long run of even currents leading to the lie. A member in the audience called out, "You just described the Little Lehigh River." It's north of Philadelphia. James Leisenring lived and worked in Allentown. The Little Lehigh was his home stream.

In the 1971 Crown edition of *The Art of Tying the Wet Fly*, Pete Hidy added several chapters that he subtitled *The Art of Fishing the Flymph*. To Hidy, a wet fly best imitated an insect that was in transition, not yet a *fly*, but no longer a *nymph*. So he coined the term *flymph*.

Rick Hafele and I met Pete in the late 1970s. He showed us how to tie flymphs. He also gave us a careful and thorough verbal description of the method he used most often for fishing them. I applied it successfully a short time later against some selective brown trout rising on the Firehole River in Yellowstone Park, Wyoming, right at evening, while clumsy buffalo calves galumphed above the river and their mothers grunted and groused about it. Over the years I've taken many more trout with the method Pete described. After he passed away, I tried to track down a written and illustrated description of the method in the literature that he left. It was there, but not all in one place. I had to piece it together from sources such as Pete's obscure *Fly Fishing* and *Book of Wet-Fly Fishing*, tiny books published in 1960 and 1961 as part of the Sports Illustrated Library series.

Pete's flymph fishing method was never named, so I describe it as the Hidy Subsurface Swing. I use it far more often than I do the much more famous Leisenring Lift. It's best applied against rising trout, and often works best when they've already refused a few dry fly imitations of naturals in the air, and at times even on the water. The Subsurface Swing is designed to place the swimming fly in front of the nose of a selective trout. Here's how it's done, briefly; the method is described more thoroughly later (see Chapter 15, "Four Men and Their Methods"). First, move into position at a 30- to 60-degree angle upstream from a working trout. Second, make the cast 2 to 3 feet above the trout and beyond it. Third and most important, give the line a slight pull to tug the flymph under. Without that, the fly will be trapped in the surface film and will cut a wake as it swings around. Fourth and finally, hold the rod steady and let the tight line coax the flymph in a short arc right across the bow of the trout. Chances are you'll see a swirl when it takes, so close to the surface it resembles a rise to a dry.

Hidy's method depends more on presentation than it does on imitation. Nevertheless, it's always best to get a look at whatever natural insect might be prodding trout to feed, and select a flymph that is near it in size and color.

The late Pete Hidy, who co-authored *The Art of Tying the Wet Fly* with James Leisenring and contributed *The Art of Fishing the Flymph* as an important addition in the second edition of the book. COURTESY OF LANCE HIDY

It's a method that works wherever trout rise. The water can be swift or nearly still. It can be tumbling or perfectly smooth. The lie can be 50 feet wide and 100 feet long, or it can be restricted to a pocket just a couple of feet across. It's a wet-fly method that has wide application, and it often works well to fish a flymph through an entire pod of feeding fish, though it's usually best to single one out. I've fished a flymph on the Hidy Subsurface Swing across a tailout thriving with selective rising trout at evening, during caddis egg-laying flights and mayfly hatches or spinner falls, and have taken trout after trout without ever pinpointing any exact fish.

Polly Rosborough's *Tying and Fishing the Fuzzy Nymphs* was first published in 1965, and has been in print ever since. It was a major advance in subsurface fly theory. His flies were clearly nymphs, further along on the mystical wet-fly-to-nymph continuum from Skues's and Leisenring's soft-hackled nymphs. But a few of his flies had fur hackle collars, and led toward the development of all-fur wet flies.

I picked up the concept for all-fur wets from W. H. Lawrie's 1967 book *All-Fur Flies and How to Dress Them.* In a chapter called "On Dressing Wet Flies," Lawrie details a method for winging a wet fly with a clump of fur in the place of the normal feather wing. It's a small bit of lore with which I have yet to experiment, to this late day, but I recommend you should. Fur might make a fine wing. It would certainly be less stiff, cleave the water less like a knife blade, perhaps look more alive in the water than a rigid feather-section wing.

What caught my eye in Lawrie's fine book were notes on a hackling method first used by Captain George Selwyn Marryat around 1880, though

The late Polly Rosborough and the author on Polly's home stream, the Williamson River in Oregon. JIM SCHOLLMEYER

who knows how long it might have been in local British use prior to that. The method, condensed, called for trapping fur in a waxed thread loop, spinning it, and then wrapping it in place of a feather hackle. Lawrie didn't detail the fur in use beyond a brief note about "soft, black cat's fur-fibers; a small quantity of well-teazed seal's fur dyed black," and in another note, mohair. I was left to believe that experiments with other furs would be beneficial.

I don't know that Polly Rosborough knew about Marryat's method. Lawrie's book was published a couple of years after Polly's, so Polly didn't learn it there. It's more likely that he devised the collar hackle method independently. Polly's famous Casual Dress calls for muskrat fur, with the guard hairs left in, caught in a thread loop and wound as hackle. Muskrat is a thick fur, with long guards, and is very difficult to incorporate into wet flies smaller than size 8 or 10 unless the guard hairs are plucked out. But the combination of Polly's notes overlaid on Marryat's method as revealed in Lawrie's book led me to play with shorter furs such as gray and red squirrel, which are better for wet-fly collars down to about size 12 and 14.

Pine squirrel, a by-product of the marten trapping trade in Canada, is the ultimate short fur for smaller all-fur wets, and I use it most on size 14 to 18 flies. Experiments with mole and other short-haired furs make it possible to tie even tinier wet flies with all-fur collars, though the colors you can find are limited.

These fiddlings with fur-hackle collars led to a small series of what I call all-fur wet flies, which will be detailed in a later chapter (see Chapter 8, "Tying All-Fur Wet Flies").

Many of Polly Rosborough's "fuzzy nymphs" were tied and fished in ways that place them as close to wet flies as they are to nymphs. His Light Caddis Emergent is an example. It could be considered a very sparse soft-hackle.

Rosborough's methods, more than his flies, reflect wet-fly practice. Polly constantly used the phrase *fishing under the hatch*. He wrote that "during a hatch, the larger fish prefer nymphs, and most nymph patterns are deadliest when fished rather shallow. This is particularly true during the early part of the hatch when the larger fish are bulging just subsurface. Only the little fellows are jumping for the few adults flying."

Rosborough tied a series of rough-bodied nymphs the size, shape, and color of the ascending stages of natural insects. They were based on mayflies, caddis, stoneflies, midges, and others. His flies were clearly nymphs, rough impressions rather than exact imitations of the naturals that Polly collected from trout stomach samples. Like Leisenring's wet flies, Polly never weighted his fuzzy nymphs.

Polly's method for fishing fuzzy nymphs was based on the traditional wet-fly swing. He noted, however, that the fly should never be dragged upstream against the current. "One thing you must never do: swim a nymph upstream against the slightest current. . . . A nymph in the current is always swimming upstream, but at the same time he is going backward in the current." To duplicate this movement, Rosborough used a fly swing that led the fly across the current and drifting downstream. I watched him do it. His method was very close to the standard wet-fly presentation. Sometimes he let his fly swing freely, other times he teased it with a gentle rhythmic pulsing of his rod. He leaned forward intensely, directed his sight and all his senses into feeling what was going on out where his fly drifted downstream through its swing. Polly appeared to be coaxing the trout, tempting them into the take.

Ernest Schwiebert's *Nymphs* was first published in 1973, and has since been published as an expanded two-volume set. It's a complete guide to the nymphs and larvae of North American aquatic insects and crustaceans. Each insect is shown in a detailed drawing done by the author, with full notes on habitat, behavior, and those critical factors in imitation: size, form, and color. *Nymphs* is beautifully written and is a necessary step in any serious study of the subsurface food forms eaten by trout.

Schwiebert's notes on caddis are perhaps most interesting to the wet-fly fisherman. His patterns for small caddisflies reflect back to the Yorkshire patterns in the time of W. C. Stewart and T. E. Pritt. The latter author codified a series of soft-hackled patterns, based on Stewart's spiders, in his 1886 *North-Country Flies*. Pritt listed more than thirty dressings, most tied with slender silk bodies and sparse hackles from such land birds as partridge, grouse, starling, and landrail.

Schwiebert noted the many species of caddis pupae perfectly imitated by such simple dressings. In *Nymphs* he brought forward the appropriate Pritt patterns to match sample species across the full color range of caddis. It's a brilliant concept, and the dressings are worth noting here: for tiny olive pupae, the Partridge & Olive in size 18 to 22; for small pale pupae, the Snipe and Yellow in size 18 to 22; for brown pupae, the Partridge & Orange in size 18 to 22; and for the many minute dark caddis pupae, the Woodcock and Hare's Ear in size 18 to 22. Schwiebert's work is an example of the way old patterns can be translated into killing dressings for hatches that we fish to this day. The hatches and the trout haven't changed.

Sylvester Nemes wrote his first book, *The Soft-Hackled Fly*, in 1975. Its subject is simple: a few soft-hackled wet flies. Its treatment is simple, too: It unwinds the history of soft-hackles, tells the best ways to tie them with modern methods and materials, then describes a few tactics for presenting them. Its prose is as spare as the flies and the methods it describes. This is a rare angling book, one that both illuminates a subject and enthuses the reader. Few who read Nemes can resist rushing to the tying vise to wrap up a few soft-hackles, then heading for the stream to cast them onto trout water.

Nemes's soft-hackled flies are adaptations from Pritt's 1886 *North-Country Flies*. In his second book, *The Soft-Hackled Fly Addict*, published in 1981, Nemes had the color plates from Pritt duplicated and printed in his own work. It's another beautiful addition to the literature of wet-fly fishing, and it elaborates on both the flies and the methods used to tie and fish them.

The third work in Nemes's trilogy, his 1991 *Soft-Hackled Fly Imitations*, looks at specific insect hatches and lists soft-hackled wet flies that match them. Many of these are new dressings, tied specifically for the hatches Sylvester found in his travels and fishing on American waters. It's a brilliant concept. The flies solve problems, and take trout, during many hatches that I encounter in my own fishing.

The late soft-hackle guru Sylvester Nemes tying on a fly on the Yellowstone River. The water he is wading is suited perfectly to his flies and his methods.

Nemes also translated to trout fishing the tactics of A. H. E. Wood, outlined in Jock Scott's 1935 *Greased Line Fishing for Atlantic Salmon*. He described his own method for fishing the soft-hackled fly as if the fly were a leaf, floating freely along with the current, not influenced by drag from the line and leader. But Nemes did not neglect the traditional wet-fly swing as an effective method for fishing his soft-hackled wets. I've watched him do it to the disappointment of many trout.

In *Soft-Hackled Fly Imitations*, Nemes wrote about fishing a soft-hackled wet fly as a semi-submerged dry fly. Sometimes the fly is dressed with floatant and fished flush in the film as an emerger. Other times the fly is left undressed and fished just beneath the film as a rising nymph, a swimming pupa, or even an adult insect adrift on the current. In any case, the fly is cast upstream and fished back down with a drag-free drift, almost precisely the way you would fish a dry fly.

The effectiveness of this upstream method is not restricted to soft-hackled wets. It can also be employed with flymphs, either afloat or just subsurface, and even with unweighted nymphs that match the immature stage of whatever insect might be hatching. Those would now be called *emergers*.

Many of the tactics written about in Nemes's excellent trilogy of soft-hackle books have applications in all types of subsurface fly fishing. Another significant advance in wet-fly fishing was made in 1981, with the publication of the late Gary LaFontaine's book *Caddisflies*, though its subject was not wet flies. LaFontaine used scuba gear to dive and study natural caddis, both pupae and adults, beneath the water. He noticed that a bubble of air is often the key that triggers trout to feed on both stages. Caddis pupae trap diffused gases beneath the pupal exoskeleton. These gases help in the rise to the surface and are important in any imitation. He used trilobal carpet yarns, called Sparkle Yarns, in his flies to achieve the same reflective effect. Not only do the artificial fibers reflect light and look like bubbles of air, they also trap air and take it beneath the water with the fly.

LaFontaine observed many caddis pupal emergences and took note of the way they left their larval cases, drifted for a time along the bottom, then rose in the water and often drifted again just beneath the surface. They were appreciated by trout at all levels. Gary devised a series of weighted Deep Sparkle Pupa patterns to be fished along the bottom, and another series of unweighted Emergent Sparkle Pupa patterns to be fished just beneath the surface film.

In my own fishing, I've committed the heresy of tying and fishing Gary's Deep Sparkle Pupa nymphs without weight. Though the weighted versions fish well when used the way Gary recommends, with wet-tip lines and presented right along the bottom, I prefer to fish them up near the surface, with a floating line, because I enjoy that kind of fishing a lot more, and in truth catch a lot more trout on his patterns when I fish them as I would wet flies.

One would do well to follow Gary's instructions and tie his weighted Deep Sparkle Pupa, unweighted Emergent Sparkle Pupa, and wet-fly version of the Diving Caddis, each in four primary colors: yellow, green, brown, and ginger. In a narrow range of sizes, they would add up to three or four dozen flies—not much of an addition to the current bulk of your fly boxes, but a tremendous increase in the options you'd have to draw on during a caddis hatch.

If you followed my errant lead, you'd also carry Gary's Deep Sparkle Pupa patterns tied without weight. You'd find some trout that forgave you for it, though Gary might have scolded you. I'm not entirely sure if you'd be fishing wet flies or nymphs, but if you fished them with wet-fly tactics, then I'd guess you were wet-fly fishing.

That's what I consider myself to be doing when I do it.

Even if we were to neglect Gary LaFontaine's nymph patterns, it would be foolish to overlook the contribution of his Sparkle Yarns in our wet-fly tying. In the first edition of this book, I called for all sorts of furs, in both natural colors and dyed. In my current tying, I incorporate reflective Sparkle

Gary LaFontaine's Deep Sparkle Pupa patterns are clearly nymphs, designed to fish deep. When you omit the weight, and fish them just inches deep, they resemble wet flies a bit in the style of tying, and a lot in the manner of presentation.

Yarns in most fur-bodied dressings by simply snipping quarter-inch lengths of the yarn in the approximate same color as the fur, or in clear, which always adds a bit of brightness no matter the color of the fur with which it will be blended. I use about a 1-to-3 ratio of Sparkle Yarn to fur.

I dump the yarn and fur together into a coffee grinder, whirl them around until they're mixed, then tie them in loosely with either a spun-body or dubbing loop technique, both discussed in the chapters on tying. You can also buy dubbing mixes, in all popular colors, that have Sparkle Yarn already added.

The main thing to note here in this chapter on the history of wet flies in America is that Gary LaFontaine's contribution to wet-fly and nymph fishing cuts far beyond the patterns he left for us. His Sparkle Yarns can be blended into almost any style wet fly you tie, to give your flies some reflectance, to make them look more alive in the water, in the eyes of trout.

Soft-Hackles, Flymphs, Winged Wets, and All-Fur Wet Flies

A condensation of history leaves us with four major styles of wet flies: soft-hackles; wingless wets, or flymphs; traditional winged wets; and all-fur wets.

Traditional winged wets, especially those gaudy types tied for brook trout, were often referred to as *lures* by writers who studied the aquatic insects and felt that all flies should be tied to match them as precisely as possible, usually with floating flies. But it's not a good idea to dismiss these old ties so suddenly. Many, if not most, of our early American wet flies were indeed bright, tied to con *foolish* brookies. But wet flies were first tied to imitate winged insects that early fly fishers observed flying over and around their favorite streams, and most traditional winged wets that have continued in use today look more like natural insects than they do bright bits of drifting detritus. Because adult insect types are easiest to observe, and it's obvious that trout eat them—and often do so beneath the subsurface—it's no mistake to this day to match winged insects with wet flies.

As more is learned about the adaptations of aquatic insects, it becomes evident that many aspects of their behavior get them into consistent difficulty with trout beneath the water as adults, not just as nymphs, larvae, and pupae. As an example already mentioned, certain mayflies leave the nymphal shuck behind on the bottom and rise to the surface as fully formed duns. Another example is the variety of trout-stream caddis adults that dive into the water and swim to the bottom to lay their eggs. These behaviors have not changed, which is why traditional winged wet flies still work so often, and so well— at times even on trout feeding selectively.

The essential element of the winged wet is the wing itself. In a properly tied fly, the wing is what catches the eye. When the fly swims in water, the wing is

The four styles of wet flies: traditional winged wet, soft-hackle, flymph, and all-fur wet.

Some traditional winged wet flies can be improved upon by spreading out the hackle fibers, and by using hen hackle fibers rather than quill—stiff feather sections—for the wing. The Hare's Ear on the left is tied in the traditional style, the one on the right with spread hackles and hen fibers for the wing. You can substitute hen for quill, using an appropriate color, in any given traditional fly pattern.

also most likely what catches the eye of a trout. It's the key characteristic. No doubt the winged wet fly owes a large part of its effectiveness to its close resemblance to the great numbers of winged aquatic and terrestrial insects, living and drowned, that find their way into the bellies of those beasts called trout.

The traditional winged wet is most often tied with a tinsel, yarn, or tightly wound fur body. This compactness can be a mistake. By incorporating the spun-fur bodies of flymphs, or the fuzzy bodies of later nymphs, you can add to the lifelike qualities of winged wet flies.

The hackle of the standard wet fly has traditionally been tied in three to six wraps at the head of the fly, immediately behind the thread head. It all arises in a bunch. If this same hackle is sparsely wound over the front one-third of the fly, rather than right at the head, it looks a lot more like the legs of a natural insect, which emanate from the insect's three thoracic segments, not just from the back of its head.

The traditional wet fly has always been winged with paired sections cut from paired feathers plucked from the opposing wings of a single bird. Mallard, turkey, and hen pheasant are used most often in America. In England, the wings are usually of smaller and softer feathers such as starling, snipe, or landrail. Many patterns, such as our Light and Dark Cahills, call for wood duck flank fiber wings. I've often felt that these dressings catch so many trout because of the lifelike action of their moveable wing fibers, as opposed to stiff feather sections.

In recent years I've been incorporating wings of hen hackle fibers into some traditional winged wets. They look as good as stiffer feather-section wings. They are easier to tie and never develop the rudder effect of what is traditionally called *quill*, which, if not tied perfectly straight, often twirls the fly unnaturally through the water on the swing or retrieve. Because hen hackle fiber wings are pliant, they work well in the water, making the fly look alive.

The essential element of the soft-hackled wet fly is its hackle. Soft-hackles have slender thread, floss, or herl bodies. The body, in some ways, becomes an undercolor to the hackle's collapsing and then unfolding, working in the current around it.

Most hackles for these simple but elegant dressings are wound from water-absorbing land bird feathers, taken from the breast, the back, or the wing shoulders. Soft-hackled wet flies lack wings. They sometimes have slight turns of fur propped right behind the winds of hackle. This fur thorax causes the hackle to stand away from the hook shank at an approximate 90-degree angle when the fly is still in the vise or the fly box. In the water, the same thorax keeps the hackle fibers from collapsing permanently against the hook in a modest to strong current, where the fibers might lose their lifelike qualities.

The most popular hackle for soft-hackled wets comes from the Hungarian partridge. This game bird has been imported into the American West. Full skins are available from nearly any fly shop or catalog. Partridge breast and back feathers are either gray or brown, and have tiny black or white markings that make them look like they've been stippled with a marking pen. The legs and antennae of many natural insects are speckled with light or dark spots. When tied into a fly, nothing looks more alive than hackle from a Hungarian partridge. A soft-hackle tied with this feather looks like it might drop out of the vise and begin crawling across the tying table. It has that same look of something living when in the water, and that's a large part of the reason trout take soft-hackles so eagerly.

Other soft-hackled wets are tied with feathers from such land birds as grouse, woodcock, snipe, and starling. A few are tied with feathers from the breasts or wings of water birds such as water hen in Britain, closely related to the American coot. I've yet to learn of soft-hackled ties incorporating the common coot into successful dressings. I'm sure I'll hear about them now, and want to. Common hen neck hackle, now available in nearly any color you can imagine, can also be used on soft-hackled flies, though it's not as traditional as winding them with land bird feathers.

The hackle is the focus of a soft-hackled fly. The body at times becomes little more than an undercolor to the hackle. There is no wing to distract from it. The liveliness of the fly depends entirely on the workings of the hackle. If it's tied too thickly, the fly becomes a brushy, knotted blob of material adrift in the water. The most effective soft-hackles are tied sparsely, so that each fiber is free to work with the current. I can still hear Sylvester Nemes criticizing my earliest soft-hackled efforts, based on his famous first book. "Too much hackle, Dave," he said. "Not sparse enough!" He was right.

Soft-hackled flies can be tied to imitate caddis pupae, a wide variety of drowned mayfly duns and spinners, caddis adults, all of the smaller stoneflies, and a few terrestrials. All of these insect types, when awash in the water, are slender and have just a few appendages waving in the current: six legs, two antennae, two or four wings. Soft-hackles tied to fish for them should be kept slender and sparse.

Wingless wet flies, now known more commonly by Pete Hidy's term *flymphs*, are tied with the focus on the body of the fly, not its hackle. The fibrous fur body entrains bubbles of air when the fly is popped beneath the surface. These bubbles give the fly a sheen nearly impossible to attain any other way. Because of this sheen, flymphs do a remarkable job of imitating caddis pupae approaching the surface for emergence, and also caddis adults diving down to the bottom to lay their eggs. Pupae trap gases inside their outer skins to aid their ascent to the surface. Adults trap gases in their hairy wings and surrounding their bodies to provide oxygen as they swim to the bottom.

Flymphs are tied with fur bodies spun on silk threads that give the undercolor you want. When spun correctly, they are very spiky, with fibers sticking out in all directions. A tier whose only goal is neatness in each finished fly might be turned away from a properly tied flymph. Trout have no interest in neatness and do not make the same mistake.

By winding the hackle in three to four turns over the front one-third of the flymph body, you can achieve the effect of legs and wings emanating from the fly's thorax, rather than just its head. This adds an attraction to the fly when you view it, as well as a liveliness when you fish it.

Flymphs can be tied to mimic many sorts of insects, but they're perhaps best thought about as what we now call *emergers*, to imitate insects in that stage that Pete Hidy termed "no longer a nymph, but not yet a fly." This makes them most useful for emerging mayflies and caddis pupae, which is not a major restriction: These are the two most important groups that attract selective feeding by trout during emergence in streams and rivers.

Stoneflies, as we already know, almost exclusively emerge by crawling out on shore as nymphs, where trout can't get at them. However, Hidy and Leisenring's famous Tup's, a soft-hackled thorax nymph that I categorize loosely as a flymph, has served me well when both nymphs and ovipositing adults of the Yellow Sally are available to trout. Hidy prescribed smaller flymphs, such as the Iron Blue Dun, for use during midge hatches. Most flymphs are less imitations of particular insects than they are impressions of many of them. This enlarges, rather than restricts, their importance.

The focal points of an all-fur wet are both its body and fur collar: in other words, the entire fur fly. The tail, if there is one, is clipped from a patch of fur,

Left: A bubble of air captured in the body fibers of a flymph. Many natural insects swim with the aid of trapped gases. The flymph won't hold its air bubbles long, but it will look very much alive while it's got them. **Right:** A size 16 all-fur wet fly, its tail, body, and hackle collar all taken from the same area on the hide of a pine squirrel.

usually muskrat or squirrel, often the same patch from which the rest of the fly is tied. The tail should include both underfur and guard hairs. When wet it tapers, and represents the back end of a slender insect's abdomen as well as its tails.

The body of an all-fur wet is also of fur, often from the same hide as the tail and collar. But it can also be sheared fur, dyed fur, or packaged fur in the color you desire. Incorporating Sparkle Yarn in the body of an all-fur wet is an excellent way to add some liveliness to the already active fly. Whatever you use for the body, dub it roughly, or use the spun-body techniques for tying flymphs. Remember that one of the primary sources for all-fur wets is Polly Rosborough's fuzzy nymphs. Polly used a hacksaw blade to rough up the bodies of his flies after he tied them. You could do this with your all-fur wets, as well, though it's faster to tie them rough in the first place.

The hackle collar of an all-fur wet is wound with fur, usually from the same fur patch or whole hide that furnished the tail and body. Include as many guard hairs as possible. Work with fur that is compatible in length with the size fly you're tying, though of course it's possible to slip out the longest guard hairs at one end, and to trim the underfur shorter at the other. But it's easier to work with short fur rather than long. Techniques for spinning the fur hackle collar will be detailed in Chapter 8, "Tying All-Fur Wet Flies."

All-fur wets are closest to the transition point, on that continuum between wet flies and nymphs, of any of the wet-fly styles. To many folks they're beyond that dividing point, and fall along the line as nymphs somewhere near the fuzzy ones tied by Polly Rosborough. I won't argue. My own definition derives less from the shape of the flies than it does from the way I fish them.

All-fur wets are not often tied to match any particular food form, but instead to remind trout about a variety of the things they've recently been eating. They do take a lot of fish, and they're wonderfully fun to tie, though at first that spun collar is not the easiest maneuver to master. Once you've got it, they become easy and fast, and their construction becomes a template on which you might build your own variations.

PART II

TYING EFFECTIVE WET FLIES

Chapter Five

Tying Soft-Hackled Flies

The essential element of the soft-hackled wet is its hackle. The body is subsidiary, usually wound of two layers of silk thread, a single layer of floss, or a winding of some sort of herl. Properly slight, the body serves as an undercolor to a hackle that thrives in the currents, opening and closing over the body.

Many soft-hackle dressings call for an optional thorax: a knot of dubbed fur tucked in tight behind the hackle. This thorax is only partly designed to look like the thorax of a natural insect, and thereby to offer trout a more enticing bite. Its larger purpose is to prop the hackle at an approximate 90-degree angle to the hook shank when the fly is dry. Thus braced, the hackle opens and closes around the thorax rather than collapsing around the body and remaining closed when the fly is fished. This gives the soft-hackle much of its appearance of life.

The hackle itself should be sparse. That is perhaps not saying it emphatically enough. The hackle should be about half as dense as you think it should be when you think you've got it sparse enough. Conventional wisdom is that you should take just a couple of turns of partridge hackle, no more. I've found that if you peel away the fibers on one side of the feather before tying it in, then the specified two turns of hackle create a finished fly that is half as dense, and also one with its hackle fibers curved elegantly rearward. A single turn of a hackle so peeled provides a truly sparse hackle, one-quarter as dense as a full hackle wound in two turns.

Materials for tying an effective set of soft-hackles can be kept as sparse as the hackles should be on the finished fly. I have an entire end of my writing studio stacked and stuffed full of fly-tying tools and materials, for the construction of all sorts of flies: drys, nymphs, wets, streamers, steelhead flies, and so on. But all the tools and materials I need to tie a successful set

If possible, buy an entire partridge skin, for the full range of feathers, rather than packaged partridge, which usually contains feathers suitable only to size 12 and larger flies. Be sure it has been skinned around the head, the area where the smallest hackles reside.

A grouse wing provides some of the finest soft-hackle feathers, well marked, in nice colors, and with the proper delicateness so the fibers work in the water when a fly tied with it is fished. Feathers in a variety of sizes can be found on a wing, the smallest on the shoulders, moving toward the largest midway to the secondaries. The larger primary and secondary feathers can be used for winging traditional wet flies if you acquire your grouse wings by the matched pair.

Soft-hackled wet flies require a minimum of tools and materials: Pearsall's Gossamer Silk Thread on a mini-bobbin, Pearsall's Marabou Silk Floss, beeswax, tacky wax to hold dubbing to unwaxed silk thread, and fur for the optional thorax.

of soft-hackled wet flies fit in an old wooden cigar box I inherited from my father.

For tying threads, and for bodies if you choose to construct them in the conventional soft-hackle manner, you'll want Pearsall's Gossamer Silk in yellow, green, orange, and crimson red. If you use standard nylon threads and floss bodies, I recommend Pearsall's Marabou Silk Floss in the same four colors. You might have to ask your local fly shop to order these exact silk threads and floss, but they are available, and your favorite shop will have no trouble finding a source for them. If they cannot, fly-tying catalogs and online sources offer them.

To construct the thorax on the soft-hackles that I'll call for in this chapter, you'll need a hare's mask, sheared and blended. I'm allergic to dander in the actual mask and cannot tie with it, so I substitute Hare's Ear Plus, a blend of rabbit fur and Sparkle Yarn, or a similar blend. It has an added bit of bright-ness to it that I like, though I've never been able to tell whether trout prefer flies tied with Sparkle Yarn to those tied with standard hare's mask, without the Sparkle Yarn added. Both the sheared fur and the pre-blends have guard hairs left in, and make a spiky dubbing when you wind them loosely onto your tying thread. If you wind them too tight, as you might for the body of a dry fly, they won't prop the hackle so well, and will also lose any life that they might otherwise add to your finished fly.

The most common hackle used on soft-hackled flies comes from the Hungarian partridge. Partridge feathers have that valuable speckling that

A male starling skin has valuable soft-hackle feathers on the breast, back, and wings. This one has been roughed up a bit, from an excess of time in a traveling tying kit, and from having many of its feathers plucked. But it still has a lot of soft-hackles left before it's done.

adds life to any fly. If you have a friend who hunts upland birds, you might have an excellent source for the feathers. If not, skins are available in nearly every fly shop. I cannot urge you strongly enough to purchase an entire skin. The smallest feathers, used to tie soft-hackles in size 16 and even 18, are located up around the head of the bird. If you buy packaged partridge, you'll get only large feathers, with which you can tie only large flies. When examining a full pelt, be sure that it has been skinned carefully to include the tiny feathers around the entire head. If the head has been chopped off before the bird has been skinned, you'll get few feathers for flies smaller than size 12.

Many of the best feathers for soft-hackles come from the wings and body of the male starling. These have an iridescent purplish cast and reflect light when the fly is in the water. Because of this, they add life to your flies. They are also very delicate feathers; their fibers work well in the water, opening and closing around a sparse body of silk or herl. Excellent small hackle feathers can also be found on the wing shoulders of the same starling. For that reason, it's again a good idea to buy an entire starling skin, complete with wings.

Other soft-hackle feathers can be found on the wings of grouse, woodcock, and snipe. You would be wise to order paired wings from each of these. Later you'll find that the paired primary and secondary feathers make excellent wings on traditional wet flies.

Although most soft-hackled wets call for feathers from the listed land birds, you'd be foolish not to consider hen chicken necks as an alternative source for hackles. Domestic hen necks come in such high quality today that many of them possess the desired sheen James Leisenring called for in his wet flies and soft-hackled nymphs, for which he prescribed rooster. Hen

An excellent experiment would be to tie and fish a simple set of four hen-hackled wet flies to match the most common colors among nature's insects, with bodies and hackles in these combinations: olive/blue dun; tan/brown; gray/grizzly; and pale yellow/ginger.

necks can be found in a wide range of colors. It's easy to select a few common insect body colors, say olive, tan, gray, and pale yellow, then come up with complementary colors in hen hackle, say blue dun, brown, grizzly, and ginger. Dub a body, wrap three or four turns of hen hackle in front it, and you'll produce a set of four simple soft-hackled wets that will take fish in a wide range of circumstances. Tie them in sizes 10 through 16. It will be an experiment for you, and you'll be coming to the idea fresh, because I've never done it and I've never read about such a simple set of flies.

I tie soft-hackles on two styles of hooks, for two separate situations. The first is a standard 1X fine dry-fly hook, which I use when I want the fly to penetrate the surface film but not sink too deeply. This hook is best used on flies for casting upstream on the smallest streams, where pools are short and not very deep. If you use a heavy-wire hook, the fly might sink to the bottom, fold its many-fibered arms, and simply sit. No trout will take it there. A fly tied on a dry-fly hook will sink a few inches, then drift slowly downstream with the current, staying at roughly the same level in the water, or else sinking very slowly. That's what you want a soft-hackled wet, fished upstream, to do on small streams.

The dry-fly hook works well for any soft-hackle that you plan to fish upstream. It's especially effective for those that you intend to cast to rising trout. This is relatively rare in soft-hackle fishing, and will arise slowly out of situations you observe, then tie flies to solve. When solving such a situation, turn to the dry-fly hook as an aid to fishing the fly in the surface film or just beneath it.

The second hook, the one I use by far most often for soft-hackles, is a standard length wet-fly hook, 2X heavy. I use it on all soft-hackles that I intend to fish on the swing, for the simple reason that it helps the fly sink far

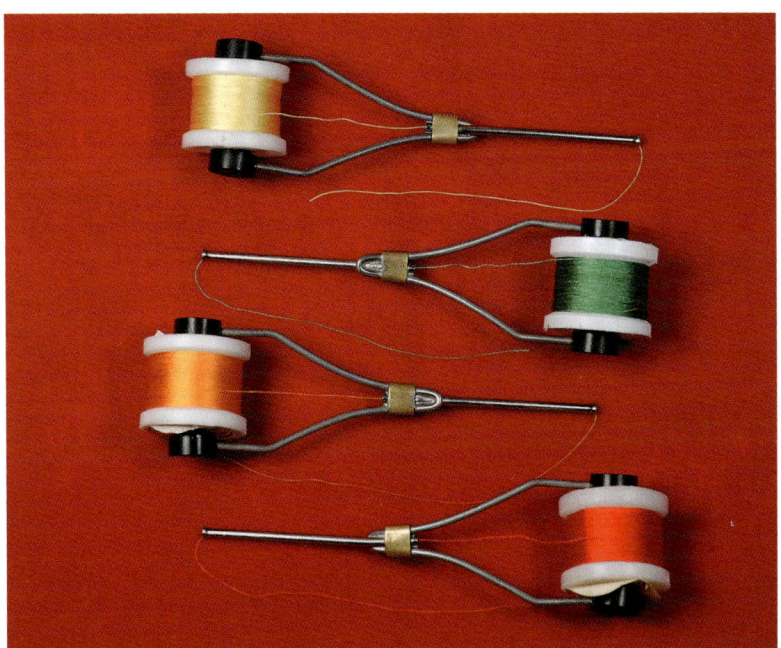

Too few tool companies now make bobbins designed specifically to hold small thread spools, such as those on which Pearsall's Gossamer Silks are wound. These are extremely handy, and it's even more convenient to keep them spooled with each of the thread colors you use most often, so you don't have to re-thread your bobbin each time you switch from one fly pattern to another. In my wet-fly tying, I always have bobbins holding primrose yellow, green, orange, and crimson gossamer silk threads.

enough to tempt trout, and also helps prevent the fly from lifting up and planing in the surface currents. Rarely will any trout but a tiddler take a waking wet fly. I tie about 80 percent of my soft-hackles on this heavier hook.

You'll need just a few specialty items for tying soft-hackles. The first is beeswax. Use it to dress the first inch of tying silk to make it stick to the shank when you start the thread. Use it again to dress the last inch of thread that will become the whip-finished head, to help seat it and hold it tight. The second is very tacky dubbing wax, to touch up the thread before applying dubbing to it. Silk is not waxed; a sticky wax applied where you need it helps you construct the spiky dubbing that you'd like in the finished fly.

The third item is a thread bobbin that will hold small spools of Pearsall's silks with the correct tension. It's not difficult to take pliers and bend the wire stems of a regular bobbin so that it will hold the smaller spools. If you must do this, do it carefully, and work at it until you've got the tension right to release thread only when you roll the spool with your thumb. Once you've got it adjusted, leave it dedicated to the small spools. Don't try to get by with a single bobbin for all of your fly tying, bending it back and forth to suit the size spool you're going to use next. You know what happens to metal when you bend it too many times.

TYING A SPARSE SOFT-HACKLE

I'll choose as a standard the Partridge & Yellow, not only because it is representative, but also because it catches lots of trout for me. I tie it in sizes 10 through 16. I fish it most often on small streams and in riffles or runs of larger rivers, in the larger sizes: 10, 12, and 14. The smaller size is trotted out only in situations where a hatch of Sulphur or Pale Morning Dun mayflies or small tannish cream caddis creates a demand for it.

You might wonder how I keep those tied on light-wire hooks separate from the standards tied on heavy-wire hooks. It's pretty easy. I tie them on dry-fly hooks most often for small streams, in sizes 10 and 12, and put them in the fly box dedicated to small-stream fishing. If I tie them on light hooks for a specific hatch, say a size 16 Partridge & Yellow for the Pale Morning Dun hatch, then they go into the box I keep specifically for that hatch, filled as well with the variety of drys, nymphs, and emergers that I fish for the same hatch.

The remaining bulk of the soft-hackles that I tie on standard wet-fly hooks go into my wet-fly box. With few exceptions, for example the Starling & Herl, all the other flies in that box will be tied on heavy-wire hooks.

PARTRIDGE & YELLOW

Hook:	#10-16 1X fine or 2X heavy
Thread:	Primrose Pearsall's Gossamer Silk or yellow 8/0 nylon thread
Hackle:	Gray partridge
Body:	Two layers of working thread or yellow silk floss
Thorax:	Hare's mask fur or natural (#1) Hare's Ear Plus (optional)

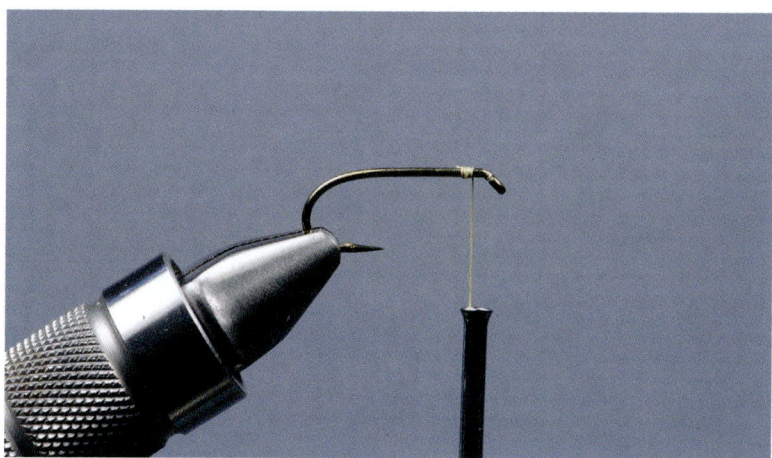

1. Flatten the barb on the hook and fix it in the vise. Dress an inch of silk thread with beeswax. Start the thread with a couple of turns over itself to lock it in, then take four to five turns forward to a point just behind the hook eye. Clip the thread tag.

2. Select a gray partridge feather from the skin. The individual fibers should be a bit longer than the hook shank, or about twice the width of the hook gap. Peel away the fuzzy excess fibers from the lower end of the feather stem, leaving only those fibers that are well marked. Hold the tip and flare the fibers from the stem. The hackle is now prepared for a traditional soft-hackled tie.

3. Hold the hackle with the concave side toward you, and peel away the fibers from the top half of the stem. This is far from mandatory, but it will result in a finished fly with hackle exactly half as heavy as a normal tie.

Note: If you live in a dry climate, and you have trouble with hackle stems breaking when you begin to wind them, run your thumbnail down the stem for a quarter inch from the tie-in point, before you tie it in. This flattens the stem and keeps it from breaking when you later begin to wrap it around the hook shank. This trick was taught to me by Barry White, noted Edmonton, Alberta, tier.

4. Tie the hackle stem to the top of the hook just behind the eye, with the concave side of the feather toward you. Tying in the hackle as the first step makes for a neater head later, and also lets you lock the stem under the body, and lock the hackle turns under the thread upon completion of the fly, thus protecting it against the teeth of all the trout you expect to catch.

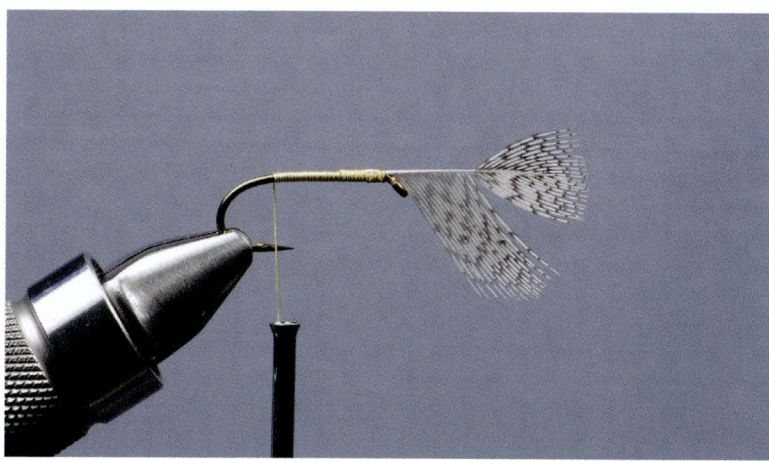

5. Take about ten turns of thread back over the hook shank and hackle stem, butting each wrap against the one before it. Clip the excess stem and continue adjacent thread wraps to a point just short of the hook bend. On most hook styles, the right place to end the body is at a point on the shank straight above the midpoint between the hook point and the back end of the smashed barb.

6. Reverse the thread wraps toward the eye of the hook, again being sure to butt them tightly together. This makes a body of two layers of silk thread. If you were to start at the back and make a single wrap to the front, the dark hook shank would show through the single layer of thread once the fly got wet, and you would not have the color you thought you had when the fly was dry. Stop the thread about $1/8$ inch behind the tie-in point of the hackle.

7. Touch up an inch of the tying thread with your tacky wax. This should be adjacent to the hook shank, not an inch or two away from it. You can use beeswax or any modern fly-tying wax, but tacky dubbing wax is best. Its purpose is to hold the thorax fur to the thread without the need to twist it up tightly. Your goal for the thorax is a loosely bound knot of fur.

8. Take a small pinch of hare's mask fur, or your pre-blended substitute, and tease it into a skein about an inch long. Touch this to the waxed thread, which should hold it. Twist the top and bottom of the skein tightly to the thread, but leave the center portion loose, or twisted just slightly, so that it adheres to the thread.

9. Take three to five turns of dubbing just behind the hackle tie-in point. It should have fibers sticking out in all directions. My rule, far from firm, is to pluck only those stray hairs—and Sparkle Yarn fibers if you're using the optional Hare's Ear Plus—that will be longer than the hackle fibers when the hackle is wound. Your thread, at this point, should be behind the hackle tie-in point. Do not take the thread in front of the hackle.

10. Fasten your hackle pliers to the hackle tip. Be sure they grip part of the stem, not just fibers. Pliers with rubber-coated tips work best with fragile soft-hackle feathers. Metal hackle pliers have a habit of scissoring through such wispy material. Take a single turn of hackle just behind the hook eye, leaving enough room for the whip-finish.

11. Tuck a second turn of hackle just behind the first, without matting down any of the fibers from the first turn. The hackle fibers should stand away from the hook shank at about a 90-degree angle, with a gentle curve toward the back of the hook. If your hackle fibers lean forward, you peeled off the wrong side of the hackle in Step 3.

12. While holding the hackle tip with the pliers, work just two or three turns of thread down onto the stem, locking it to the hook shank. Note that this is done *behind* the hackle turns, not in front of them. Clip the excess hackle tip near its tie-down point.

13. Take three or four turns of thread forward through the hackle to the hook eye. Wobble the thread bobbin back and forth as you go, thus seating the wraps without matting down any hackle fibers. This step might turn a few of the fibers forward, but this is not a problem; a natural insect awash in the water is not a neat organization. It's better to have a few fibers out of place than it is to fish a fly that comes apart after a few trout.

14. Take just enough thread turns to tidy the head without knocking the hackle fibers off their 90-degree stance. Wax an inch of thread. Place a three- to five-turn whip-finish between the hook eye and the hackle, either by hand or with a whip-finish tool.

Because silk thread is thick compared to 6/0 or 8/0 nylon, avoid taking any unnecessary turns when tying a soft-hackled fly, or any other wet fly. Doing so will add nothing to the durability of the fly, but will add awkward bulk to it wherever those extra turns are taken. For example, if you use more than a single layer to start the thread, then two or three layers to tie in the hackle, you'll end with a crowded and bulky head when you finish the fly. There's nothing worse in all of fly tying than getting to the end of the entire tying operation and discovering that you've left no room to place a whip-finish.

Extra turns of silk thread can result in lumpy bodies, matted hackles, cramped heads, and flies that in general look like tumbleweeds. They'll still take trout. Perhaps they'll take as many trout as those that are tied neatly. We all have to start tying some time, and not one of us started off tying flies that approached perfection. Set your goals for neatness and sparseness, but don't forget that trout don't always agree with those goals. Tie your wet flies as nicely as you can, but if they aren't perfect, don't let that stop you from going fishing with them. They won't let you down, and you'll get far more pleasure fishing your own flies than you will ever get out of those that somebody else ties for you.

TYING A SOFT-HACKLE WITH A FULL PARTRIDGE HACKLE

An alternative is to tie the fly with the full partridge hackle, being careful to take just one to one and a half turns. This gives an effect in which most but not all of the hackle fibers curve back. Some straggle forward in slight opposition, an effect mildly less aesthetic but not bad in terms of the way the fly fishes. It also eliminates the extra step of peeling half the hackle away. This might be the more common way to tie a soft-hackle.

1. De-barb the hook, fix it in your vise, and wax and attach the silk thread. Choose a hackle with fibers of appropriate length, and strip the fuzzy ones from the lower end of the stem. Flare the remaining fibers at 90-degree angles to the stem, and tie the hackle to the hook with the concave side toward you.

2. Wind a level body of two layers of tying thread, wax an inch of the thread, and dub a loose thorax just behind the hackle tie-in point.

3. Wind one full turn of hackle. Catch the hackle tip with your thread, and bind it down with two to three turns. Snip excess hackle. Work three to four turns of thread forward through the hackle to the hook eye, wobbling your bobbin back and forth to avoid matting down fibers. Wax an inch of thread and whip-finish.

You might come to prefer the fly finished this way, with the hackle less neat. Certainly the water will tug the hackle fibers this way and that, no matter how you tie it. You will find no difference in the way the fly takes fish, and it will take one fewer step to tie it, saving time.

TYING A SOFT-HACKLE WITH A FLOSS BODY

If you have trouble finding Pearsall's Gossamer Silk Thread, or just prefer to tie with slightly brighter floss, I recommend you use Pearsall's Marabou Silk Floss rather than rayon floss. It holds its shape better when tied and shows off its brilliant colors better when wet.

Marabou floss comes in a two-strand twist. For size 10 to 14 hooks, use both strands. For size 16 and smaller, use only one of the strands. Split them by untwisting the two strands, inserting a dubbing needle, and sliding it along the floss to separate it. To tie a soft-hackled wet with a floss body rather than Gossamer silk thread, use 6/0 or 8/0 nylon thread in a color the same as the body of the fly. For the Partridge & Yellow use yellow or tan thread.

Tie in the floss body at the back and wrap it forward, rather than tying in at the front and wrapping in a layer to the back and another layer to the front, for two reasons. First, it's not necessary to use two layers of the thicker floss for its color to dominate the hook color when the fly is wet. Second, if you begin at the forward end, wrap to the hook bend, then reverse with another layer to the front, the floss at the back end will invariably work its way down over the bend after you've fished the fly for awhile. It might not change the way the fly fishes, but it will be a bit unsightly. By tying the floss in tightly at the back, it will be anchored there, and will not creep down over the hook bend later.

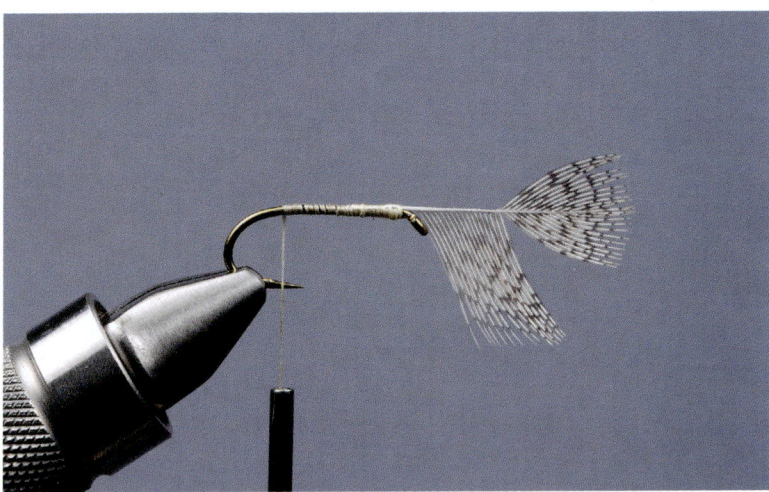

1. Place the hook in the vise, attach the thread, and prepare and tie in the hackle just behind the hook eye. Wind thread over the hackle stem about $^1/_3$ the length of the hook shank. Clip the excess stem, and continue thread wraps to the back to where you want the body to begin.

2. Clip 3 to 4 inches of floss, and divide the floss strands if you're tying on a small hook. The goal is a slender body, not a fat one. Lay the floss alongside the hook with the end extending to the point where you clipped the hackle stem. This provides an even base for the body. Tie the floss tightly to the hook shank with four or five turns of thread, then layer thread forward over the remaining floss to the end of the hackle stem, the point where you want the thorax to begin.

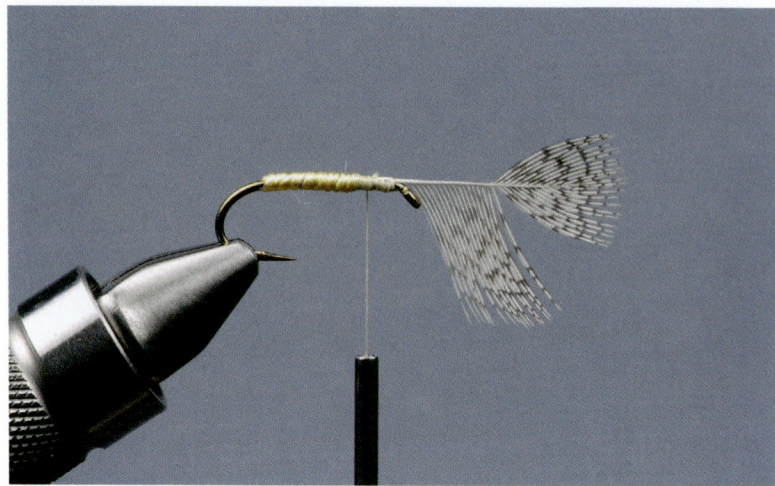

3. Wind the floss tightly forward to the thread, tie it off, and clip the excess. You can adjust the thickness of the body by twisting the floss slightly to fatten it, or untwisting it to flatten it. Either way, be sure the wraps are tightly adjacent, and the hook shank is covered, none showing through.

4. Dub a short and rough thorax. Take a turn or two of hackle back to the thread, tie off the hackle, clip the excess, and work the thread through it to the eye of the hook. Lay a neat base for the head and whip-finish. The finished fly is slightly less slender than one tied with a body of working silk, but it will fish just as well.

TYING A SOFT-HACKLE WITHOUT THE FUR THORAX

Traditionally soft-hackles, or spiders as they were originally called, were tied without the thorax to prop the hackles. A partridge or grouse pattern tied with a thorax looks buggier and has more lively hackles when fished in water with substantial current. I prefer them tied with a thorax most of the time. But you should learn to tie soft-hackles without the thorax. It's not difficult; you just leave it out. If you're a traditionalist, you'll prefer them without a thorax. A lot of it is in the eye of the beholder. It's not certain that trout have an opinion in the matter, but it is certain that soft-hackles can be tied more quickly without the thorax.

1. Fix the hook in the vise, start the thread, prepare and tie in the hackle, and clip the excess hackle stem close behind the tie-in point. If the body is Gossamer silk thread, wrap a layer back to a point at or just beyond the hook point, then another layer forward over the first to the base of the hackle.

2. Take one or two turns of the hackle, ending with the hackle tip behind the hackle wraps. Tie it off and clip the excess hackle tip. Work the thread forward through the hackle, whip-finish the fly, and clip the thread. That's it.

Alternate Step 1. If the body is floss, prepare and tie in the hackle, then take the 6/0 or 8/0 nylon thread to the end of the body, and tie in the floss with the tag end reaching the back of the hackle. Overwrap it to that point tightly with thread. Wind the floss to the base of the hackle, tie it off, and clip the excess. This forms an even body.

Alternate Step 2. Wind the hackle, tie it off, and clip the excess. Work the thread through the hackle to the hook eye, form a neat head, and whip-finish.

TYING A HERL-BODIED SOFT-HACKLE

Tying a small fly such as the Starling & Herl requires some slight increase in delicacy but is not much different from the procedures for tying a partridge-hackled pattern. You want to be sure that both the peacock herl body and the fragile starling hackle are locked into place, not susceptible to being cut by the teeth of a few trout. For a durable fly, tie as follows.

STARLING & HERL

Hook:	#14-18 1X fine or 2X heavy
Thread:	Black or iron gray 8/0
Hackle:	Starling body feather with iridescent sheen
Body:	Two strands peacock herl

1. Fix hook in the vise and attach the thread. Select a starling body feather, strip the fuzzy fibers from the butt, and tie the feather in just behind the hook eye with the concave side toward you. Starling is much more delicate than partridge; you'll need to be gentle with it. Clip the excess hackle stem, and wind the thread back to the beginning of the bend of the hook.

2. Strip two peacock herls from the peacock eye feather stem. Break off about an inch of the very fragile tips. Tie the two strands in by their remaining tips, at the rear of the hook, using very light thread turns at first to keep the thread from cutting through the herl.

3. Form a thread loop by catching the thread over the tip of your off-hand forefinger, returning the thread to the hook shank, and taking several more turns of thread around the shank, back to the tie-in point for the herl, to lock in the loop. (The end of the loop should extend beyond the length of the herl strands. For photographic purposes, the loop is shortened in this photo.)

4. Take the working thread forward to the back of the hackle. Catch the ends of the herl together with the thread loop, let the loop collapse, and twist the thread and herls together to form a herl rope. The herls don't need to be inside the loop; twisting them alongside it is fine. Don't twist so tightly that the herls break at the tie-in point. By twisting the herl into a rope with the thread, it will be locked in so that a trout's teeth cannot cut it and cause the fly body to unravel.

5. Wrap the herl rope forward to the base of the hackle. Twist the rope as you wrap it forward, to counter its tendency to untwist. Tie off the herl rope and clip the excess at the tie-in point for the hackle. Be sure to leave room for a few turns of the hackle and the head of the fly.

6. Wrap two or three turns of hackle, using a soft touch with the pliers. Take the first turn just behind the hook eye, each subsequent turn behind the turn before it. The hackle will be more attractive, and perhaps more effective, if these turns are slightly spaced rather than bunched. Catch the hackle tip with the thread, secure it with two to three more turns, and clip the tip. At this point the thread is behind the hackle.

7. Wind three to six turns of thread through the hackle, forward to the hook eye. Work the thread back and forth as you go, to avoid trapping hackle fibers under the thread. The thread is now in front of the hackle.

8. Use the fingertips of your off-hand to hold the hackle fibers out of the way. Lay an even base with minimal turns of thread behind the hook eye, place your whip-finish, and clip the thread.

I'm either a heretic or lazy: I rarely use head cement. If you use it, run the clipped hackle tip through the eye of the hook to wick off any excess cement, to be sure it doesn't dry and block the eye. This also ensures that the eye is not blocked by an oversized thread head. If anything is more frustrating than trying to thread tippet through the eye of a hook in the midst of exciting fishing and discovering that you can't do it, I don't know what it might be.

TYING A STEWART–STYLE SPIDER

You might enjoy tying and fishing spiders as W. C. Stewart might have tied them, based on those illustrated in his 1857 book, *The Practical Angler*. If you do, I promise you'll have no trouble catching fish on them. His directions call for tying in the hackle at the midpoint of the hook, then twisting it around the tying thread and wrapping it forward to the hook eye. I've tried this, but all I ever accomplish is a hackle that breaks at the tie-in point before I've got it wrapped. I might be heavy-handed, but I've found it necessary to work out a different way to achieve what Stewart illustrates.

W. C. Stewart tied his Black Spider with starling, his Red Spider with landrail, and his Dun Spider with dotteral. It's difficult today to find any but the starling. I've fiddled with substituting black, brown, and blue dun hen hackle, tying them with complementary black, brown, and gray threads. They will usually be fished shallow, in small streams; tie them on 1X fine hooks in size 12 to 16.

1. Place the hook in the vise and attach the thread. Choose an iridescent starling feather from either the body or wing shoulder. Strip fuzzy fibers from the base of the hackle stem. Tie in the hackle with the concave side toward you, the tip extending over the eye of the hook. Overwrap the hackle stem to the midpoint of the hook, and clip the excess.

2. Fasten your hackle pliers gently to the hackle tip. Take five to ten evenly spaced turns of hackle—as many as the feather will provide—back to the midpoint of the hook. Catch the hackle tip with two or three turns of thread before clipping the excess.

Note: You might want to merely twitch the hackle pliers toward the front of the hook, snapping off the tip rather than clipping it with your scissors. On occasion the stem will break behind the tie, leaving some excess tip that you'll have to sneak in and clip. Most of the time it will break off right at the thread wraps. Rarely will your hackle come unwound when you snap it off rather than cutting it off, as long as you've caught it under the thread and taken an extra turn or two.

3. Work your thread forward through the hackle to the hook eye, wobbling the thread back and forth if necessary to avoid matting down any hackle. This step is critical; without it, the fragile starling hackle stem will break and unwind on the first fish you catch. Whip-finish, and the fly is ready to fish.

Your finished spider will have hackle spread evenly over the front half of the hook shank. If all has gone well, it will be a sparse, shapely, and extremely durable tie, one that will take many fish for you, just as it did for Stewart more than a century ago.

TYING SOFT-HACKLES WITH OVERSIZED HACKLE

It's possible to use large partridge feathers to tie soft-hackles on small hooks, but it's best to avoid the necessity, by using the tiny feathers gathered around the head of the cape, if you've got one that has been skinned properly. If not, the problem is to reduce long fibers so that they are proportional on the small fly.

The solution is to tie the hackle at the midpoint or even farther to the rear of the hook shank, wind it there, then overwrap it with thread to the eye. Flare the fibers into the position they would take if a hackle were wrapped at that point. It's not perfect. The points of the hackle fibers lack much of the subtle backward curve hackles have when from a feather of the correct size. The fibers are also stiff out toward their tips.

Hackles tied in this fashion lack some of what you look for in a soft-hackled wet fly: that quivering with every ripple of current. It's never a good solution if you have an entire partridge skin available, with a full range of feathers. Nevertheless, it's a way to tie size 16, 18, or even 20 soft-hackles when all you have are larger feathers. Try it if you must. Use 8/0 thread.

1. Lay a base of thread from the eye to about the midpoint of the hook shank. Prepare a hackle feather, and tie it in near the center of the hook. (You must calculate the tie-in point so the hackle tips, after the hackle is overwrapped with thread to the hook eye, will be the right length for the size hook on which you're tying. This will naturally require some measuring practice.)

2. Take one or two turns of hackle and tie it off. Keep it sparse. Clip the excess tip.

3. Pull the hackle fibers forward, and overwind them to a point just behind the eye of the hook. Be sure to surround the hook with the hackle tips, so that when you flare them later, they will make a full collar rather than be bunched. The overwrappings of thread form the body of the fly. Use more than one layer, and adjust them where necessary to smooth out lumps from tying in the hackle.

4. Use your thumb and first two fingernails to work the fibers up into a hackle collar behind the eye of the hook. The body should brace the fibers from behind. Use a few turns of thread in front of the hackle to brace it in front. Whip-finishing completes the fly.

A FEW FAVORITE SOFT-HACKLES

The number of soft-hackles it would take to improve your fishing a lot can fit in a very small space in a fly box you already own. If you choose to add a soft-hackle box to your vest, it won't be a big one and needn't take up much room. I carry just a few soft-hackle dressings for the general run of fishing, plus a few for use during specific hatches.

Partridge & Yellow: This is the dressing listed as the sample fly tied earlier in the chapter. I use it most often in small streams, in sizes 10 and 12, for fishing plunge pools full of trout sometimes bashful about coming up to dry flies in bright sunlight. For these situations I tie the fly on a standard 1X fine dry-fly hook, to keep it from plunging right to the bottom in the slow and shallow pools.

The Partridge & Yellow is also excellent when any Sulphur or yellowish mayfly is hatching. Since most of these migrate off to the sides of the fast water where their nymphs live before emergence, I also tie those for hatches on fine-wire hooks because they will usually be fished shallow. When trout are taking Sulphurs at the edges, I often cast a soft-hackle in toward the gentle currents next to shore and coax the fly around and downstream on a very slow swing.

The Partridge & Yellow is the author's favorite soft-hackle for exploring, or searching fishing, when trout are not visibly feeding and must be sought out by fishing lots of water. But it's also excellent before, after, and even during hatches of insects such as the Pale Morning Dun shown here. Lots of the naturals fail to emerge successfully, and are taken by trout beneath the surface. A Partridge & Yellow is often just the right fly in these situations.

PARTRIDGE & GREEN

Hook:	#10-18 1X fine or 2X heavy
Thread:	Green Pearsall's Gossamer Silk or olive 8/0
Hackle:	Gray partridge
Body:	Two layers of working silk or green silk floss
Thorax:	Hare's mask fur or natural (#1) Hare's Ear Plus (optional)

Partridge & Green: This fly seems to fish best when adult caddis are in the air but trout are not taking them. I suspect it resembles many ascending caddis pupae with olive bodies, but cannot prove that with observations in fishing situations, since I'm reluctant to use stomach pumps on trout for fear of what a stomach pump would feel like if a trout used one on me. I've collected caddis pupae often, however, and a great number of species arrive in bright green dress.

Because these pupae come off in open water, often in or around riffles and fast runs, it's best to fish the Partridge & Green on a mended swing, down and across the current, in the same kind of water. For such fishing it's wise to tie the flies on 2X heavy hooks. I do tie this one in size 16 and sometimes 18 on fine-wire hooks, because it has such a resemblance to drowned Blue-Winged Olive duns.

I recall an incident on the South Fork of the Snake River, fishing with surgeon Greg Lundmark, when the Partridge & Green tied on the slightest of hooks, in size 16, worked sudden wonders. The water was broad, slick on top, gliding in great wide flats over a rocky bottom 3 to 5 feet deep. Tiny olive mayfly duns, size 22 BWOs, floated up top, and trout seemed to be feeding them. But neither Greg nor I had anything that would match them well enough to fool the fish. We arrived at approximately the same solution independently, at opposite ends of a flat that was about 100 yards long. I could look upstream and tell that Greg was into fish. He could look downstream and tell that I was into fish. Neither of us could tell what the other was fishing.

We got together later, after catching about twenty trout apiece, and compared notes. Greg got frustrated by the tiny *Baetis*, switched to a size 12 Partridge & Green fished on the swing, under the hatch. I got frustrated and fished a size 16 Partridge & Green on the swing, in the same manner.

We'd selected the same pattern based on the same logic: Trout were feeding on something olive on or very near the surface. We didn't have any dry flies that matched what was happening, but we did have subsurface flies that looked a little like what was hatching, if what was hatching got drowned before it hatched. The size in both cases was off. But the triggering characteristic must have been the color. This was not the most aesthetic solution, fishing wet flies to rising trout that might have taken drys had we possessed any in size 22 and the right color. But we didn't, and we were able to goose lots of trout into the air with those ill-sized soft-hackles fished just under the emerging mayflies and the rising trout.

I still wonder why trout were foolish enough to take my size 16 Partridge & Green, let alone Greg's size 12.

GROUSE & ORANGE

Hook:	#10-16 1X fine or 2X heavy
Thread:	Orange Pearsall's Gossamer Silk or orange 8/0
Hackle:	Grouse wing shoulder feather
Body:	Two layers of working silk or orange silk floss
Thorax:	Hare's mask fur or natural (#1) Hare's Ear Plus (optional)

Grouse & Orange: This fly fishes well when any number of natural caddis adults are out. It resembles many of the darker species in both hackle and body colors. It's also an excellent imitation of many caddis pupae rising toward the surface. Because most of this kind of activity takes place in and around relatively fast water, it's usually best to tie the fly on heavy-wire hooks.

Like the Partridge & Yellow and Partridge & Green, the Grouse & Orange also makes an excellent searching fly whenever you're fishing somewhat shallow and rumpled water, you have no idea what trout want, and you'd like to tie something on that covers lots of water and gives you a good chance to hoist a trout. All soft-hackles, fished alone or as pairs, are excellent exploring patterns. The methods with which they're fished make it easy to step-and-cast down long reaches of water, showing your wet flies to lots of potential lies.

MARCH BROWN SPIDER

Hook:	#10-16 1X fine or 2X heavy
Thread:	Orange Pearsall's Gossamer Silk or orange 8/0
Hackle:	Brown partridge
Rib:	Oval gold tinsel
Body:	Hare's mask fur or natural (#1) Hare's Ear Plus

March Brown Spider: This valuable wet fly has a rough fur body and is a combination of soft-hackle and flymph. The body should be dubbed loosely and left spiky, to make it imitative of many insects that drown, dive down to deposit their eggs, or rise toward the surface for emergence. It's not an imitation of any particular insect, but it has a rough resemblance to lots of them.

I fish the March Brown Spider often, usually as a searching pattern when nothing specific is going on, and I want to cover the water, find some fish. But I've also had success with it during evening caddis activity, and suspect it looks like the female adults diving down to lay their eggs on the bottom. I've also used it during Western March Brown mayfly hatches. It has a striking likeness to the many shipwrecked duns, unable to escape their shucks to emerge in the surface film, left stranded after a March Brown hatch.

FEBRUARY RED

Hook:	#12-16 1X fine or 2X heavy
Thread:	Crimson Pearsall's Gossamer Silk or red 8/0
Hackle:	Grouse wing shoulder feather
Body:	Two layers of working silk or red silk floss

February Red: I mentioned fishing this fly when Early Brown Stoneflies are out, starting in February and continuing on in some areas through March and April. They're small insects, on the stonefly scale, perfect for soft-hackles tied on size 12 to 16 hooks. This version of the February Red is different from the Partridge & Orange only in the color of its body and the lack of a fur thorax. You would not be making a mistake to choose between them and carry only one.

The Early Brown Stone group includes several families of small stoneflies, many genera, and more species than even an entomologist would care to identify. This is an adult Needle Fly, so named for its slender body and tightly held wings. This and its many relatives are widespread, appearing in late winter and early spring almost everywhere trout are found. A February Red soft-hackle works well when trout feed on them.

The Starling & Herl is an excellent choice whenever small, dark caddis adults are in the air and on the water. This is a gathering of size 16 Black Caddis (*Brachycentrus*) collected after an overnight frost on Montana's Bighorn River. During the daily hatch, a Starling & Herl will at times take trout that refuse floating imitations.

Starling & Herl: The dressing and steps in tying this pattern were given earlier in the chapter, on pages 65–70. It's a wonderful fly that represents many small insects, including ants and beetles that fall to the water from the terrestrial environment. But it's best during a hatch of American Grannoms or Mother's Day Caddis: small, dark, and prolific caddis in the family Brachycentridae. These hatch from May through September, in great numbers at one time or another on almost any American trout stream you could name. Trout key on them and feed selectively when hatches are heavy. They feed on them consistently, though not as selectively, when the hatches are a trickle.

I suspect the Starling & Herl is an excellent imitation of both the pupal and drowned adult stages of these caddis. I know that when they're coming off, a size 16 or 18 Starling & Herl usually does at least some wonders against trout that are snots about drys. Fish the little wet fly upstream to rises, or on a cross-stream cast that delivers it dead-drift to feeding fish.

MOTHER'S DAY CADDIS

Hook:	#14-16 1X fine standard dry fly
Thread:	Black 8/0
Body:	Peacock herl
Hackle:	Partridge, wound, then gathered over the back of the fly
Head:	Mole fur
Note:	The hackle fibers should extend a bit beyond the hook bend. To make a feather with long fibers work on a small hook, tie in and wind the hackle just behind the hook eye, draw it back and up over the body, then overwind it with thread. By tying it in farther to the front, it becomes shorter at the back.

Mother's Day Caddis: One of my fondest memories of fishing with Sylvester Nemes and his wife, Hazel, happened in early May, on the Yellowstone River near Carter's Bridge, just upstream from Livingston, Montana. Runoff was imminent, but so was Sylvester's favorite Mother's Day Caddis hatch. It's a size 16 or 18 dark insect in the same genus, *Brachycentrus*, as the Black Caddis from the Bighorn, but it's less dark, more brown than black. It often hatches in such huge numbers that floating adults form small rafts along soft edge currents. Trout naturally appreciate that.

The air was nippy, and snow still blanketed the Absaroka Mountains above the river to the east when we went out. The water was clear, though as gray as steel, reflecting dense and threatening clouds in the sky. It felt more like winter than spring, but we'd beat runoff by a few days.

Nothing happened until early afternoon, when the air and water were as warm as they were going to get that day. Then, as if turned on by magic, dark caddis adults began appearing as a speckling on the near-shore waters. Trout noses instantly appeared to approve this advent. Most trout sipped. Others fed greedily. None could keep up with the infinite supply of emerging insects.

When the Mother's Day Caddis hatch comes off before runoff, they emerge in their thousands, trout feed on them heavily, and you can have some fine wet-fly fishing, though dry flies will fool trout as well. Drys are just a lot more difficult to fish among such high numbers of naturals.

I fished dry flies, but faced that ancient dilemma: How do you follow the drift of your imitation among such a vast fleet of naturals? It gets lost among them. Soon you find yourself setting the hook to rises that you think are to your fly, but they're not, and you blow the fly out of there, frighten some fish. Or you notice a take near what you're following as your fly, realize too late that what you're watching is a natural, and that the rise was to your dry, which by then has been rejected. So it goes. I did catch a few.

Syl had none of this trouble. He tied on his Mother's Day Caddis soft-hackle, fished it on short casts that let it swing slowly down and around on those same soft currents. He felt takes when they happened, which was alarmingly often, and goosed far more trout into the air than I did. Hazel fished just upstream from us, doing approximately the same thing Syl did, with about the same results.

I had to whine a bit before I was able to borrow a Mother's Day Caddis soft-hackle from Syl. Then the fishing became easy, and it went on for two or three hours, long after the hatch itself had slowly trickled off toward nothing. Apparently a few of those caddis adults still drifted along drowned, or the trout simply remembered them well enough to be willing to continue taking the soft-hackle, because we caught fish for another hour after the last visible caddis was gone off the water.

The Mother's Day Caddis hatch happens all over the West, and in some slight modifications, in the Midwest and East as well. Sometimes it happens during runoff from snowmelt, and the chance to fish it is missed for the year. Other times it happens before runoff, and it's possible to get in a week or more fishing over it before the hatch ends, or runoff ends fishing over it. We enjoyed the same exceptional fishing for two more days, there in Paradise Valley. Then runoff hit with a smack. It didn't end the hatch, but it did end our fishing.

SOFT-HACKLED TRICO

Hook:	#20 standard dry fly
Thread:	Black 8/0
Tail:	Three or four strands clear Polypro yarn
Body:	Mole fur
Hackle:	Dirty-white hen
Head:	Mole fur

Soft-Hackled Trico: This is a Sylvester Nemes dressing, from his book *Soft-Hackled Fly Imitations*, that is well worth trying whenever you fish over those tiniest and most difficult mayflies, size 20 to 24 Tricos. Trout feed on spinners that fall in great masses in early morning or shortly thereafter. So many of the naturals land on the water at once that trout become maddeningly selective. At times they'll refuse your best efforts with any dry fly. At the same time, they'll often fall for a soft-hackle that bears a slight resemblance to the naturals, fished just inches deep.

I've been so frustrated with dry flies on the Missouri River in Montana, during an August Trico fall, that I've given up, got down near the water, watched with binoculars while trout fed during a massive presence of spinners. Such close observation revealed that most of the trout, though they sent up rise-rings that broke the surface, making it appear their takes were on top, were actually feeding scant inches deep on spinners that had drowned and were adrift in the currents.

When that happens, a soft-hackled wet fly can turn the trick.

SNIPE & YELLOW

Hook:	#16-20 1X fine or 2X heavy
Thread:	Yellow Pearsall's Gossamer Silk or yellow 8/0 nylon
Hackle:	British snipe wing shoulder feather
Body:	Two layers of working thread or yellow floss
Note:	The original Snipe & Yellow calls for British snipe wing. It's available through shops and online sources that change frequently enough that you'll have to track it down. If you're a hunter who specializes in snipe, or can get wings from a friend, American snipe is a bit different color, but I've used it and trout haven't complained.

Snipe & Yellow: This dressing is too traditional to leave off any soft-hackle list. I don't tie and fish it a lot, but it's reputation as a killer on spring creeks during hatches of tiny tan caddis makes it one to know about, and one worth trying if you get into such hatches and suspect trout feed more heavily on rising pupae than they do on floating adults.

SNIPE & PURPLE

Hook:	#16-20 1X fine or 2X heavy
Thread:	Purple Pearsall's Gossamer Silk or purple 8/0
Hackle:	British snipe wing shoulder feather
Body:	Two layers of working thread or purple floss

Snipe & Purple: This one is just too pretty to leave off the list. I don't fish it often, but its history goes back to Pritt and probably to oral traditions before soft-hackles were ever written about. All that was required to tie it was the wing off a poached British or Scottish snipe and a bit of purple yarn snitched from a sewing basket. Of course a hook was also required. Back in the misty origins of this little dressing, a hook was certainly the most difficult part of the fly to acquire. Some were bent from sewing needles purloined from the same baskets as the purple threads.

Just a small selection of soft-hackled dressings will put you into business when you might otherwise find fishing slow. Many knowledgeable fly fishers, who spend a lot of hours on the water, catch an increasing percentage of their trout on soft-hackles each season, as they try them and learn to rely on them more often.

Chapter Six

Tying Flymphs

The dominant feature of the wingless wet fly, or flymph, as tied by James Leisenring and Pete Hidy in their book *The Art of Tying the Wet Fly & Fishing the Flymph*, is the body. Unlike a soft-hackle, in which the wavering fibers of the hackle constitute almost all the action of the fly, a flymph has a loosely dubbed fur body whose fibers quiver in the current and cause the fly to look alive. The hackle is important, and is far from lifeless, but it doesn't dominate the body of the fly.

The purpose of that spiky body goes beyond its lifelike look and action in the current. In a well-tied flymph, the body and hackle entrap bubbles of air and take them beneath the surface. Many aquatic insects are buoyed to the surface for emergence by similar trapped bubbles of air. Adult insects that dive to the bottom to lay their eggs also entrap air and take it down with them. When your flymph traps air and escorts it beneath the surface, the fly looks like many of the things that trout are accustomed to eating.

A properly tied flymph body shows the primary color of any insect that is around when fish are feeding, plus some slight undercolor that shows through when the fly is wet in the water. The primary color comes from the selected dubbing fur. The undercolor comes from the thread on which the fur is spun. The two colors should harmonize with each other. They should also be in harmony with whatever insect is available to trout at the time you're fishing the fly.

Materials needed for tying flymphs are minimal. You'll use the same Pearsall's Gossamer Silk Thread colors that you used to make the bodies for soft-hackled wets: yellow, green, orange, and crimson red. These are the most common undercolors desired beneath fur bodies.

Body furs for flymphs come from a narrow array of animals. Hare's mask is the most popular and most versatile. You can shear the entire mask, put all of the fur together into a blender, tumble it until it's thoroughly blended, and you'll have a dark brownish fur with lots of spiky guard hairs in it. This color will copy a lot of the insects you encounter. The dubbing mix is so buggy that you can nearly always turn to a fly tied with it and fool fish.

You'll rarely make a mistake, for example, by tying on a March Brown Flymph when a few tan or brown caddisfly adults are in the air, which is true on most summer days when it's pleasant to be out after trout.

You can also shear various parts of the hare's mask, blend them separately and store each in its own Ziploc bag. For example, shearing the ears and half of the hair between them, called the *poll*, will give you a superb tannish dubbing with lots of spike to it. Shearing the cheeks and face will give you a somewhat darker and softer dubbing. If you shear the remainder of the poll and blend the fur to mix the guard hairs and underfur, you'll have a dubbing lighter in color than the other two. Thus you achieve a range of light, medium, and dark hare's mask dubbings, tan to brown, that covers lots of natural insect colors.

You can add clear Sparkle Yarn to any or all of the blends. Cut it into $1/4$-inch snippets, and add it to the blender in a ratio of about 1 part Sparkle Yarn to 3 or 4 parts fur.

Muskrat, or water rat as it's called in historic British books, furnishes gray dubbing of a fine texture. If you acquire an entire pelt and shear a section from the belly around to the back, then blend it, you'll have a wonderful mid-gray with underfur and guard hairs included. You can also shear a small patch of belly, a small patch at the midline between belly and back, and a patch of the dark back. Blend each separately, store them in separate Ziploc bags, and you'll have the full range of light, medium, and dark gray dubbings.

Mole fur is excellent for dark insects such as midges and the myriads of dark caddisflies that hatch all summer long. It's also available in light brown. You won't find many patterns calling for either, but it's an excellent fur to experiment with as you explore small flymphs on your own. You can shear it and blend it, but you'll get a felted fur if you do. It's then difficult to achieve a loose body with it. Instead, leave short-fibered mole fur on the skin, and clip only what you need as you spin a body or tie a body directly onto a flymph. Spread the fur onto waxed thread, spin it, and you'll have the fibrous, spiky dubbing you desire.

Australian opossum, like muskrat, varies in color from belly to back. Shear some belly and blend it; you'll have a light tan that leans toward rust or orange. Shearing the midline will give you a slightly darker tan, again with some rust in it. Shear the back and you'll have a dark brown dubbing with a reflection of red. You can blend the underfur and guard hairs together to create a range of useful colors. Mix in vibrant Sparkle Yarns in either clear or colors, and the range of possibilities with Aussie 'possum extends itself in many directions.

Many patterns in *The Art of Tying the Wet Fly & Fishing the Flymph* call for bodies spun of fur from the above listed animals. I find them useful and turn to them whenever their colors and textures are right for the fly I'm tying. But lately I've been leaning more and more toward pre-blended furs that

A complete hare's mask offers many colors and textures in its different parts. You can shear the parts, blend them, and store them separately, or keep the mask whole, clip parts of it and use it as need arises. Because your author is allergic to the dander in hare's mask, he is forced to buy pre-packaged blends, which have been washed and are therefore safe.

A cross-section of muskrat (left), from belly to back, offers shades from pale to dark gray. Mole (center) offers a short dark fur, available in black and light brown, with few guard hairs. It makes excellent dubbing for small flymphs. When spun sparsely on bright silk, it lets the undercolor show through. Australian opossum (right) has an excellent texture, and offers several shades of tan through dark brown in a cross-section from belly to back.

You can buy many dubbing blends, in a variety of textures and colors, from more than one source. For flymphs, those with the guard hairs left in are usually better, and blends with Sparkle Yarn mixed in might be best.

come packaged in the full range of the colors I'll need when I'm tying, with Sparkle Yarn already added.

My favorite blended fur for flymphs is Hare's Ear Plus. The fur used is from hare's mask, and that's an excellent place to start for any fly. It is sheared and blended, so the guard hairs and underfur are both present, giving an excellent spiky mix. The hair is washed before it's dyed, which gives the full range of colors I want. Since I'm allergic to hare's mask, the washing is a blessing, as it rids the fur of the dander that causes me to seize up with sneezing.

The largest advantage of Hare's Ear Plus is the Sparkle Yarn mixed with the hare's mask fur. These fibers add flecks of brightness. When underwater they reflect rays of light, looking slightly like bubbles. Because the yarns are designed for use in carpets, and therefore to repel water, Sparkle Yarn fibers help to entrain air and take it underwater with the fly. I've always favored the use of natural furs over synthetics, but Sparkle Yarn and fur blends let me accomplish what I want in a flymph without getting into bouts of sneezes. It's the same material used in the late Gary LaFontaine's famous Sparkle Pupa patterns.

Most flymphs that I tie have ribs, for the simple reason that their originators called for them, and I tend to follow a pattern dressing unless I have a good reason to violate it. I'm not sure tinsels add to the effectiveness of the flies, but I'm pretty sure they don't subtract from it if they're kept unobtrusive. So I use silver and gold wire on small wet flies, silver and gold Mylar on flies where I want flash, and silver and gold oval tinsel on flies where I want an added hint of weight. For most flymphs, I use narrow or medium Mylar tinsel that is silver on one side and gold on the other. Be sure to use a size that is not too wide to be nestled down into the fur body without matting it. Never use a rib that might mat down the body of the flymph you're tying. It's far better to leave the rib out than to destroy what you're trying to achieve in the rough body of the fly.

Leisenring and Hidy called for *cockerel* hackle in most of their wet flies and hackled nymphs. A cockerel is a rooster of the year, killed before its feathers are prime. The hackle fibers are not as stiff as they would be on a mature rooster. It's very awkward to walk into a fly shop today and ask for cockerel, though you might get the same quality neck if you ask for Grade #3 rooster.

Growers of super hackles today are raising and harvesting hen capes so good that hen now is better than cockerel used to be. For the hackles of most flymphs, I'm using Grade #1 hen hackles from domestic growers. It's excellent stuff, not difficult to find in the colors you need, and it often has the sheen common in the old days only on the highest-grade rooster capes. The quality hen available today is a two-edged sword, however. In the old days, you used to be able to paw through reject barrels and find prime hen necks for a couple of dollars. Now the price approaches what you used to pay for Grade #2 rooster. It's worth it. These excellent hen necks have the full range of feather sizes. Each feather is long enough to wrap a fly, with some spare turns left over that you'll regret throwing away. Save the tips for cut-wing drys, if you tie them. These excellent hen necks make tying flymphs a lot easier today than it was in earlier years. They're worth what they cost.

I recommend buying hen necks to start in brown, medium ginger, medium blue dun, and grizzly. These will get you going. As you continue your search, look for light and dark ginger, plus light and dark dun. Grab any *cree* hen cape you find: ginger or light brown mottled with black markings. This gives a lifelike effect when wound on a hook, much like the speckling of partridge hackle. A honey-dun hen crops up now and then. Grab it before I do. It will have ginger on the tips of the fibers, with a light gray center stripe. When wrapped, it gives two tones and a lifelike look. Good black hen necks are not rare, but they're not often cheap. Still, a black hen neck has many uses, and the money spent on one won't be wasted.

In truth, you should be eager to buy any hen neck that has colors appealing to you, especially if they're mottled, showing more than one color. Not all of the dressings I'll list for flymphs are set in stone, though there are certain standard patterns you'll want to tie and try. But any well-marked hen neck will produce flies that attract trout in one situation or another. The more of these necks you keep handy, the more options you'll have when it comes to making up a match for some insect you find trout eager to eat.

Though it's not stressed in *The Art of Tying the Wet Fly*, when Pete Hidy showed me how to tie his flymphs in his Boise home, he wrapped the hackle in somewhat palmer fashion, over the front one-third to one-half of each

Hen necks in brown, ginger, blue dun, grizzly, and cree.

flymph. I believe it's something that he came to prefer after the book was written, in the way that flies and the ways that we tie them evolve as we fish them. According to Pete, this was more in keeping with nature: The legs and other appendages of an insect are spread over its thoracic segments. I follow Pete in this preference, and tie flymphs and traditional winged wets with spread hackles, rather than bunching the turns behind the hook eye.

Tail fibers for flymphs are often taken from the same neck from which you get the hackle. You'll find excellent tailing material in the longest feathers at the end of the neck, or in what are called the *spade feathers* along the sides of the neck. As with hackle for collars, it's a good idea to select tail fibers marked with a couple of colors, if you can. Keep tails sparse, fewer than ten fibers in most flies. Use fibers taken toward the end of the feather, to get away from the web near the base. You'll get about the right stiffness for a flymph out of hen feather fibers that lack web.

I prefer 2X heavy hooks for all my flymphs. Though they're nearly always fished right up toward the top, flymphs are tied with such spiky bodies that they get hung up in the surface film nearly every time you cast them. A heavier hook helps them penetrate through it and get fishing faster. The little tug you'll give, in order to pop one through the surface film, will be assisted by the extra weight. When you fish a flymph on the swing, the extra weight in the hook keeps it from planing back up into the surface film, where it would leave a wake and frighten the fish.

Pete Hidy made these flymph body-spinning blocks, shown here top and bottom. The single piece of black Naugahyde can be flipped to white on the other side, for light or dark backgrounds, making it easier to get the right amount of fur, and the correct taper, on each spun body. Note the details of finishing nail placement. Also note the small piece of beeswax stuck to the upper right corner of the block on the left. When spinning bodies, this can be kept under your tongue for the correct softness of the wax. Pete kept his wax in just that spot when I watched him tie. The felt on the bottom of the block is to keep the block from sliding around.

When you choose to dress a flymph with floatant and fish it in the surface film, as an emerger, the heavy hook will rarely cause problems. The only flymphs I tie on fine-wire hooks are for fishing on top during hatches on spring creeks. Even there, heavy-wire hooks will often let the fly float, and will also do a better job holding the large trout you might hook in such water.

Hidy and Leisenring spun flymph bodies separately, on waxed silk thread, and stored them on cards. They spun a dozen or so bodies of each color fur, on each color thread, for each size fly that they might want to tie later. Then, when actually constructing the fly, they incorporated the prespun body into the fly, in the same way that you might wind a chenille body onto a Woolly Worm.

Pete Hidy gave me a body-spinning block that makes the process of creating separate bodies a lot easier than the original method, which was to spin them against your leg. Such blocks are now available in shops and online. If you're interested in constructing a block in order to tie these flies as their originators tied them, here are very truncated directions to build one. Begin with a piece of $3/4$-inch pine 5 inches long by 2 inches wide. Round off one end, sand it smooth, and stain it pretty if you'd like. Pound a small finishing nail into the block at one end, leaving $3/8$-inch of the head showing. Clip the head off with cutters, and use a file to round off any sharp edges that might fray silk thread. Tap in a pair of finishing nails close together, centered lengthwise in the block, an inch from each end. Leave the heads on these.

Use a razor blade to make a slit in the center of the block at the end opposite the lone finishing nail, in line with the two pairs of them. Make another slit on the right edge of the block, about halfway down. These two slits hold the thread while you're spinning a body.

Pete Hidy finished the block by cutting a ½-inch strip of Naugahyde, white on one side and black on the other, long enough to extend over the two pairs of finishing nails. He used a paper punch to make holes in the Naugahyde at each end so that he could slip it over the nails. This strip creates a contrasting background for threads and furs. If you're tying with dark threads and furs, turn the white side up. If you're using light colors, turn the black side up.

Pete also chiseled out a ¾-inch-wide cut in the bottom of the block, immediately below the slit that holds the thread. He inserted a razor blade into this cut, flush with the end of the block, and used wood filler to hold it in place and cover all but its razor edge. Pete used this to cut the thread at the correct length for each body. This lets you work with silk thread while it's still on the spool, and cuts down the waste of working with lengths of precut thread, from which you then have to cut the tag ends.

The following steps are for using a spinning block to make separate bodies for your flymphs. It's worth noting that James Leisenring spun bodies for his flymphs on his pants leg. The procedure is the same, but it's loaded with potential for disaster unless you practice it as often as he clearly did.

MAKING PRE-SPUN FLYMPH BODIES

1. Start with the Pearsall's Gossamer Silk color you want for the undercolor of the body. You can cut the thread, or work with it on the spool. Wax a foot of the thread, running it slowly through the softened beeswax two times. Pete Hidy kept a small piece of wax under his tongue, for the right temperature and soft consistency. Insert the end of the waxed thread into the slit in the end of the block, lay the thread between the two pairs of nails, take it behind the far nail, bring it back between the first set of nails, then fasten it into the slit on the right side of the block.

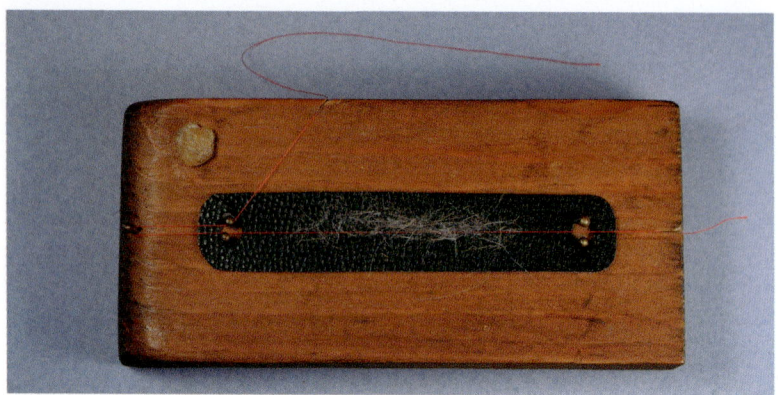

2. Choose the fur you want for the primary color of the body. Cut a small amount of it from the hide, or pull it from the package if it's pre-blended dubbing. Mix the underfur and guard hairs, if it's natural fur. Tease the fur into a skein $1^1/_2$ to $2^1/_2$ inches long, depending on the size hook you'll be winding it on later. You'll soon get a feel for the right body size if you use the spinning block consistently. The fur skein should be slightly thinner at one end, tapering up to a fullness about $^2/_3$ of the length of it, then tapering back down again. This will give you a tapered body when you wind it onto the hook later. Lay this skein on top of the waxed thread.

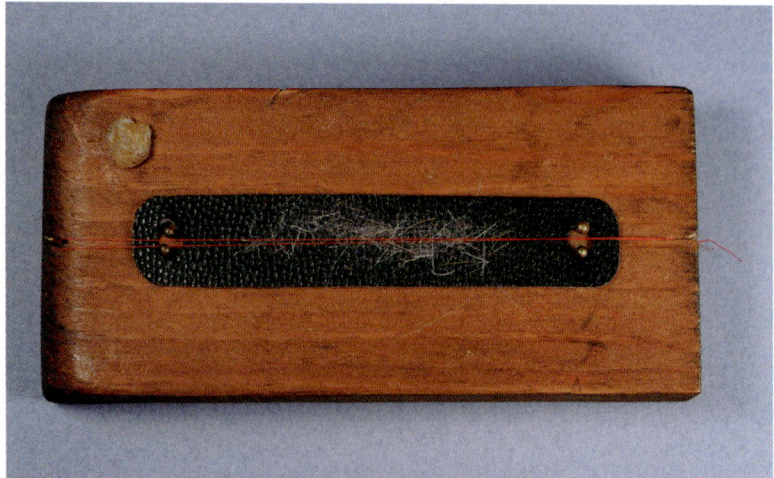

3. Remove the thread from the right-hand slit, lay the thread carefully between the pairs of nail heads, and snug it down over the fur, trapping the dubbing between the top and bottom threads. Draw the thread into the end slit, and use the razor edge in the end to cut it, or use scissors if your block lacks the blade. Now you have the body fur caught between two threads of waxed silk.

4. Pull both ends of the thread out of the slit. Keep them together and twist them several times between your thumb and forefinger. The body fur will spin into a neatly tapered fur rope, not unlike a very loose strand of chenille. The wax will set later, and this will form one of the most durable but loosely dubbed bodies possible.

5. Holding both ends of the twisted thread, lift the body from the spinning block and move it to a card cut from cardboard or any rigid plastic. Hidy used $3^1/2$-inch by $5^1/2$-inch cellulite cards. He cut twelve paired slits down the sides and thus was able to store a dozen pre-spun bodies on each card. I use 3-inch by 5-inch paper flash cards, cutting a dozen small aligned slits in each long side. They're just the right width to store the common run of size 12 to 16 flymph bodies.

Completed fur bodies are stored on separate cards until you're ready to tie with them. The beeswax sets after a few hours, and the body will not come unwound when you tie with it, as it would if you were to spin a body and immediately put it to use in tying a fly. It's important to spin a dozen or so bodies at a time, then let them sit at least overnight, or even better, incorporate them into flymphs days or even weeks later as you find need to replace those you've lost to trout.

Using pre-spun bodies is the best way to tie flymphs for the patient perfectionist. It's the traditional way to do it, and in many ways the most pleasing and also the most effective. But it takes time, which average folks today don't seem to have in excess. I suspect that Hidy and Leisenring, given today's tools and materials, might have found ways to tie the bodies into their flies as they went along, rather than pre-spinning them. But both men were perfectionists who took a lot of time at their tying. It's possible that they might do it today the same way they did it then. It's also possible that you should do it the same way today. There is something aesthetic about spinning the separate bodies, placing them on their cards, and incorporating them into finished flies later, taking all those extra steps that make our flymphs approach the desired perfection.

I get very little time to tie flies anymore, so I've devised methods that get almost the same results, but allow me to wind the bodies at the same time that I'm tying the rest of a flymph. I'll admit, though, that a flymph tied using a separate body, spun and stored on a card, ends up being prettier almost every time. I'm not sure why, because the steps in tying without the pre-spun body are approximately the same, and the results should be, too.

The following steps are for tying a flymph with a pre-spun body that you've already stored long enough on its card for its wax to set.

TYING A FLYMPH WITH A PRE-SPUN BODY

MARCH BROWN FLYMPH

Hook:	#12-16 2X heavy
Thread:	Crimson Pearsall's Gossamer Silk
Hackle:	Brown or furnace hen
Tail:	Pheasant tail fibers
Rib:	Oval gold tinsel
Body:	Hare's mask fur or natural (#1) Hare's Ear Plus

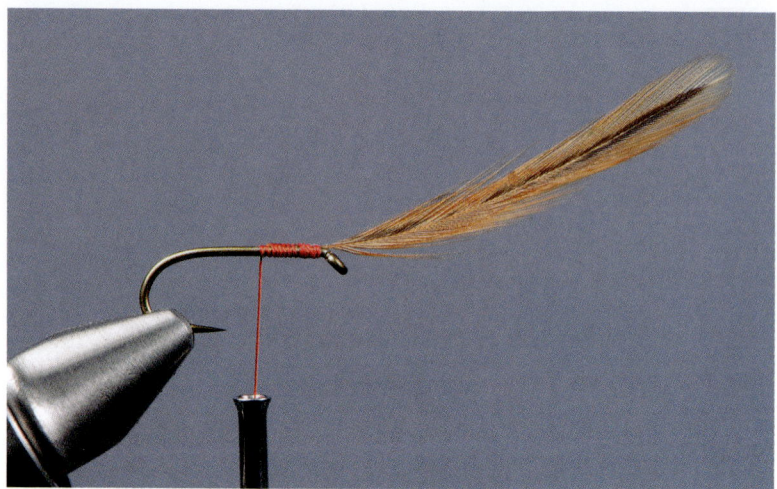

1. Fix the hook in the vise. Wax the first inch or two of the thread. Start the thread behind the eye of the hook. Be careful not to take any extra turns. Select a hen hackle feather with fibers the length of the hook shank, or about $1^1/_2$ to 2 times the width of the hook gap. Strip the fuzzy fibers from the butt of the stem, and tie in the feather on top of the hook with the concave side up, so that the fibers will slant back, not forward, when the hackle is wound later. Clip the stem. The tip of the feather extends out over the eye of the hook.

Note: Some hen necks are what Henry Hoffman, famous as the origina-tor of Super Grizzly hackle, once told me are *twisters*: They reverse when you begin to wind them, and their fibers lean the opposite way you'd expect, forward over the eye instead of back over the body. When I tie with a new neck, I try at least one turn of hackle before completing the rest of a fly, to be sure which way to tie the feather to the hook so that its fibers slant back when wound.

2. Wind thread to the beginning of the hook bend. Select three to five fibers from a pheasant tail feather, extend them straight out from the stem to even their tips, and clip or pull them from the stem. Measure the tail fibers the length of the hook shank, and tie them in with three to five thread wraps. Take one, or at most two, turns of thread under the tail, tucking this turn tightly up between the tail fibers and the hook shank. This cocks the tail slightly upward, and gives the finished flymph a rakish appearance that will surely make you fish it with more confidence, though there's no assurance trout will be similarly impressed. Bring the thread forward a few turns and clip the tail butts.

3. Clip about 4 inches of ribbing tinsel, and catch it under three to four turns of thread back to the base of the tail, leaving its tag end long enough to capture under about half the body when you wind it in a moment. This will lock the tinsel in at the rear. If you use Mylar tinsel, with one side gold and the other silver, tie it in with the gold side to the hook. When you wind it, it will reverse, and the gold side will show.

4. Remove a pre-spun body from the card on which it is stored. Tie the slender end in at the base of the tail. If you'd like to have a little of the thread undercolor show at the back of the fly, which I find pleasing, leave enough of the twisted threads exposed to take one or two wraps before the fur begins. Wrap your working thread forward over the body threads and tinsel tag, to a point about $1/5$ the shank length behind the eye. This leaves room to tie off the body and tinsel, and to wind the hackle. Clip the excess body thread.

5. Wind the body forward, keeping the turns close together, but not so crowded that the body becomes blocky and dense. A sparse flymph fishes better, and lets the undercolor of the thread come through when the fly is wet. Tie the body off behind the hackle and clip the excess threads. At first you might have some excess body, or might even come up short, which is easy enough to cure by adding some dubbing. Time and practice in the body-spinning process, rather than the tying, will solve this.

6. Wind the rib forward in four to six evenly spaced turns. If needed, wobble it back and forth to avoid matting down spiky body fibers. Tie it off at the end of the body, with just a couple of turns of thread. Reverse it, and take a few more turns of thread over it to lock it in securely. Clip the excess tinsel. Finish this step by taking your thread back to a point just in front of the mid-point on the body, in one or two long turns. The hackle will be wrapped over the front part of the flymph, back to the waiting thread.

7. Attach your hackle pliers to the tip of the hen feather. Take a single turn of hackle just behind the hook eye, leaving enough space for a thread head. Take a second turn of hackle tight behind the first. Space a third turn halfway between the last turn and the position of the thread. Take a last turn at the thread, and capture the hackle tip with a wrap or two of thread. Clip the excess tip.

8. Wind your thread forward through the hackle in four to six turns to the eye of the hook, working the bobbin back and forth to avoid matting down hackle fibers. It will now be locked in forever against the teeth of the trout that you hope to catch with the fly. Nothing is worse than catching a couple of fish on a fly, then having its hackles unwind. Use minimal turns of thread to form a base for a whip-finish. Wax an inch of thread, apply that whip, cut the thread, and your flymph is finished.

TYING A FLYMPH WITHOUT A PRE-SPUN BODY

The preceding directions are for tying a flymph the way the originators of the concept decreed. It's an aesthetic set of steps, with a bit of magic to it, ensuring that lots of affection goes into each flymph. The results will also be at least a little bit prettier than you'll get by taking shortcuts. Going for or against the patient method of creating a separate body, depending on your point of view, is the amount of extra time it takes to create all that magic.

If your life prescribes that you need to tie faster, or if you get into the sort of emergency that requires you to replenish your stock of a particular killing flymph in a hurry so that you can get back to fishing it, then there is a way to accomplish approximately the same body without resorting to a spinning block. The following steps show how to tie a body during the process of tying the rest of the flymph, rather than separate from it.

The way you tie your flymphs will reflect in some ways the way you live your life. One way is not right and the other wrong. I enjoy taking the long way around when I have time to take it. I also enjoy getting a few flymphs tied up in a hurry when I need them later the same day, or perhaps early the next. If you're on a trip, into a hatch, and want to experiment with flymphs in terms of size and color, then you'll be glad you know how to turn those experiments out in a hurry.

1. Follow steps 1 through 3 on pages 98–99 to tie in the hackle, tail, and ribbing of your flymph, preparing it for the body. Your thread should be at the base of the tail.

2. Use your tacky wax to dress 3 to 4 inches of working thread, starting close to the hook shank. Tease a small bit of dubbing into a skein 1 to 2 inches long, depending on the size hook. The skein should be tapered slightly fatter over $^2/_3$ of its length, then tapered down again. Stick the fur skein to the waxed thread. As an alternative to teasing the skein out separately and placing it against the thread, you'll eventually learn to tease the fur out of a slight ball of it held in your off-hand, right onto the waxed thread. Twist the fur onto the thread slightly at both ends of the skein, just enough to fix it to the silk.

3. Catch the thread over the forefinger of your off-hand. Return the thread to the hook shank, and use a few turns of thread to lock it near the base of the tail. This forms a thread loop, with the fur already stuck to one side of it. Be sure the fur is inside the loop.

4. Remove your finger from the loop, and collapse the threads to capture the fur. Catch the end of the loop between the thumb and forefinger of your tying hand, and spin the same fur body that is the result of using Pete Hidy's spinning block. The difference is that you've done it in place, on the hook. Take your working thread forward just behind the hackle tie-in point. Catch the thread end of the spun body with your hackle pliers.

Note: There are so many fur-spinning tools on the market, to be used in place of your fingers, that it's confusing. In my experience they all work, forming beautiful bodies quickly. I've tried many, but have discovered that, while an extra tool can get lost on my messy bench, I never have to search for my fingers.

5. Wind the spun body forward to a hook-eye length or so behind the hackle tie-in point. It doesn't hurt to leave a turn of the thread loop showing at the back of the body. The silk color is the chosen undercolor, so you want it to show slightly. Don't crowd the front of the fly; leave room to tie off the tinsel, wind the hackle, and finish the head. The resulting body should be somewhat sparse and spiky. It will also be extremely durable, because all of the fur fibers are locked between the waxed strands of thread.

6. Wind the tinsel forward in four to six evenly spaced turns, depending on the size of the fly. Tie off the tinsel by taking two turns of thread over the end, then reverse the tinsel and take two or three more turns over it, locking it before clipping the excess. Be sure to work these tinsel turns into the fur without matting down the loose fibers.

Take a moment now to examine the body of the fly. It should be roughly dubbed, with lots of loose fibers sticking out. But it often happens that maverick fibers will poke out too far, or in a color that contrasts too starkly with the rest of the fly, or so stiffly in the wrong direction that they look unnatural on the body of the fly. Take a second to tweezer any of these away. My loose rule, stated earlier, is to leave in place any fibers that will be shorter than the hackle when it's wound, and to pick out any that would be longer than the hackle. As to contrast in shade or color, it's probably more beneficial than bad. On most flymph bodies, it's not necessary to do any preening at all. Those fibers you'd like to pluck to tidy up the fly might be the very ones that would later make the fly work so well in the water, entraining that bubble of air when the flymph goes under.

7. Finish the fly now as you would one tied with a pre-spun body. Take one or two long turns of your thread almost to the center of the body. Take one turn of hackle behind the hook eye, another behind it, another halfway between the last turn and your thread, and the last turn of hackle at the thread. Bring the thread forward through the hackle, make a neat head, and whip-finish the flymph.

A FEW FAVORITE FLYMPHS

A few favorite flymphs cover a wide variety of fishing situations. It's best, when beginning to work with a pattern style that is new to you, to think of the colors that nature contrives for its insects, then carry a slight range of flies tied to cover those colors. Vary the sizes and you'll be surprised at how few flies you need to prepare yourself for all sorts of circumstances. It would be a mistake to tie all of the following flymphs, or to tie more than a few of each you'd like to try. Go out and fish a few to see which work best for you.

In my own fishing, I tend to view soft-hackled wets primarily as exploring flies, with a few used to fish during specific hatches. It's the opposite with flymphs: I tend to think of them as being imitations for specific hatches, usually, as Pete Hidy intended, for those insects that are no longer nymphs, but not yet adults . . . in another word, emergers.

March Brown Flymph: The March Brown Flymph is used as the tying example in this chapter. It's based on the ancient and effective winged Hare's Ear wet fly. It was revised by Rick Hafele, co-author of *Western Hatches*, to imitate the emerger of the Western March Brown (*Rhithrogena morrisoni* and *R. hageni*). This mayfly emerges from the nymphal shuck in the surface

Many March Brown duns fail to complete their emergence, or are swept into riffles and drowned. A March Brown Flymph can be effective when fished through a hatch, and sometimes for an hour or two afterward, as trout continue to prowl for failed duns.

The March Brown mayfly nymph swims to the surface for emergence, and usually makes the transition to a dun in the film itself. But many escape the nymphal shuck just a few inches deep, and the dun must complete the trip. It's the exact stage of an insect's life for which Pete Hidy coined the term *flymph*. The March Brown Flymph is excellent whenever this happens.

film most of the time. But some individuals jump the gun, come out as duns a few inches deep, and rise to the surface as duns. The March Brown Flymph imitates the struggling dun, but also looks a lot like the nymph swimming toward the surface. It fishes best on a patient swing through riffled water, or fairly fast runs just downstream from riffles. It should be tied on 2X heavy hooks to be sure it sinks.

The same flymph also resembles Spotted Sedges, caddis adults that dive into the water to lay their eggs on the bottom. Trout will usually be seen rising eagerly when this is going on. You see the adult caddisflies in the air and match them with a dry fly, but you can't catch a thing. The flymph represents the diving adult. Try fishing it during this hatch with the Hidy Subsurface Swing detailed in Chapter 15, "Four Men and Their Methods." Cast it just above and beyond a rising trout, then pop it under and allow it to swing right past the trout's nose. You'll be surprised how often you see the same sharp riseform that you thought was the take to a floating insect, but instead was to one submerged.

LITTLE OLIVE FLYMPH

Hook:	#12-18 1X fine or 2X heavy
Thread:	Green Pearsall's Gossamer Silk or olive 8/0
Hackle:	Blue dun hen
Tail:	Blue dun hen hackle fibers
Rib:	Gold Mylar tinsel (narrow)
Body:	Olive fur and Sparkle Yarn mix
Note:	In larger sizes, tie with silk, and either spin your bodies separately or as you tie. On size 16 and 18, tie with 8/0 thread, spinning a fibrous body as you tie the fly. Omit the rib if you'd like.

Little Olive Flymph: This flymph matches many species of small Blue-Winged Olive mayflies, the BWOs, in the widespread genus *Baetis*. It matches the dun stage, either emerging or drowned while attempting to emerge. I fish it most often in sizes 16 and 18. It also matches Lesser Green Drakes, or *flavs*, in sizes 12 and 14. It can be dressed with floatant and fished upstream to rising trout, just like a dry, and will sometimes work when a dry fly will not. It can also be left undressed and fished down and across, on a slow swing, usually through a pod of feeding fish.

I generally fish the Little Olive Flymph during BWO hatches, on fairly smooth water, when trout are feeding selectively both on top and just sub-surface. I don't dress the fly with floatant, but I do fish it upstream as a surface-film emerger. It doesn't always float, but it will if I remember to give it a couple of brisk backcasts to flick away moisture. When the flymph comes abreast of me in the currents and is about to begin dragging, I give it a slight tug to submerge it, then let it continue to fish down and around below me.

It seems that I catch about half of my trout on the flymph when it's awash in the water, on the upstream part of the drift, the other half when it's sunk, on the downstream drift and swing.

GINGER WINGLESS FLYMPH

Hook:	#12-16 2X heavy
Thread:	Yellow Pearsall's Gossamer Silk
Hackle:	Dark ginger hen
Tails:	Dark ginger hen hackle fibers
Rib:	Oval gold tinsel
Body:	Hare's mask fur or natural (#1) Hare's Ear Plus

Ginger Wingless Flymph: This tannish flymph matches many light-colored caddis species that dance over the water and often dive down to lay their eggs on the bottom. It's an excellent match for them, both because the spiky body traps air bubbles and because the Sparkle Yarn fibers in the blended dubbing reflect light and look like trapped air. Since the natural caddis adult takes air down with it, this fly works whenever you see tan caddis in the air and a few fish feeding, but you can't catch trout with a dry fly that looks anything like the caddis adults. Try this flymph on a short swing, popped under the water so that it's scant inches deep, fished to individual rising trout, or to a pod of them.

BLUE DUN WINGLESS

Hook:	#12-18 1X fine or 2X heavy
Thread:	Yellow Pearsall's Gossamer Silk
Hackle:	Medium blue dun hen
Tails:	Medium blue dun hen hackle fibers
Rib:	Silver Mylar tinsel (narrow)
Body:	Muskrat back fur

Blue Dun Wingless: The Blue Dun Wingless represents the wonderful variety of grayish mayflies, usually in the *Paraleptophlebia* genus, but also for some of the smaller BWOs. It's used most often to imitate the spinner stage, since the duns of the larger of these are not so often available drowned. To imitate the spinner, it's best to tie the fly very sparse, almost wispy. Use just enough fur to cover the silk. Spread two or three turns of hackle over the front part of the fly. Don't do anything to add bulk to the body or hackle.

If you're going to fish such sparse ties in or near the surface film, you'll have to tie them on dry-fly hooks. Tie them on heavy-wire hooks only as needed, when you want to get them deeper.

The Blue Dun Wingless can be tied in standard flymph fashion, on 2X heavy hooks, with the body more full and the hackle wound in three or four turns over the front of the fly, to represent the many Gray Sedges that bat around in midsummer sunshine over riffles and runs. These dive down to lay their eggs on the bottom. A grayish wet fly will sometimes take trout feeding on them when a dry fly fails, though a Leadwing Coachman winged wet is my preferred pattern to imitate them.

PALE WATERY WINGLESS

Hook:	#12-16 1X fine
Thread:	Yellow Pearsall's Gossamer Silk
Hackle:	Light ginger hen
Tails:	Light ginger hen hackle fibers
Rib:	Gold Mylar tinsel (narrow)
Body:	Cream and olive fur/Sparkle Yarn blend

Pale Watery Wingless: The Pale Watery Wingless has been around in various forms for a hundred and fifty years or more. It was used in Britain in the late 1800s, and crossed the Atlantic Ocean to find itself in Leisenring's fly boxes in the 1930s and 1940s. It fishes for many pale yellowish Sulphurs, Pale Morning Duns, and Pale Evening Duns, imitating both the dun and spinner stages. It should be tied fairly sparse, on fine-wire hooks, when you're using it only to imitate mayflies.

The same fly represents many pale tan caddisfly species. Most of the time the earlier Ginger Wingless will work as well or better for the caddis, so I prefer to tie the listed Ginger Wingless on 2X heavy hooks and this Pale Watery Wingless on standard dry-fly hooks. That way it's also possible to dress the pale fly with dry-fly floatant and fish it in the surface film.

GRIZZLY AND GRAY FLYMPH

Hook:	#12-16 2X heavy
Thread:	Black 8/0 nylon
Hackle:	Grizzly hen
Tail:	Grizzly hen hackle fibers
Rib:	Silver oval tinsel
Body:	Muskrat back fur

Grizzly and Gray Flymph: This is close to the old standard Gray Nymph, but tied without weight, and with the addition of a rib and tail. The hackle is wound over the front $1/3$ of the body of the fly. It resembles a lot of underwater organisms, such as rising grayish mayfly nymphs, caddis pupae, or midge pupae. I don't like to assign it to any particular set of naturals, but it looks like a lot of living things, and it certainly convinces lots of fish that it's alive and about to get away from them. It's a marvelously simple tie, and it takes trout in a wide range of situations.

RED HACKLE

Hook:	#12-16 2X heavy
Thread:	Crimson Pearsall's Gossamer Silk
Hackle:	Brown or furnace hen
Rib:	Oval gold tinsel
Body:	Bronze peacock herl

Red Hackle: This dressing might be better considered a soft-hackle than a flymph. But it was one of James Leisenring's favorite patterns, so it finds its seat here rather than in the last chapter. I've mentioned that there is no clear line separating wet flies from nymphs. The line between soft-hackles and flymphs is perhaps even less sharply drawn.

The main feature of this fly, however, is its body, not its hackle. I have a friend who calls peacock herl "trout cocaine," and swears that any fly tied with it kills fish. The herl body of this fly is clearly the largest part of what makes it a killer. It's not an imitation, or even approximation, of any single insect. I fish it as a searching dressing when I'm looking for trout, trying to find them with my fly.

The bronze peacock herl called for in the dressing can be obtained simply enough by leaving a few eyed feathers out in the sun for a couple of weeks or so; it takes longer where I grew up in the rainforests of Oregon. Just set them on the windowsill, forget them until you need them. It's kind of a secret that the fly works pretty well even if you tie it with herl that has not been bronzed, but Leisenring and Hidy specified bronze herl, and that's what you should use.

TUP'S NYMPH

Hook:	#12-16 1X long, 2X heavy nymph
Thread:	Primrose Pearsall's Gossamer Silk or yellow 8/0 nylon
Hackle:	Light blue dun hen, one size undersized
Tails:	Ginger hen hackle points
Body (back half):	Primrose yellow buttonhole twist
Body (front half):	Yellow and claret seal fur or Sparkle Yarn, blended
Note:	Buttonhole twist is a three-strand silk. For small flies you might need to untwist it and remove one or two strands. If you can't find buttonhole twist, you can accomplish the same thing with layers of silk thread or even 8/0 for the back half of the body. I use buttonhole twist because the originators, Leisenring and Hidy, called for it. I also have a few feet left of two synthetic braided yarns that Pete Hidy gave me for this fly, one yellow, the other carrot-orange. When snipped to 1/4-inch lengths and blended in a coffee grinder, the result is a pale yellowish orange dubbing that Pete used for the front half of the Tup's Nymph body. I have come to like it as well, on account of success with the fly, and I'll regret the day when I snip the last of those yarns that Pete gave me.

Tup's Nymph: This was one of James Leisenring's favorite patterns, and over time has become one of mine. It fits the description of a soft-hackled nymph, with its undersized hackle and compact body, though I fish it with wet-fly tactics, and consider it a wet, not a nymph, despite all the indications otherwise implied in its name. It's one of those dressings designed to fish *bumpety-bump* along the bottom, though it's unweighted. Leisenring, in his notes transcribed by Pete Hidy for their classic book, wrote: "Since nymphs are fished deep, the hooks for them should be of heavy wire so they will sink deep. I have no use for a weighted nymph because they do not swim naturally."

Clearly the Tup's Nymph would be a perfect candidate for the Leisenring Lift. It would sink quickly, though that is relative; it would never sink like a weighted nymph of our day, or as swiftly as one with split shot pinched to the leader above it. But Leisenring fished those long, steady current lines that led to visible trout, or very likely lies, in somewhat shallow depths. His flies, fished with his methods, on his water, achieved the depth he required to initiate his Lift.

Few of us fish such graceful streams. Mine tend to be much more brawling. But I do fish tailwaters, some of them with abundant Yellow Sally stonefly populations, and I find the Tup's Nymph deadly on those. I try to fish it in soft edge currents, sometimes just 2 or 3 feet deep, especially when trout have moved there to follow migrations of Yellow Sally nymphs in spring and early summer. If it's possible without risking a sound drowning, I work the edges by wading outside of them, casting back in toward them. Like Leisenring's favorite waters, not many are shaped perfectly for that sort of wading, either.

The cast is fairly long, at an angle almost directly in toward shore. The fly is allowed to swim downstream very slowly, on a line that is only tight enough to show some slight tightening if the nymph is stopped in the currents. That's usually a trout conducting an interview. I don't set the hook, instead letting the increasing pressure of the line set it for me. It's a little like summer steelhead fishing. On some tailwaters the rewards can be almost that large.

I've tied the fly here on a size 16 hook, because that's the size Tup's Nymph I usually fish.

IRON BLUE DUN

Hook:	#12-18 1X fine
Thread:	Crimson Pearsall's Gossamer Silk or red 8/0
Hackle:	Jackdaw wing shoulder (or substitute starling)
Tag:	Crimson tying thread
Body:	Mole fur spun on red silk

Iron Blue Dun: This fly was a favorite of Hidy's and shouldn't be left out of any treatment of flymphs. Though I haven't used it to any extent myself, it clearly would be excellent during midge hatches, and also hatches of very small, dark caddisflies in the family Glossosomatidae. These emerge in early spring, usually before major hatches of mayflies and larger caddis get going. They're so small that they're not easy to notice. Trout, however, feed extensively on both rising pupae and drowned adults.

This dark flymph, tied in its smallest sizes, is a fine imitation of both stages of the tiny caddis. Tie it on fine-wire hooks to keep it near the surface in soft currents.

The old wingless wet fly, or newer flymph, is a simple theme on which you can work many variations. The listed dressings should be considered departure points for experiments of your own. The main components are the silk thread undercolor, body fur overcolor, and hackles to represent tangled legs and wings. It's always wise to collect whatever insect trout are feeding on, get a close look at it, try to match it. But in truth, select the right size flymph, in the approximate right color, and you've usually got the fly you need to take some selective trout.

Chapter Seven

Tying Traditional Winged Wets

It's no mystery why wet flies fell so far out of use when dry flies, and later nymphs, rose to the forefront in British trout fishing. Throughout their history—with exceptions such as Stewart's spiders, T. E. Pritt's soft-hackles, and Skues's soft-hackled thorax nymphs—wet flies were tied as imitations of winged adult insects, in a fashion even those knowledgeable men called *lures*. Traditional wet flies were based on winged insects such as mayflies, stoneflies, and caddis, but tied to resemble those insects as they looked at rest, out of the water, rather than as they might look to a trout when arriving beneath the surface, tossed around by currents.

This direction away from realism in wet-fly design was encouraged when wet flies hit American shores and encountered eager brook trout. It's not the fault of the fish; they can hardly be blamed for being reckless feeders in an environment where they would not otherwise have survived. It's not the fault of our fishing forefathers, either; they tied bright wet flies because that's the kind that attracted the most trout. The later relegation of brook trout to remote headwaters, and their replacement by more selective brown trout, took place at about the same time that dry flies swept over the land.

Leisenring was the lone voice crying out for the use of imitative wet flies along our forested streams. But his quiet book, *The Art of Tying the Wet Fly*, written with Pete Hidy, got lost in the upheaval of World War II. By the time it saw a second edition in 1971, wet flies had been pushed aside once more, this time by the arrival of nymphs.

This was a mistake. Nymphs imitate many underwater forms better than wet flies do, especially immature nymphs and larvae of aquatic insects. But traditional winged wet flies are more effective as imitations for certain emerging insects, and they still make the best imitations of winged and drowned adult insects, both aquatic and terrestrial. Winged wet flies should

118

Winged wet flies work best when tied to imitate adult insects such as caddisflies, many of which swim down to the bottom to lay their eggs. They don't have this perfect form when wet and in the water, however, and you must consider what trout might see whenever you tie wet flies to fish for them.

have a place in your fly boxes. They allow you to catch trout in circumstances in which you might fail without them.

The key to tying effective winged wets lies in constructing them to look like emerging winged insects or like adult insects that have drowned, rather than the same insects as they might look while at rest on a streamside stick. It's a mistake to tie them as copies of *perfect* adults. It's also a mistake to tie them as copies of bright and stiff-winged wet-fly patterns you see in many pattern books. The standard tie for the wet fly has not changed in more than one hundred years. The average pattern plate in a book to this day shows its wet flies with tight, tapered bodies, hackles all at the head, and wings of stiff quill. These look great in photos. Get them submerged, though, and they are lifeless, their wings cleaving the water like knife blades.

For a few insects, such as adult caddis that swim to the bottom to lay their eggs, such quill-winged wet flies work well. For many other insects, they do not.

MATERIALS FOR TYING WINGED WET FLIES

The wing is the focus of the traditional wet fly. It dominates the hackle and body. It represents the upright wings of the mayfly dun, or the folded wings of the resting adult caddis. If tied right it represents them beneath the water, rather than sitting on some grass stem or leaf alongside the stream, where anglers see them but trout do not. It's better to tie the wing of soft secondary feather *quill*—the traditional fly-tying term for paired wing feather sections—if you use quill feathers at all, rather than the stiff primary feather quills that are traditionally used. It's also best not to spray them with artist's fixative, which firms them up and makes them easier to tie and look pretty. It keeps them from getting tattered quite so quickly when fished, or when chewed on by trout. But a wet fly with its wing fibers separated and working in the current usually fishes better than one that retains its perfect shape.

The wing is the dominant feature of a traditional wet fly, such as the Alder shown here. The body and hackle, and tail if there were one, are not insignificant, but it's the wing that makes the traditional winged wet fly what it is. It's likely that the wing is the feature that trout notice most, though the whole composition should be pleasing in the eyes of trout and look like something good to eat if it's not an imitation of anything specific.

When I first began tying wet flies, I used mallard primary feathers. I paired them, then cut the wing segments from the stiffest part in the upper half of the feathers, because that's what held together best, and made the fly most attractive in the tying vise. When I used mottled turkey feathers, on flies such as my favorite Alder, I sprayed them with lacquer because that kept them from separating. This was the standard advice of the time, the 1960s and 1970s.

These flies didn't catch any over-abundance of fish for me, though they worked at times or I would never have continued tying and fishing wet flies. They were pretty to look at in the hand, but they didn't look like anything that lived in the water. I began to get suspicious about them when I started studying aquatic insects with Rick Hafele, in preparation for writing *Western Hatches*. It became clear that the best way to wing a wet fly was with the softest quill. If it held together and looked pretty only until it got wet, that was fine. I preferred it to fray once it got submerged, so it looked like the disorganized wings of a natural insect when awash in the water.

I eventually began doing most of my wet-fly tying with mallard, grouse, and pheasant secondary wing feathers rather than primaries. Whenever possible I cut the wing sections from matched pairs of feathers from land birds such as snipe, woodcock, and starling. These have many markings, rather than a single, solid color. And they're fragile, which is a strike against them if you're trying to make your winged wet flies look nice, but a solid pitch for them if you're trying to tie wet flies that catch trout.

When hen necks of excellent quality became available, I began experimenting with wet-fly wings taken from the long feathers on the same necks from which I plucked the hackle feather for the fly. This made life very simple. All I have to do is tie in the hackle feather first; tie in the tail, body, and rib of the fly; then wind the hackle and wing the fly with long, soft fibers

Mallard primary feathers (top), are stiffer and less fragile than secondaries (bottom). No matter the feathers you use, be sure to cut sections from the lower, softer, ends and discard the feathers when you've reached the stiffer fibers toward the tips. Often the useful part will be just half the length of a feather. The same is true for many land birds such as pheasant, but it's especially true in waterfowl wings.

When you select a well-matched pair of feathers, such as these from hen pheasant wings, then it's wise to tape them together (top). You'll need to cut a section from each, face them, and align their tips. You can save time by taping them so their concave sides are forced together (bottom), in which case you can align them carefully before cutting, then remove the joined sections ready to measure and tie to the hook. As shown here the feathers are separated, but when the tips are brought together, they will be matched perfectly, so that a single cut will remove paired feather sections ready to tie on a winged wet fly.

from the same neck. Those long feathers at the upper end of a neck are usually wasted anyway, so it becomes a great new use for them. Because the tail, hackle, and wing usually come from the same neck, everything is sure to be in harmony on the finished fly.

The largest advantage of hen hackle wings, however, is in the way the soft fibers work in the water. Stiff quill wings don't look as alive. Hen hackle wings quiver and kick, much like soft-hackle fibers, with every ripple of current. Stiff feather sections also have a tendency to get slightly twisted, no matter how carefully you tie them in. When this happens the wing can serve as a slight rudder, rolling the fly over and over as it fishes down and around on the swing in moving water, or as you retrieve it through still water. The result is astonishing to trout. They've never seen anything swim like that. They might take the fly; they might also back away from it. I suspect that this rudder effect is part of the reason traditional winged wet flies fail more often than soft-hackles, flymphs, or wets with wings of softer materials.

You can tie any traditional wet fly with a hen hackle wing. Just select a hen hackle feather in the correct color, strip a substantial bunch of fibers from it, and tie it in, replacing the more normal feather-section wing. Instructions are given later. Try it yourself and see which way you, and perhaps the trout, prefer your favorite winged wets. If you have hen saddle patches, you'll have a ready supply of wing fibers that will last almost forever.

The hackle collar on a traditional wet fly is dominated by the wing, but it's still important. If the fly is tied right, which is to say somewhat sparsely, then the hackle becomes even more important, though it's still not the focus of the fly.

The traditional wet fly is most commonly tied with three to five turns of hackle right behind the eye of the hook. The wing is then tied in over the hackle, and a whip-finish completes the fly. This can cause extra bulk at the head, especially when you tie with thicker silk threads. It's a problem in tying because it's hard to finish the fly without an oversized head. To make the hackle more effective, and to eliminate the problem of finishing with a bulky head, use the same half-palmering technique covered in the preceding chapter for tying flymphs. Tie the hackle feather in behind the eye as the first step in tying the fly. When the tail, body, and rib have all been wound, then wrap the hackle over the front one-third of the hook shank. This spreads it out in a more natural fashion, and also allows you to lock it under several turns of thread. Just as important, it places the bulk of the hackle behind the head, rather than bunched up behind the whip-finish.

Finish the fly by tying the wing butts over the front turns of the hackle. Just a few turns of thread hold it down, and the whip-finish locks it into place. The result is a neat head, with the bulk of the hackle in the thorax region, where it should be.

The tail of the wet fly is not so important that it's worth dwelling upon. I usually use fibers from the same neck that furnishes the hackle. Keep the tail sparse, just five to ten fibers. For a livelier fly, take a turn of thread under the tail to cock it upward, though this is more for your own pleasure than it is for the satisfaction of trout. But don't overlook little things that please you. They'll make you fish any fly with more confidence, which means you'll fish it more effectively.

Ribbing on a wet fly is optional. It's said to reflect light and therefore look like bubbles of air. I'm never sure whether tinsel looks like air when underwater, or if it adds much attraction to a wet fly. But it does not detract any unless you make it obtrusive. Use narrow Mylar tinsel on size 10 to 14 wet flies and wire ribbing on smaller hooks. If you'd like a little extra weight on the fly, use oval tinsel, either silver or gold depending on which color harmonizes best with the body color you've chosen. Whatever you use for a rib, be sure to work it into the fur of a dubbed fly so that it does not mat the body fibers against the hook.

The bodies of traditional wet flies, especially those tied for brook trout, have typically been floss in yellow, red, or some other showy color. It's far better to tie your wet-fly bodies with fur in the same range of colors as natural insects. Peacock herl also works well. Its tiny fibers reflect points of light. Flies tied with peacock herl look especially alive.

When you use fur, tie it in with a silk thread color that you'd like to have show through as an undercolor. Either spin bodies separately and store them for later use, or twist them up in the same fur rope used for a flymph, as you tie each fly, to give a durable but very fibrous body. When using herl, twist it into a rope with a thread loop, following the instructions as given for tying the Starling & Herl in Chapter 5 (pages 65–70).

On size 14 and larger hooks, I usually use Pearsall's Gossamer Silk to furnish the undercolor of choice. On smaller hooks, however, the thicker silk can bulk up quickly at the head if you use any extra turns. With some experience you'll have no trouble tying small flies with the thicker silk. At first, though, you'll do better using 6/0 or 8/0 nylon.

Traditional winged wets are nearly always fished on the swing in moving water, and on the retrieve in still water. Consequently, it's best to tie them on heavy-wire hooks, for the extra sink rate. In fast water a heavy hook helps the fly get beneath the surface and keeps it from planing up into the film, leaving a wake. In slow water a heavy hook lets you sink a wet fly a few inches to a foot or two deep, if it's tied sparsely enough. In a lake or pond, the weight of the hook helps the fly penetrate the film and begin the slow sink that in itself can be the best way to entice cruising and feeding trout.

TYING THE TRADITIONAL WINGED WET FLY

It's best to learn to tie wet flies with traditional quill, or feather-section, wings. It's an easy step from there to tying with hen hackle wings, instructions for which are later on page 135. If you buy mallard or pheasant wing feathers packaged in pairs, make sure they're actually paired: from opposite wings and about the same size. I prefer to buy paired wings because I can pluck primaries or secondaries matched for size, tape them together, and know that they'll meld into perfect wings. Hen pheasant wings are not always available, but be sure they're matched pairs if you buy them. I've found whole hen pheasant skins a good bargain. They offer some fine soft-hackle feathers in the breast and back of the cape, though few established patterns call for them. The wings, when attached to the skin, are certain to be paired.

You can experiment with other wings and wing feathers. Starling, crow, partridge, and quail come to mind. Be sure that whatever you use is legal to possess and legally acquired.

Winged wet flies, up to the point of tying in the wing, are similar to flymphs, or as they used to be called, wingless wets. In some cases, if you stop at the wing, you've got a flymph. The following Hare's Ear Wet is not far off from the March Brown Flymph tied in the previous chapter. It could be tied with a separate body built on a spinning block and stored on a cellulite card. The two flies could even be fished in the same way. But I usually fish flymphs as imitations of emerging or drowned insects, high in the surface film and most often to rising trout, while I more often fish winged wets for insects either drowned or actively swimming down to lay their eggs, not deep, but most often on the swing.

The fly in the following photos is tied with Pearsall's Gossamer Silk, on a size 12 hook. If it were any smaller, I would want to tie it with 6/0 instead, to give me more margin for error with my thread. If I lacked a lot of practice tying wet flies with the thicker silk, I would also want to tie it with the thinner thread. The result might be a bit less revealing of the orange undercolor, but it would be a lot easier to tie, and I might feel a bit more confident about the durability of the fly.

Choose between silk and nylon based in part on your experience, and in part on the size hook on which you're tying. Silk is more traditional and requires a bit more focus when you're tying. Nylon is more modern, lets you be a bit more hurried, and gets you back on the water sooner—perhaps with a few more flies in your box. Which thread you choose in some ways reflects what you're doing at the moment: relaxing at the bench at home or on a trip and into fish.

It also might reflect your personality: patient, meditative, enjoying your time at the vise, or anxious to be out on the water, capturing and matching what's going on out there, catching trout. Let's hope you can find a way to be a bit of both of those. I'd hate to have to separate them out in my own life.

HARE'S EAR WET

Hook:	#12-16 standard wet fly or 2X heavy
Thread:	Orange Pearsall's Gossamer Silk or orange 6/0
Hackle:	Brown or furnace hen
Tail:	Five to ten brown hen hackle fibers
Rib:	Oval gold tinsel
Body:	Hare's mask fur or natural (#1) Hare's Ear Plus
Wing:	Hen pheasant wing feather sections

1. Wax an inch of silk thread, and start it with a few turns, leaving about a hook-eye length for the later head and wing tie-in point. When using silk thread, don't take extra turns; it builds up quickly. Select a brown or furnace hen hackle with fibers the length of the hook shank, or $1^{1}/_{2}$ to 2 times the width of the hook gap. Strip fuzzy fibers from the base of the feather, and tie it in with the concave side away from you, so that when it's later wound, its fibers will slant back, not forward. Clip the excess hackle stem.

Note: Some hen necks twist the opposite way; it's always wise to take an experimental turn of the hackle to see which way it will lay before clipping the stem and continuing to tie.

2. Wind thread to the bend of the hook. Select five to ten brown hen hackle fibers from a long feather at the back or side of the neck. Even the tips of the fibers before pulling them or scissoring them from the stem. Measure these fibers the length of the hook shank, and tie them in at the bend of the hook with three or four wraps of thread. Take one or two turns of thread under the tail to cock it upward.

3. Clip 3 to 4 inches of tinsel from the spool. Lay the tinsel alongside at least half the length of the hook shank, to lock it under the body of the fly. Tie the tinsel in with thread wraps from the base of the tail to the midpoint of the hook shank.

4. Touch 3 to 4 inches of thread with tacky dubbing wax. Tease the fur, or fur and Sparkle Yarn mix, into a tapered skein $1^1/_2$ to 2 inches long, depending on the size fly you're tying. Lay this skein against the waxed thread. Twist just the first and last $^1/_4$ inch of the skein to attach it to the thread.

5. Catch the working thread over the forefinger of your off-hand and bring it back to the hook shank, creating a thread loop. Secure the loop with several turns from the bobbin around the hook shank, working it back to the base of the tail. Take the working thread forward almost to the tie-in point of the hackle, where the body will end.

6. Catch the end of the thread loop between your right thumb and forefinger. Twirl the fur and thread into a dubbing rope. Twist enough to lock the fur in, but leave it fuzzy; don't twist until the fur is bound tightly. Fasten hackle pliers to the end of the fur loop.

7. Wrap the body forward to the hackle tie-in point. I like to leave a wrap or two of thread showing at the back, enhancing the undercolor effect. The body should be spiky when finished, and should taper slightly from back to front. Don't crowd the head. If any fibers stick out that will be longer than the hackle when the fly is finished, pluck them out, but don't tidy the body too much.

8. Bring the ribbing forward in three to five evenly spaced turns. Tie it off at the end of the body with two or three turns of thread before bending the tinsel back over itself and taking two or three more. Clip the excess tinsel. It's now locked in at both ends. Before beginning to wrap the hackle, take your working thread back ⅓ of the shank from the eye, and dangle it over the body at that point.

9. Take one turn of hackle at the tie-in point. Make a second turn tight behind the first. Make a third halfway between the hook eye and the dangling thread. Finish the hackle with one more turn at the thread. Capture the hackle tip with two to three thread wraps, then either clip the excess tip, or draw it forward to snap the stem. Your thread is now at the back end of the spread hackle.

10. Work your thread through the hackle in four to six turns to the eye of the hook. If necessary, wobble the bobbin back and forth, seating the thread wraps without matting down hackle fibers. Hold the front of the hackle back out of the way with your off-hand thumb and fingertips, take the thread to the hook eye, then wrap a layer of thread back against the hackle. This forms an even thread base for the wing tie-in, and also holds the hackle in the proper swept-back wet-fly posture. End with the thread tight against the hackle; that's where you want to take the first turn over the wing.

Note: If you're tying with 6/0 thread, it might take two to three layers to make this base and hold the hackle in position.

11. Snip sections about one hook gap wide from the same point on matched wing feathers. Join these sections with their concave sides toward each other and their tips together. Hold them between the thumb and forefinger of your tying hand, and position them at the eye of the hook. Measure the wing to the midpoint of the tail. If you're tying a fly with no tail, the wing should extend just beyond the end of the hook.

Note: You can tie the paired wing sections with their tips down, in traditional wet-fly fashion, as shown here, or with their tips up, as shown in the next step.

12. I usually prefer to tie quill-winged wets with the wing tipped up at the end, as shown. The reasoning is the same as with the turn of thread to cock up the tail: The finished fly looks racier to me, and I fish it with more confidence. But the wing will tatter as soon as you fight a fish with the fly, and which way you tilt the wing tips of a wet fly is of little concern to the trout you're about to catch with it, so you should please yourself.

13. When the wing is measured to the midpoint of the tail, take hold of it gently but firmly between the thumb and forefinger of your off-hand. Hold the wing in place right behind the hook eye, perfectly upright, married sections together. The back end of the wing is now out of sight under your grip, which is why you measured it for length with the tying hand, then transferred it to the off-hand to tie it in. The thread should be tight against the hackle, so your first turn of thread over the wing will be the farthest back.

14. Tie the wing in with a *soft loop*. To execute the soft loop, slip the thread straight up between the forefinger and thumb of your off-hand, on the near side of the wing. Pinch the thread above the wing, then bring the thread back down between the forefinger and thumb on the far side of the wing. Take the thread straight below the hook shank. You're now in position to draw the first turn of thread directly toward you with the bobbin.

Note: In the photo the loop is exaggerated and the thumb is drawn back to show it. In practice the loop would be pinched firmly between forefinger and thumb.

15. Draw the thread toward you on the underside of the hook, allowing the loop to draw down on the wing, collapsing it onto the hook shank. If done correctly this will stack the individual fibers of the feather sections on top of each other and bind them tightly to the hook shank. Take two or three turns of thread toward the hook eye, to secure the wing in place.

Note: If you have trouble with the wing tilting over in the direction of the thread turn, correct it by tilting the wing slightly toward you before drawing the soft loop tight.

16. Trim the excess wing butts as close as you can to the thread wraps. Take enough wraps to cover the protruding wing butts and to make a neatly tapered head. Wax an inch of your thread if it's silk, whip-finish, clip the thread, and the winged wet is ready to fish.

Note: If you were to wrap any turns back over the wing toward the hackle, after pulling the soft loop home, they would push the wing over in the direction of the turns. That is why you make the soft loop at the back of the head and all subsequent turns forward of that first turn of thread.

I just took Helen Shaw's beautiful 1989 book *Flies for Fish and Fishermen* down from the shelf to refresh my research in the matter of the downswept versus up-tilted wet-fly wing. The winged wet fly reached its pinnacle at her vise, and in the pages of her book, with exceptional step photography by her husband, Herman Kessler. In the color plates, every quill-winged dressing has the wing tipped up, not down. If your interest is in the traditional winged wet, and you desire to tie them beautifully, this might be the single most important book, if you can track it down.

Bergman's plates, in his classic *Trout*, show more than half of traditional wets with their wings tips-up. But the plates are painted, not photographed, and though they're beautiful, might reflect the preference of the artist over that of the fly tier.

Roger Fogg's more recent British book *Wet-Fly Tying and Fishing* shows most, though far from all, of its winged dressings with the tips down, in what I consider the more traditional position.

I have a set of a dozen favorite wet flies tied by Davy Wotton (see Chapter 16). He has his wet-fly tying and fishing roots in Wales, but now guides on the White River in Arkansas. Most of the flies he tied for me have their wings with tips down, the same as Roger Fogg's.

TYING A TRADITIONAL WET FLY WITH A HEN HACKLE FIBER WING

To tie the Hare's Ear Wet with a hackle fiber wing, you need the same set of materials except for the pheasant wing feather sections. Substitute a clump of pliable brown hen hackle. The wing will be far less showy, and also less pretty, but it will be more active when worked by currents. It will never have the rudder effect that can be caused by stiff quill, especially when it's been sprayed with fixative so that it holds together in the water.

Nothing could be simpler than substituting hen hackle for feather sections. If you try it for no other reason, it makes a wet fly much easier to tie. Begin by tying the fly through the steps to the point where it's ready for the wing. Tie in the hackle, tails, ribbing, and body, following the same procedures in the previous Steps 1 through 10.

HARE'S EAR WET (HACKLE FIBER WINGED)

Hook:	#12-16 standard wet fly or 2X heavy
Thread:	Orange Pearsall's Gossamer Silk or orange 6/0
Hackle:	Brown or furnace hen
Tail:	Five to ten brown hen hackle fibers
Rib:	Oval gold tinsel
Body:	Hare's mask fur or natural (#1) Hare's Ear Plus
Wing:	Brown or furnace hen hackle fibers

1–10. Prepare the Hare's Ear Wet for the wing, just as you did when tying it with feather sections.

11. Select a long feather from the back end of the cape, or from a saddle patch. Stroke about $^1/_2$ to $^3/_4$ inch of fibers so that they stand at a 90-degree angle to the feather stem, with their tips even. Be sure that these fibers are long enough to reach from the head of the fly to approximately the midpoint of the tail. Some hen necks do not have feathers with fibers long enough to tie wet-fly wings larger than about size 12. You can solve this problem by buying combination necks and saddles and taking the wing material from the saddle feathers, or by buying India hen saddles with plenty of long fibers.

12. Strip the selected fibers from the feather, keeping the tips even, and roll them into a bunch. Hold the bunch between your thumb and forefinger and lay them over the hook eye. Measure the ends of the fibers to the midpoint of the tail. If there is no tail on the fly, measure the wing to a point just beyond the end of the hook.

13. Holding the wing bunch in place, transfer your grip from the right to the left hand. Hold the wing firmly over the hook eye, and use a soft loop to lock it in place. Take a few more turns of thread to secure it. You need not worry about making your first turn the farthest back. As long as you hold the wing in place while you wrap it, to keep it from getting knocked off center, you can go back over the wing at will.

14. Clip the excess wing butts, and lay a base of thread over the butts to cover them and form a neat head. Wax an inch of thread if you're using silk, whip-finish the fly, and clip the thread.

It's much easier to tie a wet fly with a hen hackle wing than it is to use quill. The wing will never cause the fly to roll over and over in the water or to rudder from side to side as you retrieve it. The fibers will also work in the water, responding to the current or to your retrieve. In my experience, the hen-winged wet is not only easier to tie, but also at least as effective to fish.

TYING A WINGED WET FLY WITHOUT HACKLE

Some of the most effective wet flies fish as well or better without any hackle at all. It's an option to keep in mind for all of your winged wet flies. It's also a method worth considering when experimenting with your own patterns. The dubbing fur for the body is left rough at the thorax, or even picked out, to represent the legs of an insect.

I tie the Hare's Ear Wet most often in this fashion. It works well on lakes and ponds, during hatches of Speckle-Wing Quill mayflies in the widespread genus *Callibaetis*. Trout seem to mistake the wet fly for a rising nymph. It's most effective just before and also during a heavy hatch when cast out, given a moment to sink, then retrieved shallow with short, staccato strips. Pauses during the retrieve sometimes incite trout to strike while the fly is on the sit.

HARE'S EAR WET (WITHOUT HACKLE)

Hook:	#12-16 standard wet fly or 2X heavy
Thread:	Orange Pearsall's Gossamer Silk or orange 6/0
Tail:	Three to five pheasant tail fibers
Rib:	Oval gold tinsel
Body:	Blended hare's mask fur or natural (#1) Hare's Ear Plus
Wing:	Hen pheasant wing feather sections

1. Attach thread to the hook, wrap it to the bend of the hook, and tie in three to five tail fibers about the length of the hook shank. Take a turn or two of thread under them to cock them up. Clip excess tail butts. Tie 3 to 4 inches of ribbing tinsel in at the base of the tail. Secure the tinsel with thread about half the length of the hook shank.

2. Apply tacky wax to your thread for $1^1/2$ to $2^1/2$ inches, depending on the size fly you're tying. Tease a skein of fur into the proper length, then press it against the waxed thread. Twist just the tips of the fur onto the thread to hold it in place. Be sure that the fur is thick and loose in the lower $1/3$ of the skein, which will become the thorax and in this case also the legs of the finished fly.

3. Catch the thread over the forefinger of your off-hand, and return the thread to the hook shank to make a dubbing loop. As an alternative shown here, use one of the many dubbing-twisting tools available. Spin the loop into a fur rope. This should be slender at the top but much wider and thicker in the bottom $^1/_3$. It will be better if many spiky fibers stick out. Take the working thread forward to a point just behind the hook eye.

4. Wind the fur in close turns to a point just behind the eye of the hook, leaving room to tie in the wing. Tie it off there. Clip the excess thread. In time, you'll be able to build a body of the precise right length and thickness. At first, however, you'll come up with extra fur rope on some flies, and find yourself needing to add fur to your working thread on others. Don't worry about it. Just be sure the front portion of the body is spiky and loosely dubbed.

5. Work the ribbing forward in three to six evenly spaced turns. Be sure it seats well into the fur and does not mat many fibers down. Tie it off at the head of the fly with a couple of turns of thread, turn it back, and take about three more turns of thread before clipping it off. Before tying in the wing, lay a base of thread from the end of the body to the hook eye and back again, creating an even under-layer for the wing tie-in. Finish with the thread at the rear of the head. Your first wrap on the wing should be the farthest back.

6. Select paired feathers from matched hen pheasant wings. Clip sections from opposite feathers equal in width to the hook gap, and join them together with their concave sides facing each other. Measure the wing to the midpoint of the tail. Again, you can tie the fly with the wing tips curved either down or up, depending on your own sense of aesthetics. I'm tying with them down here, in the more traditional manner.

7. Switch your grip on the wing to your off-hand thumb and forefinger, hold the wing upright over the hook shank, then use a soft loop to draw the wing material directly down onto the hook shank. Secure it with two to three more turns of thread, none of them behind the first turn of the soft loop.

8. Clip the wing butts, make a layer of thread to cover them, then whip-finish the head. If the thorax region of the fly does not have enough loose fibers sticking out to represent the legs of an insect, use your bodkin or dubbing-roughing tool to pick out the fur. If the fly looks neat when you're finished, you're not finished. Make it scruffy and you'll have it right for fishing.

A FEW FAVORITE WINGED WETS

I do not use an extensive array of traditional winged wet flies. Many of those that I do use are tied with hen hackle for wings, rather than stiffer quill. For example, the Blue-Winged Olive wet can be tied with mallard or teal wing feather sections, or with a clump of blue dun hen hackle fibers. In either form, it makes an excellent imitation for the many mayfly duns that fail to reach the surface during a BWO emergence, or that get drowned by rough water after attaining the top. If tied sparsely, it also represents the spinner of the same species. This adult is rare among mayflies in that, like many caddis species, it lays its eggs on submerged sticks and stones. It crawls down them frequently, rather than swimming, but it's often knocked loose in the currents, and trout often take BWO spinners submerged rather than spent and floating on top.

The bulk of my fishing with winged wet flies is done when adult caddis are in the air, either emerging or laying their eggs. It's difficult to tell which one they're doing unless you catch a trout, take a throat sample, and find pupae dominant. It's likely that they could be emerging and depositing eggs at the same time. I've already mentioned the two groups that dive to the bottom to complete this last mission in their little lives: Gray Sedges (*Rhyacophila*) and Spotted Sedges (*Hydropsyche*). Since these are among the most abundant trout-stream caddis, it's wise to keep in mind that adults seen in the air are often an indication to fish a winged wet fly, not a dry.

The first of my favorites, which you should guess because it's the sample fly tied in three versions in this chapter, is the Hare's Ear Wet. I fish it in its standard version, with a feather-section wing, or tied with a hen hackle wing, interchangeably. It's an excellent pattern to fish for the ubiquitous Spotted Sedges, which are the most abundant trout-stream caddis group on more than a few trout waters. They come in sizes 12 though 16, and those are the hook sizes on which I tie and carry the fly.

LEADWING COACHMAN

Hook:	#10-16 standard wet fly or 2X heavy
Thread:	Black 6/0
Hackle:	Brown or furnace hen
Tag/Rib:	Silver Mylar tinsel
Body:	Peacock herl
Wing:	Mallard wing feather sections

Leadwing Coachman: I prefer this traditional tie with the standard mallard quill wing, though it can also be tied with dark blue dun hen hackle fibers. It often works better than a dry fly when large Green Drake duns are out, both on the water and under it. It's even better when Gray Sedges return to lay their eggs by diving down to sow them on bottom stones. These adults are best imitated with wet flies, not drys. They're winged, and I prefer the quill-winged Leadwing Coachman to imitate them.

LIGHT CAHILL

Hook:	#12-16 standard wet fly
Thread:	Tan 8/0
Hackle:	Ginger hen
Tail:	Ginger hackle fibers
Body:	Light Cahill dubbing
Wing:	Wood duck flank fibers

Light Cahill: I consider the Light Cahill wet fly almost exclusive for Yellow Sallies and Pale Evening Duns. It's effective in size 16 during Pale Morning Dun hatches as well. Don't overlook it as a general searching wet fly, especially if you're looking for a pale wet to pair with a darker wet in a brace that offers trout a choice between the two. This choice can reveal the trout's preferences much more quickly. Though it's a traditional winged wet, its wing is flank fibers, not feather sections. If the body is tied roughly, this traditional wet could almost be considered a flymph with a few fibers added on top for a wing. It's an easy fly to tie.

BLUE DUN

Hook:	#10-16 standard wet fly or 2X heavy
Thread:	Gray 6/0 or 8/0 nylon
Hackle:	Medium blue dun hen
Tail:	Medium blue dun hen hackle fibers
Rib:	Silver Mylar tinsel (narrow)
Body:	Muskrat belly fur
Wing:	Mallard wing feather sections

Blue Dun: This wet fly is so popular that it must be honored, though I don't fish it often any more. It's not that it wouldn't work; it's just that I solve the conditions in which I used to use it with other dressings instead, and haven't gotten it wet the way I did in my past. That past was often spent fishing small Coastal Mountain lakes in late spring through mid-summer. Heavy hatches of speckle-wing mayflies, followed by similar abundant spinner falls, would get trout up and working at or near the surface. When they did, my dad would call out, "They're taking those blue duns!" And he'd tie one on. And he'd catch lots of trout.

For many summers I followed his lead, and the Blue Dun wet, simply cast out and retrieved, or trolled slowly behind a pram if trout were not rising steadily, solved most of those situations for me. Then I made the mistake of getting interested in aquatic entomology. During a hatch I collected a few "blue duns," peered at them through a magnifying glass, and discovered that they were brown with some hints of olive tossed in. I also discovered that a dry fly tied in the right size and color—not blue dun—would interest those rising trout as often as the wet, and give me a greater sense of having outsmarted them when they took it.

Spinners of the speckle-wings are pale gray. There is little doubt that the Blue Dun wet would fool at least a portion of the trout feeding on them. But it doesn't represent their behavior at all, and I prefer experiments with dry flies, though in truth I do poorly enough that I ought to give up and just go back to the wet.

There is no question that if Dad were still fishing those ponds, he'd be doing it during speckle-wing hatches with a Blue Dun wet. He'd catch trout, and I probably would not.

BLUE-WINGED OLIVE

Hook:	#12-18 standard wet fly or 2X heavy
Thread:	Olive 6/0 or 8/0
Hackle:	Light blue dun hen
Tail:	Light blue dun hen hackle fibers
Rib:	Oval gold tinsel (optional on small sizes)
Body:	Olive fur, or fur and Sparkle Yarn mix
Wing:	Mallard or teal feather sections, or hen hackle fibers

Blue-Winged Olive: Tied in sizes 16 and 18, this wet fly represents spring and fall hatches of BWO mayfly duns. In larger sizes, 12 and 14, it also imitates mayflies that are variously called Olives, Lesser Green Drakes, and *flavs*. Various species hatch East, Midwest, and West, all spring and summer. In some places, especially the high elevations of the Yellowstone Plateau, they continue into autumn.

In its small sizes, the Blue-Winged Olive wet is little more than a Little Olive Flymph with a wing added. In its larger sizes, it's essentially a Blue Dun tied with an olive body. In the full range of sizes from 12 to 18, it manages to cover a lot of the natural insects that trout feed on throughout the season.

BLACK GNAT

Hook:	#10-14 standard wet fly or 2X heavy
Thread:	Black 6/0 nylon
Hackle:	Black hen
Tail:	Red hackle fibers
Butt:	Red floss
Body:	Black dyed fur, or fur and Sparkle Yarn mix
Wing:	Dark gray mallard wing feather sections
Note:	To get an appropriate dark wing for this fly, it's usually necessary to pair the wing feather sections with their dark sides out. This generally causes a flared pairing, the tips separating slightly rather than melding. This is not detrimental unless the wing is set at an angle, which would cause it to rudder. Black hen hackle is an excellent substitute.

Black Gnat: This wet fly is an excellent solution when winged ants and the general run of terrestrial beetles and other dark insects trundle around near the water, and often plummet into it, almost always during the heat of summer. They sink quickly. The black wet fly is usually a better solution than any dry fly when these insects are out.

We always saw winged ant dispersal flights in May and June on the same forested lakes that my dad fished so eagerly with his Blue Dun wet. When those ants were in the air and falling to the water, he'd switch to the Black Gnat, and it would work. When we would arrive at the same stillwaters and find them lifeless, we'd often tie on the same fly as an exploring pattern, to be cast around fallen logs and along the shoreline, or towed behind a pram, trolling slowly. Intervals between takes were often long, but we never did get evidence that anything would work any better.

ALDER

Hook:	#10-12 standard wet fly or 2X heavy
Thread:	Black 6/0 nylon
Hackle:	Dark furnace or black hen
Body:	Peacock herl
Wing:	Dark turkey wing feather sections or furnace hen hackle fibers

Alder: This ancient dressing, devised by Reverend Charles Kingsley in 1858 for an alderfly hatch on the River Itchen, is still effective in its original tie, with a turkey feather section wing. I sometimes tie it with a black or furnace hen hackle wing because of the vibrancy the softer material lends to the fly. It's also difficult to find turkey feathers in pairs that match and make good wet-fly wings. When you find a good set, spray them with artist's fixative and let it set before tying with them, or they'll tatter before they even get wet.

The Alder is a dressing that takes a lot of trout for me each season to this day, much more than a century after it was first tied by its originator. The adult alderfly is out over forested stillwaters, and streams as well, from the time the sun warms things up in May until the oppressive heat of July. The naturals are so dense that when they land on water, they soon sink. A wet fly simply cast out, allowed to sink a bit, then retrieved slowly with thoughtful pauses, is more effective than any dry fly.

The Alder is shown here, in honor of its originator, with a turkey feather wing, which is still the way I tie and fish it most often.

Though I supply a short list of favorite winged wet flies here, remember that you can vary the style to match anything you see in nature, or in addition, anything that might meet your fancy. Those bright wet flies that our fishing forefathers used for brook trout would probably surprise us on occasion by working as well now as they did then, if only we'd give them a chance.

When you see caddis adults in the air, especially over broad riffles such as the one shown at right on the Bighorn River in Montana, suspect that trout taking with splashy rises are feeding on the pupae as they rise for emergence or on adults as they swim down to lay their eggs. If a dry fly fails to take the trout, don't wait long before tying on a winged wet fly, approximately the size and color of the naturals in the air. Fish it on a patient swing, down and around with the current. Don't let it move too fast; trout aren't used to seeing the naturals swimming boldly.

Chapter Eight

Tying All-Fur Wet Flies

Polly Rosborough's book *Tying and Fishing the Fuzzy Nymphs* sowed the first seeds for my thoughts about what I've come to call *all-fur wet flies*. He was the guru of the fibrous, working nymph. *Fuzzy Nymphs* is considered a classic for its original research into the ways aquatic insects move, the reasons trout take them, and the ways artificial flies can imitate those insects and fool trout into taking them for the real thing. Polly's concept of *fishing under the hatch* is brilliant. He tied many of his fuzzy nymphs to represent insects, mostly caddis pupae and swimmer mayfly nymphs, approaching the surface for emergence.

His philosophy was that most trout, and almost always the largest of them, continue to feed subsurface on these rising immature forms throughout a hatch, letting little trout tip up for the adults. It's not always true, but it's true often enough that it's wise, as we've already decided, to have representations of those emerging insects.

Many of Polly's nymphs were tied as imitations of specific naturals. Others were general patterns that looked like lots of things that trout eat. Whether specific or generic, Polly's patterns were tied with rough bodies. They did, and still do, look alive in the water. Polly's methods for fishing his fuzzy nymphs were based on the oldest and most efficient wet-fly techniques. When I watched him fish on his home Williamson River, he cast at an angle slightly upstream, gave his fly plenty of time to sink, then fished it down and around on the swing. Polly never weighted his nymphs, another reason his flies and tactics fit our current concept of wet flies more tightly than they do our present thoughts about nymphs. He did use sinking-tip lines, which took his flies down 2 to 3 feet in the moderate currents that he fished most often.

Polly Rosborough's Casual Dress is clearly a nymph, not a wet fly. But its fur collar, as a concept, has applications in wet-fly tying. This one is tied on a size 12, 3X long hook. That is large for trout, but about as small as it can be tied with muskrat fur and still keep the guard hairs in proportion to the rest of the fly.

One of his best dressings is the Casual Dress. Polly tied it large: size 2 and 4 for bass, 6 and 8 for trout, 10 and 12 for panfish, all on 3X long, 2X heavy hooks. Part of the reason for such large sizes is the difficulty tying a small fly with a fur collar constructed with muskrat. It has very long guard hairs. It's difficult to tie a decent muskrat collar on a hook smaller than size 12, and have any of the guard hairs left in. Polly's size 12 for panfish would just be getting down toward the sizes I fish most often for trout, whether in wet flies or nymphs.

When thinking about wet flies, Polly's fur hackle intrigued me. A fly tied with one would be buggy, would have plenty of movement in the water, and would, as Polly put it, look alive. That's our goal with wet flies, but I had no idea how to achieve it in smaller sizes until I later came across some research that reflected back to a time much earlier than Polly's.

In the late 1970s, I read W. H. Lawrie's 1967 book *All-Fur Flies and How to Dress Them*. It had a chapter on wet flies, which interested me. It described a method for tying fur hackles that intrigued me. It probably came down through oral tradition, but in print was apparently first used by Captain George Marryat, recorded by G. E. M. Skues in the late 1800s, and later translated for dry-fly use by Frederick Halford. It's a tangled trail on paper, and probably even more so at the bench and on the water. I've often wondered if Polly Rosborough was aware of the long history behind the fur collar. I didn't think to ask him, and he didn't mention it. I'm inclined to believe he came up with the idea on his own.

Marryat split his thread, inserted the fur between the strands, twisted it together to form the fur hackle. Halford lay waxed thread on a surface, spread the fur on it, captured it by drawing the thread back over it before spinning it. This is similar to the spun-fur method used in Hidy and Leisenring's flymphs. Polly was a student of fly-fishing literature; it's possible he was aware of not only the earliest applications, but also those techniques recorded in the 1941 edition of *The Art of Tying the Wet Fly*.

Lawrie doesn't mention the types of furs used in the earliest works, beyond mohair and cat. Neither material solves the problem of tying in small sizes. Interestingly, Lawrie notes that Marryat and Halford spun their fur hackles several inches long and tied each fly with a segment of it, much as we might tie several dry flies from a single long saddle hackle in this day, or several bodies from a dubbing brush.

I always try to incorporate materials in the process of tying a fly, rather than constructing something separately and reaching for it when it's time. It's easy, however, to create a spun-fur collar into the tying of an individual fly, just as it is to tie a flymph with the body spun on the hook rather than on a block, though there are always arguments for doing it either way. If you're already making dubbing brushes, then you'll find it easy to apply the same techniques to fur collars. I don't tie hackle collars that way, and will show the methods I use.

Fox and gray squirrels have fur and guard hairs somewhat shorter than muskrat, and lend themselves to tying fur hackles down to size 14, and not necessarily on long shank hooks. Fox squirrel fur, with its white-tipped guard hairs and underfur that varies from reddish orange to gray, makes a fine mottled collar, and perhaps an even more attractive speckled body, when the guard hairs are left in the mix. The most famous use for this fur is in Dave Whitlock's Red Fox Squirrel Nymph, which belongs in every fly box. But it's a nymph, and for some reason I've bypassed fox and gray squirrel furs in most of my own wet-fly experiments. I'd encourage you to correct that in your own tying. Both furs give an excellent mottled coloration to a finished fly.

Most of my tying and fishing with all-fur wets has focused on flies tied with pine squirrel. The hair itself is shorter, and the guard hairs are in nice balance with the underfur, in terms of both length and density. However, pine squirrel hides are far from all the same, or even similar, in length and texture of the fur. One killed in summer will have mostly short guard hairs, with little underfur. Another killed in autumn will have a nice balance of long and short hairs. A squirrel trapped in winter, especially in the far north, will have dense underfur and sparse guard hairs.

Each of these hides will provide perfect fur for a different range of fly sizes. The average will be just right for sizes 12 and 14, and with some trimming will work on size 16. As I've recommended for most things along the way, it's wise to buy an entire skin. It will have a range of shades, textures, and lengths as you move from belly to back, and from head to tail. Somewhere in that carpet of fur, you'll find just what you want. I also recommend you sort through pine squirrel hides whenever you get a chance, and buy any that will tie a range of fly sizes you don't already have covered.

I've found pine squirrel skins dyed olive over the natural color, but the fur is so dark to begin with that the olive doesn't show well. I once found a hide that had been bleached and then dyed light brown, and found it so useful

All-fur wets can be tied with gray squirrel (left) and fox squirrel (right). Both result in fine flies, with nice mottling that is effective on trout. I haven't done a lot of experimenting with these furs for wet flies, having focused instead on the use of shorter pine squirrel fur.

A section of pine squirrel hide that has been used consistently for tying all-fur wet flies. Note that the fur has been cut to form a shelf. This prepares it for holding down the fur with the off-hand and sliding the scissors under a wide but thin section of it. After it is snipped, the tying hand can lift the section cleanly from the hide, then transfer it safely to the pre-formed waxed dubbing loop.

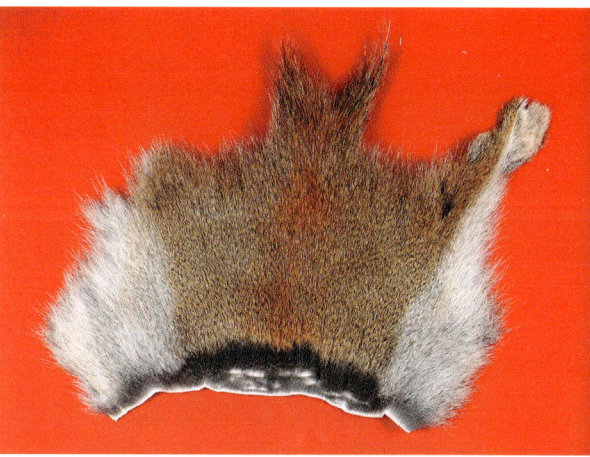

I used it all and haven't been able to replace it. I'm putting in a request here for some supplier to take on the task of bleaching and dyeing pine squirrel hides in a pleasant array of colors: tan, brown, olive, black, and what we call medium blue dun when we're talking about hackle.

The perfect source for dyed pine squirrel can be found in Zonker strips. One strip will provide what you need for quite a few fur-hackled flies. In some ways it's easier to use for a fur collar because the thin, wide section has already been created for you, and all you have to do is hold it while cutting it from the strip, then transfer it to a pre-formed waxed thread loop. You could even nip the length of strip you desire, trap the fur in the loop, and trim it from the hide after it's trapped. An advantage of using Zonker strips is the

Tanned pine squirrel hides take the dye color much better than dark natural hides. These, in light olive and rust, have been pre-cut into Zonker strips and might make the ultimate material for fur-hackle collars in the range of sizes most useful in all-fur wet flies for trout, size 12 down to size 16, with some careful scissoring of the butts.

ease in trimming the butts of the fur to a length suitable to the size fly you're tying, in the process of cutting the fur from the hide. Depending on the length of the fur on the strip, you might cut it full length for a size 12 fly, leave a bit of butts on the hide for a size 14, or cut away the guard hairs and just half of the underfur to create the collar on a size 16 hook.

Feather-Craft Fly Fishing in St. Louis, Missouri (www.feather-craft.com), has tanned and dyed pine squirrel half hides in an array of thirteen colors, pre-cut into Zonker strips. These colors open the concept of all-fur wets to all sorts of experiments that I haven't had time to make yet. I'm starting with light olive and rust, because so many caddis pupae come in those two colors, but everything from black through red to fluorescent chartreuse might be found of interest to trout. Not every all-fur wet needs to imitate something in nature; trout are as experimental as we are. A half pine squirrel hide will tie a lot of all-fur wets.

Mole fur makes fair hackles for all-fur wets in size 16, with some trimming down to 18, and with some struggling in the tying, perhaps as small as 20. However, mole has only soft underfur, no guard fibers, and it comes only in black and tannish brown. They are both nice colors. I tie a very short list of what I think of as all-fur wets with them. But I'm never quite sure if I'm fishing a wet fly or nymph when I get them into trout water. I'll let you decide.

It's important to note that all-fur wet flies are a concept, far from a new one, but also one that hasn't seen much experimentation yet. You might decide that they're nymphs, not wet flies, and desire to move on to the next subject. Before you do, however, I recommend you at least learn to tie a fur

Olive and rust all-fur wets tied with pine squirrel Zonker strips. These are tied on size 14, 2X heavy wet-fly hooks. The guard hair and underfur has been cut from the strip a bit short. If it's left at normal length, it will tie a size 12, and if cut shorter, a size 16.

Mole fur in black and tannish brown, the only two colors I've found, can be used to tie some small all-fur wet flies, which will be useful when trout are interested in small caddisflies, either in the pupal or adult stages. Note that the fur has no guard hairs, so the resulting hackle collar will be of an even length, lacking the spikiness squirrel furs have. Mole is a very soft fur; wet flies tied with it will have lots of movement in the water.

hackle collar. You'll find it fun after working with the idea, perhaps after some blow-ups when you first start sticking patches of fur to thread. You might find it useful, whether you apply it to tying all-fur wet flies, or to the nymphs that lie just a bit farther along on the continuum of fly types.

TYING ALL-FUR WET FLIES

The fur-hackle method is similar to the spun bodies of Leisenring and Hidy. I've fiddled with forming hackle collars separately on a spinning block, and working them into all-fur wets after the body has been completed. The results are fine, it just takes a lot of extra time. As with those spun bodies on flymphs, it's a more contemplative way to tie. It also might be beneficial because it encourages giving bodies and fur hackles an appropriate undercolor of silk thread that is a different color from the fur. But that can be accomplished as well by tying with gossamer silk rather than 6/0 or 8/0 nylon. I haven't gone in that direction yet, but recommend you get ahead of me on it.

Nothing is set in stone in the all-fur wet style. I tie just a few patterns in a narrow array of colors, and use them when appropriate. Most often that use is for searching situations, when I don't know what trout are up to. More rarely it's to imitate a specific stage of a certain insect species.

A fur hackle must be formed with patience and care, especially at the beginning. If it doesn't work out it can explode off the thread into a ball of fur in the air, which can be another form of fun. It takes several tries before creating a fur hackle becomes anything like routine. I've been tying with them for years and still suffer occasional blow-ups. They seem to be most frequent when I demonstrate the technique in front of an audience at a wet-fly-tying workshop.

The following sample all-fur wet shows the steps in tying a fly with the tail, body, and hackle all taken from the same pine squirrel skin. It has the advantage of being one of my favorite wet flies. The critical steps are in forming the hackle collar, which will be used in each following all-fur wet.

PINE SQUIRREL ALL-FUR WET

Hook:	#12-16 standard wet fly or 2X heavy
Thread:	Brown 6/0 or 8/0 nylon
Tail:	Pine squirrel fur with guard hairs
Body:	Pine squirrel fur with guard hairs
Hackle:	Pine squirrel fur with guard hairs

1. Wrap a layer of thread from the eye to the beginning of the hook bend. Clip enough fur from the hide for a thick tail. Winnow out some of the shortest underfur, but leave most of it in. Tug out any maverick long guard fibers from the tip end of the patch. Measure the tail about $^2/_3$ the length of the shank, hold it in position, and nip off the butts about $^1/_3$ the shank length behind the hook eye. Tie in the tail. Overwrap the butts forward with thread, then back to the base of the tail.

2. Cut a substantial fur patch, leave all the guard hairs in, place the patch in the palm of your off-hand, and rough it up into a loose ball with your tying hand forefinger. You can *direct dub* the body, twisting the fur onto the thread, or catch it in a dubbing loop and spin it into a dubbing rope, just as you would for a flymph. Either way it should be loose and spiky, not tight. Dub a fur body covering about $^2/_3$ of the hook shank.

3. Use your tacky wax liberally on about three inches of thread. Catch the heavily waxed thread over the forefinger tip of your off-hand, return the thread to the shank, and capture it with enough turns to create a dubbing loop. You can let this loop dangle; the wax, if sufficient, will cause it to remain open. I prefer to catch the loop in the materials holder on my vise barrel. Pre-form this loop so you don't have to form it after you've cut the fur for the hackle.

4. Clip a ¹/₂-inch wide but thin section of pine squirrel fur directly from the hide. To do this, place the forefinger of your off-hand on the hide side—the back side—of the fur patch, and use the thumb on the fur side—the near side—to pin a *shelf* of fur between the forefinger and thumb. The fur will then be held tightly to the hide, presenting a smooth surface. Slip one blade of your scissors under the fur, against the hide, and slide that blade about ¹/₂ inch along the fur. Keep the blade shallow; your goal is to cut a ¹/₂-inch wide thin slice of fur from the hide.

5. Clip the slice of fur. Keep the slice locked in with your off-hand thumb and forefinger. Bend the hide away from the scissor cut with your tying hand. This lifts the butts away from the hide, allowing you to get ahold of them between the thumb and forefinger of your tying hand. The goal is to separate the cut butts so you can get a grip on them and remove them from the hide in the same wide but thin strip in which you've cut them.

Note: If you have any wax on your tying hand fingers, you're pointed toward disaster. I make it a habit to swipe my thumb and forefinger along my pants leg at this exact point, to ensure they're free from anything that might cause the fur to stick to them. Because I keep my scissors on my tying hand ring finger, without ever setting them aside, I have to be careful not to spear myself in the leg when I do this.

6. Pinch the butts of the slice of fur between the thumb and forefinger of your tying hand, and remove it from the hide. Retain its full width, and keep it as even as possible, the tips aligned and the butts aligned. If the fur is just the right length for the size fly you're tying, you can skip the next step, and insert the fur into the waxed thread loop. If it's too long, you'll need to shorten it, as shown in the next step. The fur in this photo needs to be shortened for the size hook on which the hackle will be wound.

7. Transfer the slice to your off-hand thumb and forefinger, being sure to keep the butts aligned. Calculate the length you want, and take a single cut across the butts to shorten them to that desired length. All of this is approximate, and comes with time and practice. The length of the fur hackle you're after is the same as that for a feather hackle: $1^1/_2$ to 2 times the hook gap. The fur slice should be shortened to about twice that length if it's too long when cut from the hide, which will be most often.

8. Lay the fur against the waxed side of the thread loop. Collapse the loop onto the fur by letting it slip slowly between the forefinger tip and ball of the thumb of your off-hand. This captures the fur between the two waxed threads. The fur should be caught about halfway between butts and tips, and should be spread on the thread exactly as it was removed from the hide. If it's not, push or pull the fur butts or tips, coaxing them into alignment. If the fur is not spread evenly on the thread, tease it out until it's a length that will give you two or three hackle winds.

Note: If the fur for the hackle is trapped precisely in the center of the thread loop, then the butts sticking out one side and the guard hairs on the other should both be the length of the hackle you want. It's best to trap the hackle a bit longer on the guard side, so that when wound, the guards stand above a core of underfur. In this case the guard fiber side should be the length of the hackle you want. Practice will make you perfect.

9. Spin the loop end to form the fur hackle. It should look like a bottlebrush. If the fur is captured off-center, with the guard hairs a bit longer than the underfur, you'll see now that the hackle has a darker and thicker core, with the guard hairs sticking out from it. Capture the end of the loop with your hackle pliers.

10. Moisten the thumb and forefinger of your off-hand and stroke the fur back. Take one turn of fur hackle at the end of the body. Use your moistened forefinger and thumb to sweep back the fur for the next turn.

11. Make the second turn of hackle between the first and the eye of the hook. On some flies, and with some fur hackles, this second turn will fill in all the space and create a full hackle.

12. On most flies you'll need a third turn of hackle. On some you'll use a fourth. Treat them as the first and second, stroking the fur back before making the hackle wrap. With a bit of practice, you'll end with the right amount of hackle for the size fly you're tying, each time you spin a hackle loop.

Note: If you have more hackle than you have room on the hook, tie it off and trim the excess behind the eye. If you end up short, just add a bit of the same fur as dubbing between the last turn of hackle and the eye. It will look like you did it on purpose, and trout won't mind.

13. When you've finished winding the hackle, stroke it all back and hold it out of the way with your off-hand. Take two or three layers of thread between the eye and the hackle to brace the hackle back, and to form a neat head. Tie it off with a whip-finish.

14. As a final step, comb the fur hackle back gently with your fingers. At this point you can tidy up the fly and shape it to suit you. Pluck any over-long guard fibers out of the fur. If you feel the fur hackle is too thick, prune it until you like it better. Don't get brutal; just meld the fly into final shape, and remove any fibers that are not locked in. The finished fly should look very graceful, like it might go out and chase a trout. That fur hackle will give it lots of movement in the water.

TYING AN ALL-FUR WET WITHOUT A PRE-FORMED LOOP

An alternative method for a fur hackle simplifies procedures by omitting the pre-formed loop, and using a dubbing tool, though you can use your forefinger as usual. This method increases the danger that things will blow up, because it becomes necessary to form the loop after you've applied the fur loosely to the thread. If you slip while forming the loop, you'll twang the thread like a guitar string, and you know what the fur will do.

1. Prepare your fly for the hackle by tying in the tail and dubbing the body. Wax 2 to 3 inches of thread liberally with tacky wax. Beeswax won't hold the fur to the thread.

2. Clip a thin but wide slice of fur from the squirrel hide. If it's too long to form the right-sized hackle, shorten the butts. Gently—I should say gingerly—place the fur slice against the waxed thread. It should stick there. Don't sneeze.

3. Even more carefully, attach your dubbing loop tool to the thread, bring your bobbin up to capture the fur between thread and thread, and form the loop with a few turns around the hook shank. With excellent wax and lots of practice, you'll be able to do this fairly consistently, but expect the slice of fur to fall, spring, or explode off the thread occasionally when you make any slight mistake. After you've securely captured the fur and formed the loop, you can breathe a sigh of relief and also adjust the fur, spreading it inside the loop and aligning the tips and butts.

4. Twirl the fur into the bottlebrush that will form the fur hackle, just as you did when tying with a pre-formed dubbing loop.

5. Finish the fly by winding two to four turns of fur hackle, stroking the fur back between turns. Whip-finish, tidy the fly a bit if you wish, and it's done.

FORMING A FUR HACKLE WITH A DUBBING LOOP TOOL

Dubbing loop tools are made especially for capturing fur between two strands of thread. They have two wires with hooks at their ends. You wax the thread, form the loop by capturing the thread with the two hooks, place the fur on the waxed thread, and collapse the loop by pulling down on the tool. It works very well. Like anything else, if you use a tool and get used to it, you'll get faster with it, and you'll also find that you can fine-tune your fur hackles as time and experience march onward.

I keep tools to a minimum in my own tying and have never gotten used to dubbing loop tools, though I recommend you at least try one or two. There are a variety of them on the market. All work well in some areas, less well in others. Each works perfectly for some tiers but causes problems for others. The following photos show one of them at work.

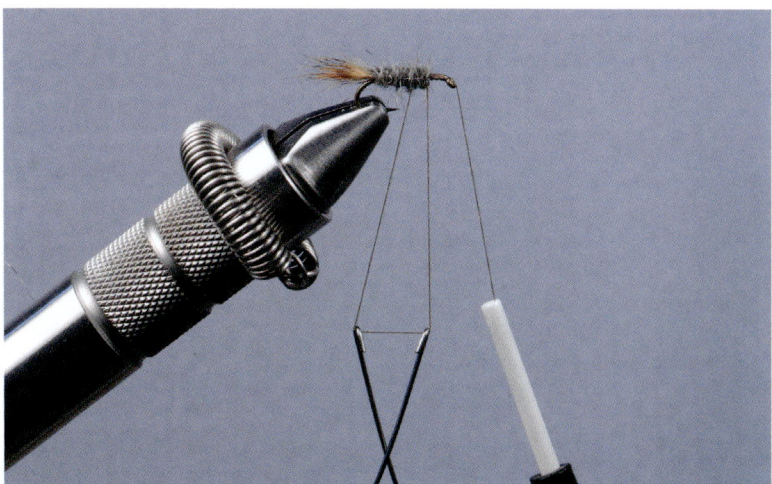

1. Wax several inches of thread. Capture the thread in the two hooks of the dubbing loop tool. Form a loop by running your thread to the hook and taking several turns over the shank. My minor problem with this sort of tool for an all-fur wet is that it's necessary at this point to let the tool dangle while I cut the fur for the hackle. Sometimes the tool takes on tasks of its own while I'm away, collapsing the loop, even twisting itself up. This reflects my lack of patience to work out those details.

2. Cut a wide and thin slice of fur from the hide, shorten it if necessary, and insert it into the loop that is held open by the tool. Hold the fur in place and tug the tool downward to collapse the loop. If all goes well, you can adjust the fur to spread it and to align it within the loop that has captured it.

3. Twirl the tool itself, and the fur hackle will twist into that familiar bottle-brush. Use the tool to complete the fly by winding the needed turns of hackle to the eye. As an alternative, slip the loop off the tool, capture the end in hackle pliers, and wind the fur hackle as shown earlier.

TYING AN ALL-FUR WET FLY WITH MOLE FUR

Mole fur is short, fine, and has no guard hairs. You can tie flies in sizes 16 and smaller with it, though you'll have to clip the butts shorter the smaller you go. I find it useful on sizes 16 and 18. If I want a fly smaller than that, I give up calling it a wet and just tie a nymph, with a dubbed fur thorax rather than the fur-hackle collar.

You might consider it easier to do that in sizes 16 and 18 as well. I won't blame you. These are so close to that border between wet flies and nymphs that I'm not sure which they are. I do know they're effective when trout feed on the wide variety of tiny caddisflies that are sometimes mistakenly called *microcaddis* by fly-fishing writers. True microcaddis, as entomologists use the term, vary from size 28 to smaller than size 32, the smallest hook that's being manufactured. If I'm tying something in those sizes, it's not going to be an all-fur wet fly.

It's worth having a few small all-fur wets tied with mole, so I'll show the procedures here. They are no different from tying with larger fur, just on a smaller scale and executed more carefully. A sparse list of favorites follows.

DARK MOLE & HERL

Hook:	#16-18 standard wet fly or 2X heavy
Thread:	Black 8/0
Body:	Peacock herl
Hackle:	Mole fur

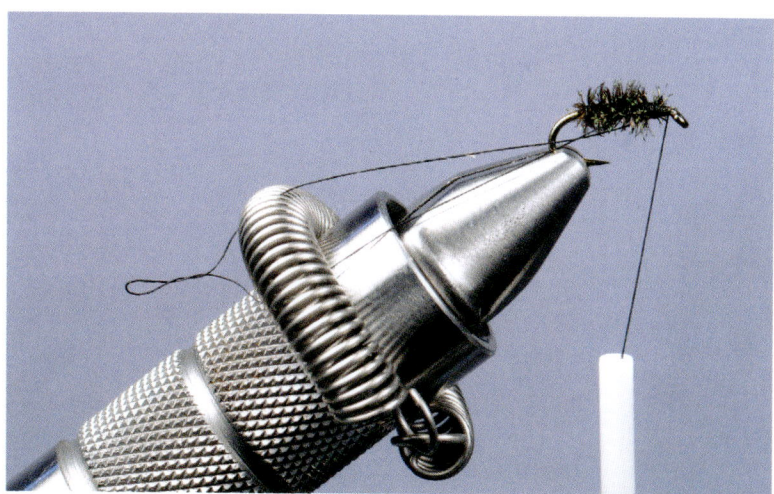

1. Make a peacock herl body, using the thread loop method to be sure it's secure against the teeth of trout (see Chapter 5, pages 65–70). Apply tacky wax to an inch or two of thread. Form a short loop, and secure it in the materials holder on the vise.

2. Clip a thin but wide slice of mole fur from the hide. Shorten the butts proportionate to the size hook on which you're tying, for a fur hackle 1¹/₂ to 2 times the hook gap. Lay this against the waxed side of the thread loop, and collapse the loop to capture it. At this time you can align and spread the fur inside the loop if you need to.

Note: To be sure the tips of the fur dominate in the finished hackle, it's best to capture the fur in the loop with about ²/₃ on the tip side, ¹/₃ on the butts side of the thread.

3. Twirl the fur into a bottlebrush for the hackle.

4. Wind two to three turns of hackle, stroking the fur back between turns. Gather all stray strands back from the hook eye, hold them out of the way, make a base of thread for the head, and whip-finish the fly.

TYING AN ALL-FUR WET FLY WITH THE SPLIT-THREAD METHOD

Forming a fur hackle might be best accomplished by splitting the strands of your tying thread, inserting the fur between them, collapsing the thread onto the fur, then spinning the thread to create that desired bottlebrush. You can use the same method for dubbing a body. It accomplishes the same thing as a dubbing loop, but uses less thread. It also can take fewer steps and even be easier if you use the method consistently enough to work it into your tying routine, which I, unfortunately, have not.

The split-thread technique requires thread that can be separated. Uni-Thread, with its bonded strands, does not lend itself to the method. Since that's the thread I use most often, I've failed to practice enough to do any more than introduce the subject here, for your own experimentation. Most other threads can be used, some as fine as 12/0 and even 16/0, though the target for your needle becomes smaller as the thread gets finer.

In order to separate the strands, it's helpful to flatten the thread, making it easier to get the point of a needle between the strands. All common fly-tying threads flatten when you twist the bobbin counterclockwise and tighten when you spin it clockwise. It takes close observation, as well as good light and sharp eyesight, to notice when the thread visibly flattens against the hook shank. If you use the technique a lot, a light with a magnifier might be what you need to make the method work.

It also helps to run the thread between your thumbnail and forefinger. Start close to the hook shank, pinch the thread, and stroke it, repeating once or twice. Then hold it within $1/4$ to $1/2$ inch from the shank to maintain the spread. Poke it with your dubbing needle or bodkin, which must have a fine point. Separate the strands by running the needle point down to your bobbin, then open the distance between them and insert your forefinger, just as you would with a dubbing loop. Tease out the dubbing, or clip the fur hackle, position it inside the split thread, and let the strands collapse onto it. Then spin the thread clockwise to tighten the thread. It will capture the fur into the type of spiky body you would get from a spinning block, the same kind of fur hackle you'd get in a dubbing loop.

Pearsall's Gossamer Silk Thread is excellent for the split-thread technique because it's easy to split. It is wound of three strands, which are not difficult to separate. I've used silk in the following photos, in part because it's thicker and shows up better, in larger part because it's easier to work with than finer threads. It also has the advantage of showing through as an undercolor when the fly gets wet if the body fur is sparse enough.

Pearsall's Gossamer Silk is twisted in the opposite direction from all other threads. To flatten it and separate the strands, twist it clockwise. To tighten it and capture fur into a dubbed body or fur hackle, spin it counterclockwise.

LIGHT MOLE & OLIVE

Hook:	#16-18 standard wet fly or 2X heavy
Thread:	Primrose yellow Pearsall's Gossamer Silk
Body:	Olive fur and Sparkle Yarn mixed
Hackle:	Light mole fur

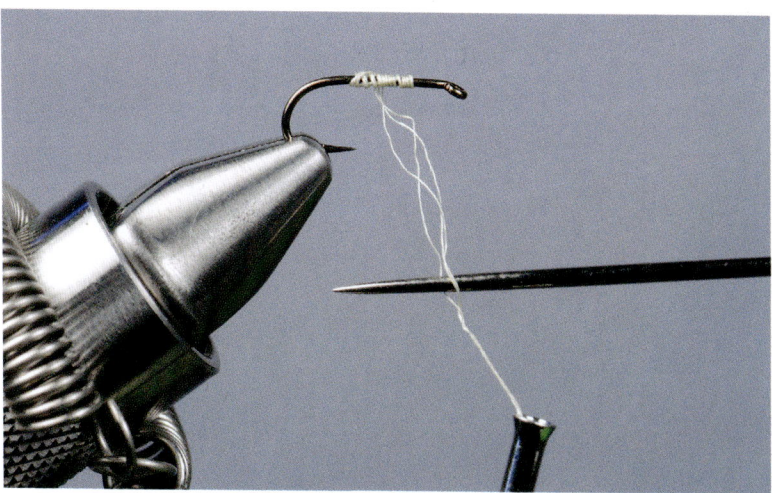

1. Start the silk thread well back from the hook eye, to allow bare shank when you separate the strands later for the fur hackle. Layer the thread over about half the hook shank length, allowing you to avoid the hook point when separating the thread strands for the body. Spin the bobbin clockwise to flatten the thread. With three-strand silk and the right flattening, you can separate the strands just by lifting up on the bobbin, creating slack in the thread. Probe with your needle point to find an opening in the strands.

Note: If you're using regular thread, spin counterclockwise, and center the needle in the flattened area close to the hook shank.

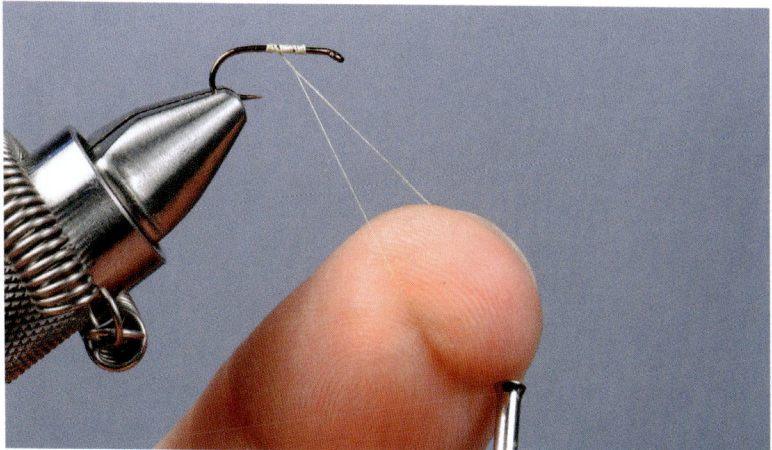

2. Run your needle down to the bobbin, between strands of silk. Hold the strands apart with the needle, and slip the forefinger tip of your off-hand between the strands to keep them separate. This forms, in essence, a thread loop.

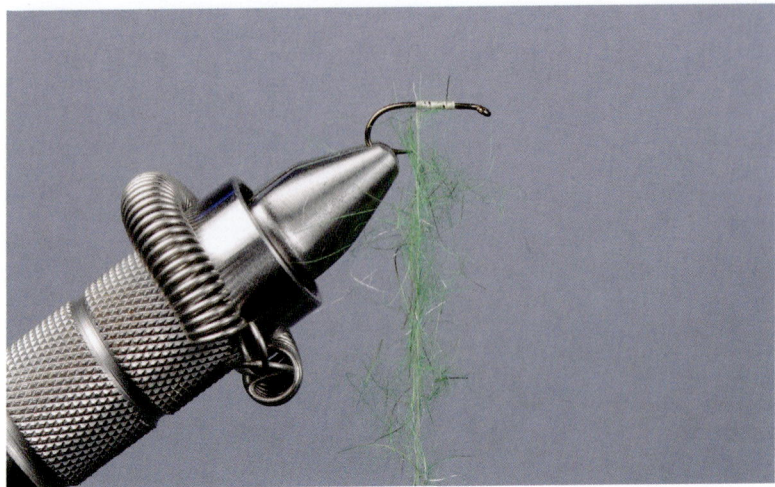

3. Work out a sparse skein of dubbing in the appropriate amount for the size hook on which you're tying. Insert the dubbing between the thread strands, and let them collapse on it. This will hold it in place. At this point you can tug the fur around, adjust the thickness and taper of it to suit you.

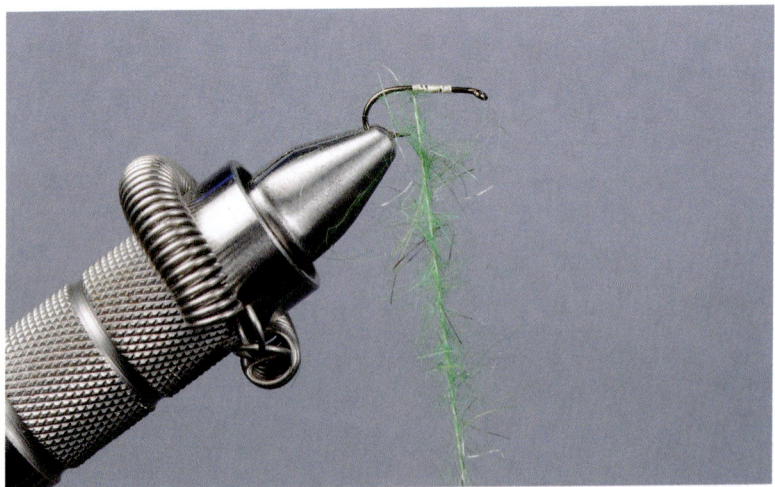

4. Grip the thread between the bobbin and fur with your forefinger and thumb tips, and hold it. Spin the bobbin barrel with a brisk counterclockwise twist, and let it spin to twist the thread. When the twirling bobbin begins to lose momentum, release the thread. The dubbing will spring magically into a very nice spiky dubbing rope. It will look very much like a flymph body spun separately on a dubbing block.

5. Wind the thread back to the hook bend, calculating to arrive there just when the fur dubbing reaches the hook shank. Wind the body forward to a point approximately $1/4$ to $1/5$ the shank length behind the eye, leaving room for the fur hackle.

6. Spin the thread clockwise to flatten it, separate the strands with your dubbing needle, and insert your forefinger between them to form a dubbing loop, as in steps 1 to 3.

7. Clip a small slice of fur from the hide, shorten it if necessary with a cut across the butts, and insert it between the strands of thread. Let the thread collapse to capture the fur. You can adjust it to align the tips and butts, and also to spread the fur for the hackle.

Note: To ensure that the hackle is the right length for this size 16 hook, the short mole fur has been placed well off center, with the tips long and the butts short, so that when wound, the hackle will be $1^1/2$ times the hook gap.

8. Spin the bobbin clockwise to twist the fur into a fur hackle.

9. Wind the hackle forward in two or three turns, stroking the fur back between turns to form a swept-back hackle. Leave room for a few turns of thread for the head, whip-finish, and tidy up the fly if you feel the need.

A FEW FAVORITE ALL-FUR WET FLIES

I use just a few all-fur wets, and even those are far from set in stone. It's good, however, to cover the most important colors that natural insects show to trout, and that trout get used to eating. That calls for flies in olive, hare's ear, cream, rust, and of course peacock herl. If a specific hatch is happening, especially an uprising of caddis pupae, one of those colors will usually cover it.

I've already listed a few favorites to illustrate the tying steps: the Pine Squirrel All-Fur Wet, Dark Mole & Herl, and Light Mole & Olive. I'll add the Light Mole & Cream here first, to get the mole dressings out of the way.

Pupae of the prolific little Black-Horned Sedges (family Glossosomatidae) are found in so many moving-water habitats and are so abundant that trout often watch for them in spring and early summer on trout streams across the continent. A small cream-colored all-fur wet will often make fools of those trout.

LIGHT MOLE & CREAM

Hook:	#16-18 standard wet fly or 2X heavy
Thread:	Tan 8/0
Body:	Cream or light cahill dubbing
Hackle:	Light mole fur

Light Mole & Cream: Peacock, olive, and cream colors cover a lot of small caddis pupae. In the small sizes you can tie with mole, trout are often more concerned with size and shape than they are with color, and you can get away with one of the listed dressings even when it's not quite right.

PEACOCK ALL-FUR WET

Hook:	#12-16 2X standard wet fly or 2X heavy
Thread:	Green Pearsall's Gossamer Silk or green 6/0
Tail:	Olive-dyed pine squirrel guard hair
Body:	Peacock herl
Hackle:	Olive-dyed pine squirrel

Peacock All-Fur Wet: Every line of flies should have a peacock herl body in it. Trout fall for it in drys, nymphs, wets, and streamers, so it would be foolish to tie all-fur wets without including it. Because I own an olive-dyed pine squirrel hide, I use it for harmony here. If you don't have squirrel in any shade of green, it will fish fine when tied with natural pine squirrel fur. If you have dyed pine squirrel Zonker strips, it will be even better.

HARE'S EAR ALL-FUR WET

Hook:	#12-16 standard wet fly or 2X heavy
Thread:	Orange Pearsall's Gossamer Silk or orange 6/0
Tail:	Hare's poll guard hair and fur (or substitute pine squirrel fur)
Body:	Hare's mask fur, mixed, or natural (#1) Hare's Ear Plus
Hackle:	Pine squirrel fur

Hare's Ear All-Fur Wet: For much the same reason as the peacock, every line of flies finds need for a hare's ear body. The material has the advantage of resembling many natural insects that trout eat, among them caddis pupae rising toward the surface for emergence, and caddis adults diving toward the bottom to lay their eggs. It must also remind trout about many of the things they've eaten recently, because it makes a good searching dressing, fished on a very slow swing, when the situation offers you no hints about what fly to try.

OLIVE ALL-FUR WET

Hook:	#12-16 standard wet fly or 2X heavy
Thread:	Green Pearsall's Gossamer Silk or green 6/0
Body:	Caddis-green fur and Sparkle Yarn, mixed
Hackle:	Olive-dyed pine squirrel (or substitute natural pine squirrel)

Olive All-Fur Wet: Many caddis pupae get caught heading toward the surface wearing bright green bodies. These include the net-spinning Spotted Sedges (*Hydropsyche*), the Gray Sedges (*Rhyacophila*), both in size 12 and 14, and most American Grannoms and Mother's Day Caddis (*Brachycentrus*) in size 16 and 18. All can be imitated in the pupal stage with the Olive All-Fur Wet.

Because I use it most often when caddis pupae are active, I'll show it tied without a tail, and manicured into roughly pupal form. In this case, the fur collar is left full on the sides and bottom, to represent the wing cases of the natural, and pruned on the top, again to give it that pupal shape.

If you weighted this fly, it would clearly be a nymph. It might even be one as it's tied. It's certainly close to being a nymph, but I fish it as a wet, so I call it one.

AMBER ALL-FUR WET

Hook:	#8-16 standard wet fly or 2X heavy
Thread:	Orange Pearsall's Gossamer Silk or orange 6/0
Body:	Rust or amber fur mixed with Sparkle Yarn
Hackle:	Fox squirrel fur (#8-10) or pine squirrel fur (#12-16)

Amber All-Fur Wet: The only reason for this rusty-orange dressing is the many caddis pupae that arrive in just that color, including the big Fall Caddis (*Dicosmoecus*), but also many that are much smaller. They're common in moving water. You don't see them often unless you're an entomologist and carry a pair of dissecting scissors just to tweak natural pupae out of their retreats. But trout see them much more often. Amber caddis pupae are also common on lakes and ponds, usually leading toward later adult Cinnamon Sedges (*Limnephilus*).

CREAM ALL-FUR WET

Hook:	#12-14 standard wet fly or 2X heavy
Thread:	Primrose yellow Pearsall's Gossamer Silk or yellow 6/0
Body:	Cream or light cahill fur and Sparkle Yarn, mixed
Hackle:	Fox squirrel fur and guard hair

Cream All-Fur Wet: This dressing extends the Light Mole & Cream into larger sizes than those covered by the all-fur wet tied with shorter mole fur. Most cream-colored caddis pupae are in those smaller sizes, and the mole dressing is probably more useful. But the naturals are at times as large as size 12, and it won't hurt to have a pale fly in those sizes, or at least to know how to tie one if you ever need it.

I'm not suggesting that you tie and fish all of the above all-fur wets; it would be wiser to select two or three of them—a light and a dark, a large and a small—and give them a try. That will introduce you to the methods used in tying them and allow you to conduct experiments with them to suit your own fishing situations. For example, you might get into frequent hatches in which trout take ascending caddis pupae just beneath the surface. The average of them will be either olive or tan, size 14 or 16. An abundance of them, in the Grannom group, will be size 16 or 18 and so dark they're almost black.

If you were to tie the Olive All-Fur Wet and Cream All-Fur Wet in size 14, and the Dark Mole & Herl in size 16, you might find solutions to problems that have eluded you in the past.

You might also consider the listed all-fur wets as nothing more than departure points for your own experiments, the subject of the next chapter.

Chapter Nine

Experiments with Wets

We've seen the four basic styles of wet flies: soft-hackles, flymphs, winged wets, and all-fur wets. To experiment with them, it's necessary to change them. Something changed often becomes something different. A wet fly might become a dry fly if it's designed to fish in the surface film to imitate an emerger. It might become a nymph if it's weighted to fish deep. It might become a streamer if it's tied on a hook so long it makes the fly resemble a baitfish. These dangers are both real and imagined. To wet-fly traditionalists, it's horrifying to contemplate a wet fly that has crossed the border into some other sort of fly. To a trout, there are no definitions, and if it looks good to eat, they simply eat it.

To experiment with wet flies, it's necessary to define them. I looked in all my books about them and found nothing more tidy than a couple of pages describing what wet flies are not: They're not dry flies, not nymphs, not streamers. Roger Fogg's excellent British book *Wet-Fly Tying and Fishing*, published in 2009, is the first I've found that talks about a continuum of fly types, and defines wets' place along it. I thought I'd invented that continuum myself, but Fogg pre-dates me. I suspect I read it in his book, the idea made sense and stuck, but I forgot where I'd read it. So I'm hereby giving him the credit. His book is valuable for that continuum and for more substantial reasons. For example, the British are far ahead of us on stillwater fishing, with wet flies or any others. I've already confessed that I don't fish lakes with wet flies to any great extent. Fogg's book has chapters on lake flies and lake tactics, which should work on our waters as well as they do on his.

No definition of wet flies was needed until the advent of nymphs. Before G. E. M. Skues started experimenting with his subsurface imitations on the Rivers Itchen and Test, anything sunk was a wet fly . . . unless it was a streamer. Skues's originals, shown in the sparse plates in his 1921 *The Way of a Trout with a Fly*, show their own roots in wet flies. They have undersized and sparse hackle collars, or short hackle fibers, for legs. They have wing cases that if not tied down over the thorax would stand up as wings. They're nudged along the continuum, away from wets and into the new category called nymphs, by just a couple of changes.

It's interesting and important to note that none of our wet-fly gurus ever weighted any of their flies. That starts with the soft-hackle, from Stewart and Pritt to Sylvester Nemes. It includes Hidy and Leisenring, who called some of their wet flies "soft-hackled thorax nymphs" and fished them *bumpety-bump* along the bottom. It even includes Polly Rosborough, whose fuzzy nymphs were predecessors to all-fur wets. He considered it a crime to weight his nymphs. All of these writers were so insistent on this matter of weighting that it becomes reasonable to include it in any definition of wet flies.

That definition of wet flies should be short, say a sentence; define what they are; and separate them from what they're not. They're not cows, houses, or planetary objects, so we'll begin by declaring they're flies.

Wet fly: An artificial fly tied on a short, standard length, 1X, or 2X long hook that is unweighted, hackled, and designed to be fished just subsurface or in the upper layers of the water column.

I think that with these few words we've described it as a fly, but not a dry fly, nymph, or streamer. There is room for error. A wet fly can be tied on a longer hook without becoming a streamer. It can be fished in the surface film without becoming a dry fly. It can be tied without weight, but so sparsely and on such a heavy hook that it sinks like a nymph, without becoming a nymph.

If this leaves you dissatisfied as a concise and precise definition of wet flies, let me defend it by referring you to Webster for definitions of a creek, stream, and river. The best you'll discover is that all are moving liquids, that a creek is a small stream, a stream is a small river, and a river is a stream larger than a creek. Each is described in terms of the others, and therefore none are ever truly described. Webster does not define wet flies.

As we begin experimenting with wet flies, let's stipulate that some folks will be offended, and I won't take offense at that. Many will consider that we've simply moved out of wet flies and into nymphs. I won't disagree with that, either. Some will consider any change from the way things were once done a violation of tradition. I spoke recently with an advocate of the soft-hackle, and mentioned that I used a mix of fur and Sparkle Yarn when tying the thorax. He scolded me for adding the Sparkle Yarn. I was okay with that. I didn't mention that in their origins, soft-hackles didn't come equipped with thoracic segments at all, and therefore the thorax itself is a violation of tradition. That's how it goes: Things change a bit, the change becomes the tradition. Trout are bemused by it all.

The Little Olive Flymph on the left is tied with dyed rabbit fur straight from the pack. The one on the right is tied with the same rabbit fur mixed with Sparkle Yarn in a coffee grinder. I'm not sure that trout would take one and refuse the other. The bits of yarn look like tiny bubbles of air underwater, or at least I think they do. The one with sparkle appeals to me, adds some shine to my life, and for that reason, if for no other, I'm going to fish it more often and with more confidence.

Olive-dyed rabbit fur with clear Sparkle Yarn mixed in. It's far more lively, at the vise and in the water, than dyed rabbit fur without the added bits of brightness.

WET FLIES WITH SPARKLE YARN

I add clear Sparkle Yarn to almost all my furs for subsurface flies, if I don't buy them pre-mixed. Rabbit is the most common base fur, soft and easily blended. Squirrel is also excellent. You could shear your own hides and also dye them, but it's only worthwhile if you're into production tying, and I doubt it's worth the time and mess even then, unless you happen to enjoy the process. I tried it in my early tying days, and decided first that I'm never going to tie commercially, and second that dyes can cause permanent stains on the kitchen counter if you're not careful, which I'm often not.

Adding Sparkle Yarn to pre-dyed dubbing is a straightforward and simple process. It requires a coffee grinder, which should be dedicated to fly tying.

A Ginger Flymph with a body of clear Sparkle Yarn spun on yellow gossamer silk. The three-strand thread is easy to split, and it's thick enough that it adds an undercolor of yellow to the finished body. The result violates tradition but might trigger takes from trout keyed on bubbles and brightness in the naturals upon which they're feeding.

The same Ginger Flymph, tied with a clear Sparkle Yarn body, held underwater. Note that the body fibers become a sort of cloud that looks like a bubble of air. Note also that the yellow undercolor of the thread shows subtly when the fly is wet.

I've kept the same one on my bench for decades. I put a clump of fur in the grinder, snip in Sparkle Yarn in $^1\!/_4$- to $^1\!/_2$-inch lengths until the proportion is about 3 or 4 parts fur to 1 part yarn. Then I push the button and whizz it around until it's mixed. I usually blend a particular fur for a specific dressing, or more likely for a set of them, say the olives or the ambers. It can be stored in a Ziploc, film canister, or anything else. It's wise to use a container that allows you to see the color inside, and to label the mix so you can repeat it next time if trout like it enough to bite anything you tie with it.

It's possible to go further into apostasy with Sparkle Yarn by tying an entire body with it. I've carried these experiments out at the vise, but not yet onto water. That will be up to you. I can lay down the theory here. I've tried it only with flymphs, because they have that set goal of capturing a bubble of air and taking it underwater with them. If Sparkle Yarn looks like air, then a body made of it would not need to be backcast until it's dry between presentations. The concept, however, could as easily be used for the thorax on a soft-hackle or the body of a traditional or all-fur wet . . . but then it would no longer be an all-fur fly.

To tie a wet fly with a Sparkle Yarn body, use either the dubbing loop or split-thread method. Tie in the hackle at the hook eye, lay a base of thread to the hook bend, and tie in the tail if there is one. Then either form a thread loop or split the thread with a needle or bodkin point. Rough up a very sparse amount of Sparkle Yarn in the palm of your hand, so that its fibers are aimed in all directions rather than aligned. Insert it into the loop or between the split strands, collapse the thread onto it, twist it up, and wrap it forward. It will be unruly. You'll probably need to gather overly long fibers between the thumb and forefinger of your off-hand, lift them above the body, and nip them all at once. Then wind the hackle.

Remember that those maverick fibers are the ones you're after. Don't trim them much shorter than the finished hackle, or you'll defeat the purpose of using Sparkle Yarn. It need not be clear yarn. Any other color will give you a body that is bright and has lots of sparkle. You'll have to tie flies, fish them, and see how well trout approve. It's certain that wet-fly traditionalists, with whom I have a high degree of sympathy, are going to disapprove.

TYING WET FLIES WITH BEADS

This, I'll admit, gets into fun. I enjoy tying with beads. So long as the purpose of the bead is to provide a bit of brightness, not excess depth—as if sinking deep were some sort of sin!—I believe we can stay within the definition of a wet fly. That usually means glass beads, and that's the kind I usually incorporate into wet flies. When the purpose of adding a bead becomes weight, especially when the beads are tungsten, then I have to believe that the fly has been pushed along the continuum into the category of nymphs. That doesn't mean it shouldn't be tied. It's clear that such a fly would fish deeper and be pleasing to trout; I just don't know that it can still be called a wet fly.

To deflect some criticism here, and also to enlighten your further exploration in this direction, I'm going to recommend Allen McGee's 2007 book *Tying & Fishing Soft-Hackled Nymphs*. This fine book is mostly about wet flies, despite its title. It covers soft-hackles and flymphs, though not winged wets nor all-fur wets. It contains a lengthy section on how to fish wet flies that is nicely done, and adds some new methods, especially for those tied with weight and designed to be fished more deeply than our definition of wet flies covers here. A large benefit of the book is that it gives permission to take traditional wet-fly tying methods and experiment with them. Because Allen has named his flies *nymphs*, he has instantly removed any reservations about the use of beads and weight and bodies made of wire. He also removes any guilt you might feel about violating wet-fly traditions, because you're no longer tying wet flies, you're tying *soft-hackled nymphs*.

I'm going to show you one way to add glass beads to wet flies. You can use the same method to add any sort of bead your conscience—or your own demarcation point between wet flies and nymphs—allows.

AMBER ALL-FUR WET (WITH BEADS)

Hook:	#8-16 2X long, 2X heavy, or standard wet fly
Beads:	One clear and one amber glass bead
Thread:	Orange Pearsall's Gossamer Silk or orange 6/0
Body:	Rust or amber fur mixed with Sparkle Yarn
Hackle:	Fox squirrel fur (#8-10) or pine squirrel fur (#12-16)
Note:	For smaller sizes (#14-16), use just one bead of either color.

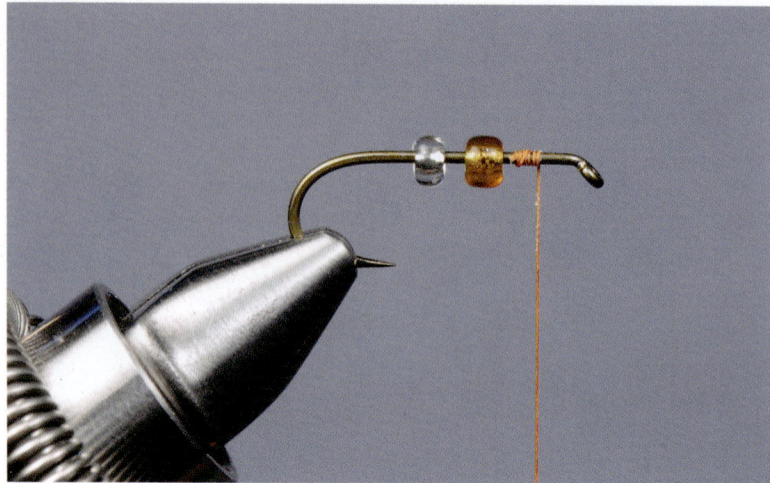

1. De-barb the hook. Slip one or two glass beads over the hook bend to the center of the shank. Fix the hook in the vise. Wax an inch of thread and start it behind the hook eye, leaving a bit of bare shank to split the thread later for the fur hackle.

2. Secure the front bead in place. To do this, run thread wraps against the front of it until you have it where you want it. Brace the back of the bead with the forefinger nail of your off-hand. Bring your thread around the bead and catch the thread between the forefinger and thumb of that hand. Continue the thread around the back side of the shank, while holding a short loop. In essence you're forming a soft loop, the same one you'd use to tie in a tail or any other material, but behind the bead.

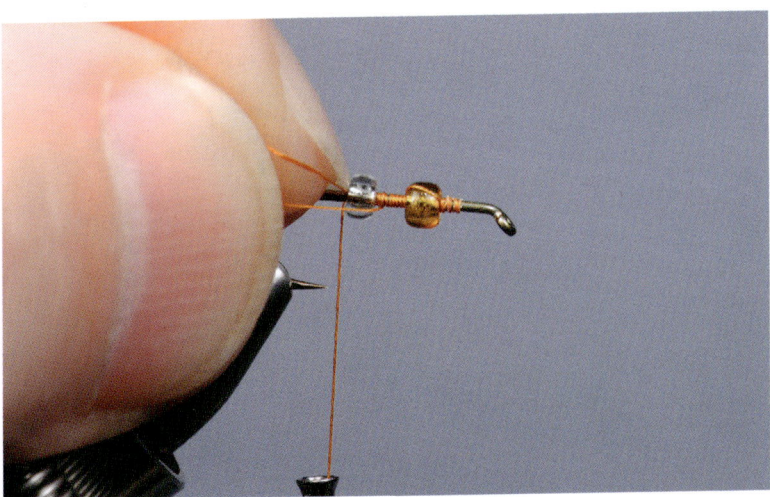

3. Let the loop slide between your thumb and forefinger. It will slip into the gap between your forefinger nail and the bead. This is a temporary placement, holding the bead in place until the fur body locks it in. Position the second bead with the forefinger nail of your off-hand, and take wraps back against it until it is in the position you want. Repeat the process of forming a loop behind the bead and holding it between thumb and forefinger of your off-hand.

4. Let the loop slip behind the bead, locking the second bead in place. Continue thread wraps to the bend of the hook. The beads are now held in place by a single loop of thread over each. They won't migrate much, but you can position them slightly forward or back as you wind the fur body between them.

5. Split the thread or make a thread loop, place a loose skein of fur between the strands, and twist it into a spiky dubbing rope.

6. Wrap the fur rope forward to the back of the rear bead. Use the forefinger nail of your off-hand in front of the bead to hold the bead where you want it on the shank. It should be braced between the fur rope behind it and the fingernail in front of it.

7. Take a loose wrap of fur rope around the bead, using your forefinger to place the fur. Take one or two turns of fur rope between the beads. The first turn should be tight against the front of the rear bead. The second turn, and third and even fourth if necessary, should take the fur loop forward to a brace behind the front bead.

8. Take a loose wrap of fur rope around the bead, using your forefinger to place the fur, as you did the first bead. The beads are now locked in fore and aft by the body material. The body itself should be loose and spiky.

9. Wind the rest of the fur rope ahead of the front bead. Be sure to leave space for the fur hackle. Sweep the unruly body fibers back with your off-hand forefinger and thumb, and take a few wraps of thread in front.

10. Finish off the fly with a fur hackle, just as in the previous chapter on all-fur wets. I've used the split-thread technique on this fly, with fox squirrel guard hairs and underfur. Form a thread head and whip-finish the fly. Tidy it up a bit, if you desire, but not too much. It should look rough, and the beads should barely show.

A bead can be placed on any wet fly using the same procedure. It can be set on the butt of the fly, representing an egg sac. It can be placed in the middle of the fly, offering that bit of flash that mimics a bubble of air. It can be placed tight behind the hackle, perhaps replacing the fur thorax on a soft-hackle. It can be placed at the head of the fly, just as you would on a bead-headed nymph, which might be what you're tying when you do it.

IRON BLUE DUN (WITH BEAD BUTT)

Hook:	#12-18 standard wet fly
Butt:	Red glass bead
Thread:	Crimson Pearsall's Gossamer Silk
Hackle:	Jackdaw wing shoulder (or substitute starling)
Body:	Mole fur spun on red silk

HARE'S EAR WET (WITH CENTER BEAD)

Hook:	#12-16 standard wet fly or 2X heavy
Bead:	Clear or amber glass
Thread:	Orange Pearsall's Gossamer Silk or orange 6/0
Hackle:	Brown or furnace hen
Tail:	Three to five pheasant tail fibers
Body:	Hare's mask fur or natural (#1) Hare's Ear Plus
Wing:	Hen pheasant wing feather sections

MARCH BROWN SPIDER (WITH BEAD THORAX)

Hook:	#10-16 standard wet fly or 2X heavy
Bead:	Clear or amber glass
Thread:	Orange Pearsall's Gossamer Silk
Hackle:	Brown partridge
Rib:	Oval gold tinsel
Body:	Hare's mask fur or natural (#1) Hare's Ear Plus

OLIVE ALL-FUR WET WITH BEAD HEAD

Hook:	#12-16 standard wet fly or 2X heavy
Bead:	Green glass
Thread:	Olive 6/0 or 8/0
Body:	Olive fur mixed with Sparkle Yarn
Hackle:	Pine squirrel

Rick Hafele playing a cutthroat that intercepted his soft-hackled wet fly, fished on a slow swing across a broad and bouldered but shallow run on Idaho's Lochsa River. The water, and the tactic, were right out of Sylvester Nemes's classic book *The Soft-Hackled Fly*, and I thought the fly was as well, until I got a good look at it later. Its body was wound with Ice Dub.

TYING WET FLIES WITH FLASH

I fished Idaho's Lochsa River in a recent October with Rick Hafele, who is known better as a nymph fisherman, author of *Nymph-Fishing Rivers & Streams*. We encountered the usual range of fall weather that high in the Rockies: rain and hail and even some accidental sunshine. Most of the time the air and the water were both cold, but trout were fairly active. They responded with eagerness to a size 22 Blue-Winged Olive hatch that happened almost every afternoon, in the usual way of mayflies, coming off in good numbers except when the sun was out. We caught fish on tiny dry flies and were happy at those moments. But the hatch was short, from half an hour to maybe an hour on the best days. The rest of the time Rick fished nymphs and I fished wet flies, and we each did well enough to be content.

In a puzzling and punishing switch the evening of the last day of the trip, I fished nymphs fruitlessly in a deep and difficult pool, going after the big ones I knew must be down there, while Rick swung a soft-hackle pleasantly across the long, shallow run into which the pool tailed out. He didn't exactly hammer the fish, but a few of them intercepted his wet fly. A couple were 16-inch cutthroats, in beautiful colors and excellent condition. I caught as many trout, the same size as his, but worked twice as hard to get them.

I asked to fish a few casts with his rod, but caught no more trout when he generously allowed me to use it. It was near enough to dark that I reeled up, nipped off Rick's soft-hackled wet, pinned it into the day's page of the

Bodies wound with flash and with a few tendrils of it left as antennae or tails or whatever else you and the trout might imagine can be incorporated into any style wet fly, from the soft-hackles shown here to flymphs, winged wets, or all-fur wet flies.

The soft-hackle that Rick used on the Lochsa was tied with October Caddis pupae loosely in mind. It was size 12, small for the species, but in its golden body and brown hackle, it had the colors of the natural. Trout might have mistaken it for a Fall Caddis pupa on the currents, or they might have simply been enticed into taking it because of its brightness and the lifelike movement of its hen hackle fibers.

pocket notebook I carry on every trip. It's there to this day. I just pulled it out and looked at it under a magnifying glass. The body is wound of golden brown Ice Dub. Rick is no traditionalist when it comes to wet flies.

Ice Dub might be as heretical as you can get when thinking about wet flies and traditions. But the tradition in wet-fly tying and fishing, from Stewart through Skues to Leisenring and Hidy and Allen McGee, is toward using available materials and methods to tie flies that more closely resemble natural insects, and that also more often fool trout. If Ice Dub adds sparkle to a fly and that sparkle makes the fly more attractive to trout, those traditionalists would likely have used it, had it been available in their day.

I suspect that's the best way to look at recent innovations. If a material or a method improves the performance of a wet fly—or any other kind of fly—then you ought to at least try it. Today's experiments are apt to become tomorrow's traditions.

Ice Dub comes in an array of colors from black through white, with stops at brown, tan, several shades of olive, yellow, and even pink. You should try all of them. In some circumstances, I'm certain each will catch trout.

In the same vein, it's easy to tie several strands of Krystal Flash or Flashabou at the bend of the hook, as if it were floss or fur, in any of an almost infinite range of colors, and wind a body with them. Use four or five fibers, twist them lightly, and the body is thin. The fly will sink but not abruptly. Use ten or twelve fibers, twist them tightly together when winding, and the body becomes stout. It will sink faster than any unweighted wet fly tied of more traditional materials.

If you leave a few strands of the flash unclipped at the end of the body, you open up a whole new set of experiments. They might look like an insect's antennae. They could be tied in as tails, and look like a flashy trailing shuck. I've played with these ideas more at the bench than I have on water. If I were to list any dressings, they would be what I call *paper patterns*: tied and pretty in the vise but not proven against trout. The world of fly-fishing literature has more than enough paper patterns. These experiments with flash as bodies and trailing fibers are yours to make.

WET FLIES WITH WIRE BODIES.

A couple of seasons ago, I came up with a pattern to imitate pupae of early fall Black Caddis (*Brachycentrus*) on the Bighorn River in Montana. It did well enough during that hatch, but it was more fun to fish dry flies over those hyper-selective trout at times when they would take them, so I only got a few chances to fish the wet fly.

A season later my wife, Masako, and I fished Oregon's famous Yamsi Ranch, in the spring-creek headwaters of the Williamson River. John Hyde, a member of the family that owns the ranch, was guiding. He spotted a few nice trout working the bottom in a wide stretch of water with modest flows over 3- to 4-foot depths. The fish moved boldly back and forth, sometimes shooting to take something, but never rising more than inches above the bottom. It was impossible to approach them from downstream; any cast that lined them in that clear water would have sent them sailing. So upstream nymphing with indicator and shot was not an option.

Masako tried a streamer from an upstream position, the standard method on the stream, one that had been working well for us all day. She cast it well above the trout, allowed it to sink, then animated it slightly as it swam near the bottom and approached the trout. One showed interest, followed the streamer, but turned away. After that, the streamer only succeeded in parting a path through the four or five trout that we were able to see. While she continued to cast over them, I lengthened my 10-foot 4X streamer leader with a foot of 5X and about 4 feet of 6X tippet. When I searched my fly boxes, I noticed the unnamed black caddis pupa that I'd tied for the Bighorn River, calculated that it would sink about as fast as any wet fly I owned, and tied it on for no other reason.

The author with a brook trout that took a wire-bodied Yamsi Special fished near the bottom in spring-creek currents so slow they were almost still.

When it came my turn to fish, I did about the same thing Masako had been doing. I cast the size 16 fly about twenty feet upstream from the position of the feeding trout, which had slowly backed down out of the way of her streamer, but continued to move and feed along the bottom from time to time. I tossed a couple of upstream mends, then followed with the rod tip and let the fly sink and drift toward the fish without hindrance. When I felt it had reached their position, I stopped the rod, then did nothing more. The fly, in that slow water, began to swing slowly across in front of the fish and at the same time to lift upward in the water column.

I felt a bit of a pull, refrained from setting the hook, finally felt the weight of a trout that was displeased by the sting of what it had just eaten. I didn't need to set the hook; I didn't dare to set it on that fragile 6X. The trout bolted in the other direction.

It was a brook trout, but no monster, especially for the stream from which we caught it. But it was pretty enough, and it felt so good to have fooled it with such an old wet-fly technique, essentially the Leisenring Lift, that I decided I'd been wet-fly fishing, not nymphing. You might not be so sure, since the fly in question was tied with a body of wire.

I named that fly, designed for the Bighorn River, the Yamsi Special. It was size 16, tied on the heaviest wire hook I could find, a 2X heavy curved scud hook. The body was two strands of Ultra-Wire—one copper, the other light green, both size Brassie—tied in together and wound side by side. The hackle was black mole, tied in the style of an all-fur wet fly. Its mission, violating my own definition of a wet fly, was simply to sink. I'll show the brief steps in tying it here. You can make further experimentations along the same lines, if you'd like.

YAMSI SPECIAL

Hook:	#14-18 2X heavy curved scud
Thread:	Black 8/0
Body:	Copper and olive Ultra-Wire (Medium for #14 and Brassie for #16-18)
Hackle:	Black mole

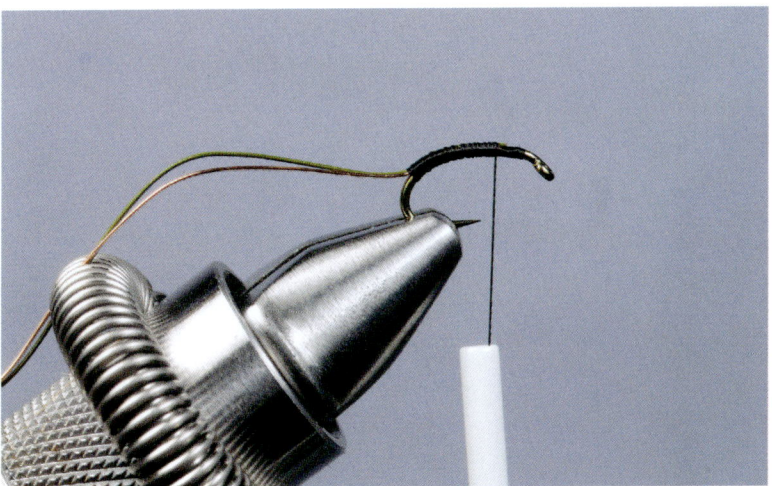

1. Cut 3 to 4 inches of olive and copper wire from the spool. Lay them side by side on top of the shank, and overwrap them with thread from front to well down on the bend of the hook. Bring the thread back to the front of the wire. Leave about a quarter of the shank for the fur hackle. Laying the wire the length of the body adds a bit of extra weight, and also forms a smooth underbody.

2. Wind the wires forward together, side by side, to form a distinctly segmented body. I don't know that the trout care about this, but it makes the fly more appealing to me, and captures the colors inherent in the caddis pupa for which I first tied the fly. Tie the wire off, and either bend it back and forth until it breaks, or dull your scissors by cutting the excess.

3. Form a thread loop, wax it well, and capture a wide but thin patch of mole fur between the strands of the loop.

4. Twirl the fur into the bottlebrush that will become the fur hackle. The fibers should be a bit longer than the width of the hook gap.

5. Wind two to four turns of hackle from the end of the body to the eye of the hook, leaving enough room for a thread head. Stroke the hackle back as you wind each turn. Whip-finish the head, and the fly is ready to fish.

When fishing the Yamsi Special as originally intended, during a hatch of Black Caddis, I usually target a particular trout that is rising, as they do on the Bighorn, in a pod of them. I position myself either straight across from the trout, or slightly upstream. The cast is placed 4 to 6 feet upstream from the selected trout, the fly sinks a foot or so, then it's animated, hopefully right in the eyes of the trout I'm after. If that fish takes, I'm delighted. If it lets the fly go by, then I continue to fish the fly on a slow swing through the rest of the trout in the pod.

About as often as I hook the trout that I've pinpointed, I catch one that is not on my radar. I don't usually mind, unless the one that lets the fly pass by is big and the one that takes is a tiddler.

The olive, copper, and black mole combination is not the only one I tie, but it's the one I use often enough for it to have a history worth mentioning. If you were to try a different combination, say black and silver Ultra-Wire and just a tuft of black mole, you'd have something approaching a Zebra Midge. It might be a wet fly, or it might be a nymph. But it would work. It's likely there are more than a thousand combinations and permutations of wire and fur colors. I hope you can see why I haven't tried them all. They would all work at one time or another.

TYING WET FLIES WITH WEIGHT

In the first edition of this book, I covered a few kinds of nymphs, named them as such, and mentioned *underweighting* them. I'll continue that sin in this edition, with the codicil that the flies are nymphs according to my new definition, but I fish them as wet flies. They're Gary LaFontaine's Deep Sparkle Pupa patterns, from his 1981 book *Caddisflies*. Gary tied them heavily weighted, to tumble along the bottom. I tie them very lightly weighted, to penetrate the surface film and to fish just beneath it. I only tie and fish them in a couple of colors, olive and ginger, though Gary listed four primary colors and about a dozen secondary combinations. If you do your own insect collecting, which is always wise, you might find trout feeding on a caddis pupa best imitated with colors I'm not going to list. You'll know how to substitute the right ones.

The following underweighting concept could be applied to many of the wet-fly types in this book, in particular the all-fur wets. According to my loose definition of wet flies, they would then clearly be nymphs. That wouldn't keep trout from eating them. I use them most often in ginger and the Brown & Bright Green Sparkle Pupa shown in the following steps.

BROWN & BRIGHT GREEN SPARKLE PUPA

Hook:	#12-16 standard wet fly
Weight:	Eight to ten turns undersized non-lead wire
Thread:	Brown 6/0 or 8/0
Overbody:	Light olive Sparkle Yarn
Underbody:	Bright green fur and Sparkle Yarn mix
Hackle:	Dark grouse fibers
Head:	Brown fur dubbing

1. Fix hook in the vise. Select weighting wire that is finer than the hook shank. Standard weighting wire is the same diameter as the shank. Wrap eight to ten turns of the wire. Start the thread and lock the wire in with thread turns over it to the back and again to the front. Build slight thread shoulders in front and back of the wire, then take the thread to the bend of the hook.

2. Separate two strands out of four-strand Sparkle Yarn. Comb one strand to separate its fibers, and tie it in on top of the hook shank. Comb a second and tie it in on the bottom of the shank. When brought forward, the two strands should form a somewhat sparse bubble around the body.

3. Use tacky wax to coat a few inches of thread, and use a dubbing loop to wind a slender, rough body to the end of the weighting wire. Leave plenty of room for the fur head of the fly.

4. Draw the top strand of yarn loosely over the body. Tie it off with two to three slightly loose turns of thread. Use your bodkin point to draw the yarn back and to tease it into a sheathe around the top half of the body. At this point you can tug the yarn forward or back under the thread wraps until you've got it the way you want it.

5. Draw the bottom strand of yarn under the body. Tie it off with two to three loose turns of thread. Use your bodkin point to draw it back and tease it into a sheathe around the underside of the body. If your vise is rotary, rotate the fly to examine its off-side. It should be sheathed the same as the near side. I always tease out a few yarn fibers and draw them to the back, more as a *trail* than as a tail for the fly. Clip the excess yarn strands at the front.

6. Tie in a few grouse breast, back, or wing fibers on each side of the body, for the legs of the natural. If you don't have grouse, brown partridge fibers make a nice substitute, and trout have never been noticed to complain.

7. Dub a tapered head from the front of the body to the hook eye. Form a thread head, whip-finish, and the underweighted fly is ready to fish whenever caddis pupae are rising or, less intuitively, when Spotted Sedge or Gray Sedge adults are in the air, indicating trout have been seeing their pupae recently.

TYING WITH MEDALLION WING

The late Shane Stalcup, in his 2002 book *Mayflies: Top to Bottom*, offered a wet-fly style to represent drowned duns and spinners. The concept was new and experimental to him when he wrote the book. It's even more so to me. I haven't tied and fished it at all. Yet it appears to be on the cutting edge of where wet flies might be going, so I'm going to offer a look at it here.

MEDALLION BIOT WET FLY, OLIVE

Hook:	#14-18 3X long, curved shank
Thread:	Olive 6/0 or 8/0
Tails:	Brown partridge fibers
Underbody:	Fine dubbing, tapered up to thorax
Abdomen:	Olive turkey biot
Thorax:	Olive dubbing
Wings:	Dun Medallion sheeting
Legs:	Brown partridge fibers
Head:	Olive dubbing
Note:	Soak a few biots in advance. Tie in the tails, then the biot, then lay a tapered underbody of fine dubbing, thin at the tail, thicker toward the thorax. Wrap the biot forward to the end of the underbody and tie it off. Dub a thorax and tie the wings on either side of it. Tie in a few leg fibers on each side, dub the head, and whip-finish the fly. As a last step, trim the wings to a rounded mayfly shape.

As a style, Shane's Medallion wet fly can be varied to match any mayfly dun you encounter. Since olive and Sulphur/PMD are the two most common colors in the moving-water mayfly world, it wouldn't be out of line to suggest that you start with just those, give them a try, and experiment from there.

Each tied in a narrow range of sizes, 14 to 18, on the long shank hooks called for by the originator, will cover the most common hatches in the olive and pale yellow colors.

The purpose of this chapter is to offer a few ideas for your own experiments, some ways to play with new materials and work your own variations. If you're a traditionalist, you won't want to go anywhere with them; you'll want them to go away. But those who laid down today's traditions were experimenting with the modern materials of their own day. It's likely that if they had all the new materials that we have available, they'd be breaking their own rules and creating some new traditions.

WET-FLY METHODS

Chapter Ten

Tackle for Fishing Wet Flies

I'd like to advise that you're required to go out and buy special tackle just for wet-fly fishing. For example, if you're not fishing a bamboo rod, British reel, and silk fly line, trout are going to turn away from your wet flies with great disdain. Of course it's not true. I fish bamboo, most often when I know I'm setting out to fish wet flies, and I arm the rod with an old Hardy reel when I do. Most of the time I select my tackle based on the broad run of dry-fly, nymph, and wet-fly fishing I might do on any day, on whatever stream, river, lake, or pond I intend to fish. I don't own a silk line, which doesn't mean I wouldn't like to. I've just never seen a reason for one, in practical terms, in my own wet-fly fishing, which doesn't mean you won't find an excellent reason for one in yours. Tradition can be an acceptable compelling reason.

The tackle I carry on any given day, on any chosen trout water, might have to turn over a bushy Royal Wulff dry fly, set a tiny imitative dry delicately just upstream from a rising trout, fish a nymph rig complicated with indicator and shot, or even toss a small weighted streamer. About a third of the time, I'm going to arrive streamside and discover I want to fish wet flies. The tackle I'm carrying has to handle that, too. But I'm not often going to select tackle perfect for wet-fly fishing, and only that. Most of the time, I want to carry an outfit that will execute almost any order I might give it.

The rod you choose for a day astream should probably be chosen as much for the size water on which you'll use it as for the type of fishing you plan to do that day. Small streams can be best fished with 7- to 8-foot rods. Since you're far more likely to use dry flies than wets on small waters, you'd be better served by a fairly fast dry-fly rod than you would one with a fairly slow wet-fly action. If the water you intend to fish is anywhere from a medium-sized trout stream through a small river, and on up to a large one,

You don't need a special rod for fishing wet flies. However, you do want one that is not so fast that you have no control over your casting loops. Often, when fishing wet flies, you want an open loop rather than the tight loop that is more often prescribed as right. Though the author is fishing here on Idaho's big Lochsa River, he's casting a pair of wet flies upstream, and he's armed with his favorite old Leonard Duracane bamboo rod.

then you'll want what I consider an all-around rod, longer, and with a more versatile moderate action.

Several graphite rods I own fall into the category of all-around trout rods. I'm nearly always armed with one or another of them on anything but a small stream. Two are 4-weight rods, one $8^1/2$ feet long and the other 9 feet. Two are 5-weight rods, again $8^1/2$ feet and 9 feet. These rods have a single thing in common: They're not so stiff that I can't cast them short, or with an open loop, if I choose to. I often lament the trend toward graphite rods as stiff as pool cues. They're great for casting over the horizon, but most of the trout I catch are nearer to me than that. I think 6-weight rods and up should be designed for distance casting, because casting long, or in wind, is usually their main function. But for lighter rods, versatility becomes the primary purpose, and a slightly softer rod will do more things well, while a stiff one will only deliver distance.

By slightly softer, I mean a rod that would have been called moderate, or even fast, in the old days, which were not very long ago. I'm among a large group of trout fishermen I know who preferred "fast" rods thirty years ago, but who now like "slow" rods. But the rods we like haven't changed at all. It's just that the definition of "fast action" has accelerated to the point that it's more meaningful to apply the word "stiff." The trend now is toward designs that go off the chart past fast. Their tapers are designed by tournament casters.

You won't do a lot of tournament casting on the average trout stream. If you're after summer steelhead, fishing a big stillwater, or casting into a Patagonian gale, you'll be glad to have one of those distance rods. Most of the time, on trout water, they're more handicap than help.

It's an aside, but perhaps important in more than just your wet-fly fishing: Most of the rods that I prefer for versatility on trout streams and rivers are constructed from IM6 graphite, a material about three generations old as I write this. Many fine rods are still made of it, and many of those rods have actions that are about two generations behind the stiff ones that are better for distance but not always better for fishing. You should never buy a rod without casting it first. The material from which a rod is made will go some distance toward predicting the action it will have.

To add wet-fly fishing to your list of tactics, get a rod on the slow side of fast. Then you'll have a rod that works well for presentation fishing with dry flies of average to small size. It will also propel the mix of split shot, strike indicators, and two-fly nymph rigs without getting them all tangled. If you try to cast all that puffery 45 feet with a stiff rod, you'll learn the true meaning of the word *tangle*.

When I know I'm going to fish only wet flies, I love nothing more than to trot out to the stream with my old Leonard bamboo. It's $7^1/2$ feet long, carries a 5-weight double-taper line easily out to 50 feet, and will handle 60 or even 70 feet of line if I ask it to. It slides slightly off the slow end of the chart, even on the old scale. It's soft, gentle, graceful. It lofts a wet, or a brace of them, into a high backcast with an open loop that prevents the line, leader, and flies from getting together and quarreling in the air. After a single backcast to change the direction of the presentation, it places the fly or flies back onto a broad riffle or run with most of their moisture still entrained. The wets sink and commence tempting trout right away.

That old Leonard rod has had a long list of accidents. When I broke one original tip, I had it replaced by Thomas & Thomas. It turned out to have the same moderate action as the first one, perfect for wet-fly fishing. I recently broke the second—the last!—original tip, and had it replaced by Glenn Brackett of Sweetgrass Rods in Twin Bridges, Montana. I asked if he could tweak it just a bit faster, to suit both dry-fly fishing and wet. I just got it back. It's sweet, perfect for presentation dry-fly fishing to rising trout, and just as nice when trout refuse those drys and I switch to wets to show them something just subsurface.

When wet-fly fishing is all I want to do, that rod is the one I want to use, and I fish it far more often now than I did in the days when it had both of its original tips. But it's rare for me to go out fishing with a firm conviction about the way I want to fish. Instead, I approach any water, whether moving or still, with the intention of letting it inform me about the way it ought to be fished, letting its trout tell me what they want, rather than trying to dictate to them what they're going to get. I want to carry tackle that allows a broad array of responses—dry, nymph, wet fly, or streamer—to any situation. I'm not fond of fishing nymphs or streamers with bamboo. That's why it's usually best to be armed with an $8^1/_2$- to 9-foot graphite rod that carries a 4- or 5-weight line, and lofts it with a moderate-fast action, the sort of rod that lets you slow your stroke and open up your loops if you'd like to.

Lines for wet-fly fishing are easy to describe. The goal is control—control of the cast in the air and control of the line once it's landed on the water. The line type that offers the most control is the double-taper floater. Get a good one; it's the core of your fly-fishing outfit. It's the line you'll use for most wet-fly fishing on moving water.

Weight-forward tapers are better for distance casting. It's rare that you'll need distance in wet-fly fishing. In fact, distance can cost you control and also make it more difficult to detect takes and set the hook. So in the end, distance can cost you fish. But you don't have to cast a weight-forward line for distance, and at times, in situations where distance will help you cover more water, it might gain you a few fish.

For example, when you're fishing lakes and ponds, the need for line control drops but the benefits of distance increase. The farther you cast, the more trout you reach that haven't been alarmed by your presence. So a weight-forward line is a good decision for the days you spend on lakes. The same might be true for big rivers, with broad riffles and runs, where distance can at times outweigh the advantages of line control.

Many modern weight-forward lines are built with long heavy sections in front of the lighter running line. The old standard was 30 feet of head, which is sufficient for control of wet flies on small streams, but not on broader waters. Weight-forward tapers with 40 feet and more of heavier head are available, and are an excellent compromise between the constant demand for control over your line on the water, and distance in the cast when you might need it.

Another good reason to select a weight-forward floater as your primary line, as opposed to a double-taper, might be the way it pleases a particular rod. It's quite common that a rod feels good and casts well enough with a double-taper 4-weight, but is suddenly far more alive and pleasing when armed with a weight-forward 5-weight. This boils down to aesthetics, feel, and other stuff that's easy to understand with a rod in your hand, but difficult to describe, even to somebody standing next to you. That person might even prefer the rod with an entirely different line than you do. If it's your rod, always fish it with the line that feels best to you, whether it's a weight-forward, double-taper, triangle taper, or any other.

It's also important to know that you can slow a stiff rod down a little by using a line that is one weight heavy. A fast 4-weight dry-fly rod might become a fine moderate wet-fly and nymph rod when loaded with a 5- or

Distance is more often critical on lakes and ponds than it is on rivers and streams, especially when trout are rising way out there, and you want to reach them with a wet fly. If you can't reach them, you're not going to catch them. Set aside all of your requirements for loop control in the air and line control on the water. Use gear designed for distance when you fish stillwaters with any kind of fly.

even 6-weight line, double-taper or weight-forward. The heavier line will cause the rod to bend farther down into its mid-sections, and therefore open up its loops, leading to fewer tangles. I gave a rod away once because I got so many tangles with it the first time I fished it that I never wanted to fish it again. Jim Schollmeyer, then guiding on the Deschutes River, strung it with a line one weight heavier than that recommended by the rod manufacturer, and used it for many years as a client rod. It was often better than the one the client brought to the water, and that was often because the client's rod was underloaded, and therefore too fast to cast without constant tangles.

I've been doing more and more of my wet-fly fishing in recent years with intermediate sinking lines. I prefer them in visible but subdued colors for streams, so I can see them and tend to the drift by leading the fly or flies, by feeding line into the drift to slow it or to lengthen it, or even by mending the instant the line lands on the water, before the line begins to sink, if the shape of the water calls for a mend. In lake fishing, I do about half of my subsurface fishing with a clear intermediate line, whether it's with wet flies, nymphs, or streamers. I've encountered an increasing number of times that I've fished the same flies at the same depth and with the same retrieve, using floating, clear intermediate, and sink-tip lines, which can all achieve the same depths if you vary the sink time. For reasons I'm not able to explain, the clear intermediate usually brings many more trout to the net, whether I'm casting and retrieving or trolling. It's a line I'd never be without when fishing any lake or pond.

There are, of course, myriads of sinking line types designed to achieve greater depths. They merit consideration in all of your nymph and streamer fishing, especially for stillwaters. But my subject here is wet-fly fishing. If I stick with my arbitrary definition of wets as flies to fish at no more than moderate depths, then I'll stop my discussion of line types at the slow-sinking intermediate.

Leaders for wet-fly fishing can be elementally simple, but they can also get quite complex. When you're fishing a dry fly and want to switch to a single wet, most often you can just nip off the dry fly, tie on the wet you want to use, and you're ready to fish again. A typical dry-fly leader is 9 to 12 feet long, depending on the size and smoothness of the water you fish. The same leader will be the perfect length for the wet fly you want to fish on that same water. Be sure that your tippet is at least 2 feet long. If it gets shorter than that, replace it just as you would when dry-fly fishing.

The tippet should balance the size fly you're casting. For size 6, 8, or 10 flies, use 3X or 4X tippet. For size 12, 14, or 16 wet flies, use 4X or 5X tippet. If you go down to size 16, 18, or even 20 wet flies, then 5X or 6X tippet will be best, depending on the type of water you're fishing. It's so rare for me to drop below 6X, for drys or wets, that I don't clutter up my vest with a spool of 7X unless I'm going to be on a spring creek or tailwater.

It's quite common to fish a pair of wet flies on the same cast. This lets you try two different sizes or colors or types of flies. It can cut in half the time it takes you to figure out what trout want. Using two flies is not a way to catch two trout at once, or to double the number of trout that you catch, though those are occasional inadvertent outcomes and not necessarily disappointing when they happen.

View the two-fly setup as an exploratory tool. Once you've figured out what the trout prefer, it's usually best to go to that single fly and cut off the other. It reduces tangles and keeps you from catching your own thumb on the loose fly that jerks about when you land a fish. Using a single fly makes it easier to release a trout quickly and unharmed.

There is a big *however* attached to the above advice to remove a second wet fly if it's not hooking any trout. It often seems that trout are attracted by a two-fly setup, even if they consistently take only one of the two flies. If you remove the one that's not catching fish, you suddenly begin catching nothing on the one that's left. A lot of reasons might apply: Trout notice a bright one or big one, but then accept the drab or small one near it; they think the big one is going to eat the little one if they don't get to it first; or they see two, get greedy, but usually take the smaller or less bright one of the brace. I don't know what's in their minds. I just know that a two-fly rig often entices more trout than a single fly. This applies to all sunk-fly fishing, whether with wets, nymphs, or streamers.

Many ways have been devised to tie dropper flies onto the leader above the point fly. The easiest, and the one most often recommended, is to leave the tag end of your tippet knot uncut and about six inches long. Always leave the heavier of the two strands, clip away the lighter, and tie the fly to the

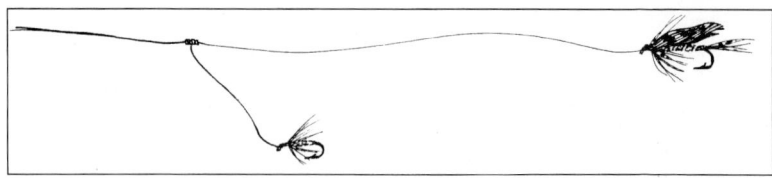

When using more than one wet fly on the same leader, offer trout a choice by choosing a large pattern and a small one . . .

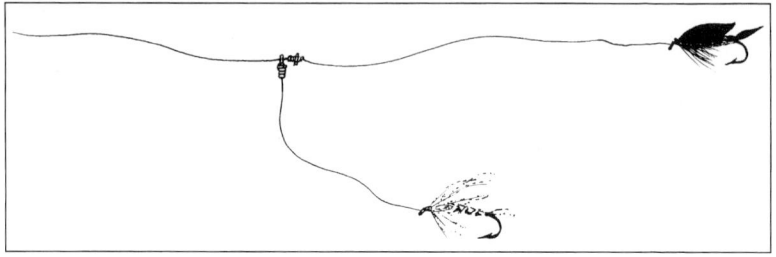

. . . or by using one fly that is dark and another that is light.

stout tag end. The stiffer leader will help prevent tangles, though no dropper rig is going to keep the fly from wrapping around the leader on occasion. I use this method for droppers most often. Be sure that your tippet to the point fly is at least 2 feet long, in order to separate the flies when they're adrift in the water. This separation also helps prevent trout from tangling in both hooks during the fight. Such tangles can injure them.

Often I'll decide to add a dropper when my tippet knot is already tied, with its tag ends trimmed, and my point fly is already attached. I just nip about eight inches of material from a spare spool of tippet a size stouter than the tippet already on the leader, and tie this tag to the leader with a clinch knot, the same knot used to tie the dropper fly to the other end. Tie the dropper above the tippet knot, then simply slide the dropper knot down to jam against the tippet knot, and the fly is fixed in place.

If you're using a knotless leader and want to attach a dropper, you have a couple of choices. You can form a loop in the main leader where you want the dropper, then make a loop in the end of the dropper and attach it to the leader loop. That's easy. But it puts a loop in the leader, and I have no fondness for bulky loops in my leader.

I normally clip the leader where I want to insert the dropper, then tie it back together with a surgeon's knot, leave the stronger end uncut, and tie the dropper fly to that. This method creates less leader bulk at the tie-in point.

It's possible to fish two, three, or even more dropper flies. The standard setup in the 1800s consisted of at least three wet flies, sometimes as many as eight or nine. I know, however, if I rig any more than two wet flies on the leader that I'm going to spend time untangling them at least twice every

Tackle for wet-fly fishing should generally be the same rod, reel, and line you'd use for other types of fishing on the same size stream. That way when an emergence starts and trout get eager for dry flies, you can switch to please them. If it turns cold and trout stay deep, you'll be armed to rig a nymph-and-indicator setup and go down to dig them out. When conditions are right for wets, or you just get overwhelmed with a desire to fish them, then you're geared just right for them as well. On this medium-sized mountain stream, with its fairly open canopy, you'd do fine with any rod between 7^1/$_2$ and 9 feet long, with a floating line. If you were on a smaller stream, you might want a shorter rod. If you were fishing a larger river, you'd probably be best equipped with the same rod that would work well on this one: your favorite trout rod.

hour. That's not fun. I rarely use more than two wet flies on a cast. The exception is when I rig an 11-foot slow rod with three flies specifically to fish Davy Wotton's methods on broad riffles and runs (see Chapter 16, "Keeper of the Flame: Lessons from Davy Wotton").

I use multiple wet flies less often than I probably ought to, considering the advantage gained—the time saved trying to figure out what fly the trout want. To gain that advantage, you've got to be sure your two flies are different. Try one light, one dark, or one large, one small. Try one soft-hackle and one winged wet or flymph, or a traditional wet paired with an all-fur wet. Try all sorts of different combinations, but make sure that the two flies are in contrast, and thereby amount to an experiment. Give the trout a choice. Let them make it. Once they do, reduce your tangling potential by nipping off the fly that isn't catching anything. If both flies catch trout, leave both on the leader. If you clip one off and the one that was working ceases to catch trout, tie the other back on.

That's all I have to say about wet-fly tackle, because I usually select what I'm going to use based on the water I'm going to fish, for a wide variety of methods, on that day, for that water, not just for wet flies. One of the great sorrows of wet-fly fishing is that it provides only a mild excuse to rush out and acquire a bunch of brand new gear.

Chapter Eleven

Fishing the Traditional Wet-Fly Swing

We know how nature treats natural insects: just tosses them onto the water and lets them tumble along, at the whim of every current. We also know how our fishing forefathers fished their wet flies: just tossed them out there and let them swing down and around, at the whim of every current. Though that method is now derided as *chuck-and-chance-it*, it's difficult to miss the similarity between what happens to natural insects and the way our elders fished their early wet flies. It was no accident that those old wet-fly fishermen caught lots of trout.

Nature hasn't changed tactics with the foods she shows to trout. You'd be foolish to neglect the traditional wet-fly swing today.

The downstream swing calls for inserting yourself into the water along the edges of a stream or river, then wading downstream, casting not just to the most likely water, but to *all* of the water. It's a method for exploring, to find out the sort of water in which trout might be holding. If you cover all types of water, and by doing that discover that trout are only in one of those types, say in riffles, then you should begin to restrict your focus to just that kind of water. Many times trout will be sprinkled in runs, under current tongues and on tailouts in pools, as well as in those riffles. In that case you'll want to continue covering all of the water.

To oversimplify the traditional wet-fly swing, cast quartering downstream across the current, fish the fly—or if you prefer, the pair of flies—down and around. Let them dangle straight below you, take a step or two downstream, lift the line, cast across the currents at a downstream angle again, and fish out the swing again. No method is easier. Few methods show wet flies so thoughtfully to every possible holding lie down the entire length of a piece of trout water.

In the old days, wet flies were sometimes given a vigorous and rhythmic retrieve as they swam across and downstream. This tactic can be useful at rare times, for example when you fish wet flies in slow water that holds lots of large swimmer mayfly nymphs. For the most part, though, it's not effective to give wet flies much added action because few natural insects swim boldly, especially in fairly fast or broken water, which is where the traditional wet-fly swing works best.

I've done quite a few experiments with adding action to the wet-fly swing. The most calculating was in a broad riffle on Montana's remote Smith River. The water was a couple of feet deep, flowing briskly in an even sheet 200 feet wide and 300 feet long. The bottom consisted of softball-size and larger rocks, so the surface was lumpy, though no rocks protruded through it. Trout were not working visibly, but it looked like a good holding riffle to me, on account of all the lies such rocks form along the bottom. So I tied on a size 12 all-fur wet fly with a cream body and tan fur collar.

I entered at the head of the riffle, worked out about 50 feet of line, and cast it at an angle about 45 degrees down and across the current. On the first cast I let the fly swim around without any action added. On the second cast I gently lifted and lowered the rod tip, a total movement of perhaps 6 inches each time. It was a slow, steady pulse, just enough to swim the fly in darts rather than a steady pace. A 12-inch trout thumped the fly on that second cast. I thought, "Aha, action on the fly is better!"

I continued to alternate the pulsing swing with swings lacking action. By the time I got to the end of the riffle I'd released eleven trout, all around a foot long. Six took on the animated swing, five on the one without action. The results in that particular situation were too near to separate. They do nothing more than point to the possible benefits of experimentation. Had all the trout taken on one sort of retrieve, I might not have caught any had I used only the other.

Most of the time, in most types of water, I prefer the constant swing, with no swimming movement added by pulsing the fly rod, simply because I've studied enough aquatic entomology to know that the preponderance of insects are helpless when cast loose in currents. The steady swing is more in keeping with the action of those natural insects. I find few times when an active swing adds to my catch, but lots of times when it kills any hope of catching trout. If fishing is slow, however, it never hurts to add some swimming action every few casts, as a test, to see if movement might not be the secret at that particular moment, on that bit of water.

The old chuck-and-chance-it method can take lots of trout for you. Use it as an exploratory tool, when you don't know where trout hold, and you don't know what they're doing. Try it with a brace of wet flies, again offering

The traditional wet-fly swing is an excellent method to use when you're new to the water, want to explore it, and would like to know where its trout hang out. You can insert yourself into it, cast to cover all of it, take long strides to move quickly downstream through it. Somewhere along the way you'll begin catching trout and learn what type of water might hold most of them, and therefore might be best place to focus your fishing. RICK HAFELE

more than one size, color, or style. It works best in water with substantial movement, least well in water that is ponded nearly to stillness. You can use the method to explore downstream through a wide variety of water types: riffles, runs, flats, and pools. It's most effective on streams and small rivers that are about a cast across, because you can cover every potential holding lie, from the far bank to the near. But it's also excellent for covering broad riffles, runs, and even smooth or chattery flats on big rivers. You'll rarely use the traditional wet-fly swing on tiny streams, because they're too narrow to cast across in most places, too cramped for a downstream swing.

If the water you're about to fish is broken by rocks and boulders and pockets, so much the better. Fish the brace of wet flies down and around all of them. Show the flies to every bit of water. You're bound to find some willing trout.

Take a step or two after fishing out each cast. Once you've lengthened your line to the right distance to cover the water, continue with the same amount of line in the air, and use your own downstream stepping movement to show the flies to new lies. If you're using a single fly, cast long with a tight loop. If you're using two flies, or even three, use a slower, more open casting loop to reduce the chance of tangles.

There is often some magic to setting the hook with wet flies fished on the swing. Trout will often climb onto the fly and set the hook themselves. You feel a yank, and your arm, without instruction from your brain, yanks back. That's fine, but don't yank too hard. Just as often, however, a trout will simply intercept the fly as it comes to it on the current. You'll feel no more than a slight increase in pressure on the line. Or you might feel nothing while the line begins to belly strangely in the current, as if you've hung on a snag high in the water column, where there are no snags. This means that a trout has stopped the fly, hasn't reacted to the hook, but can't get rid of it. The current has usually drawn the hook into the corner of the trout's jaw, and there it hangs.

If you set the hook to this kind of take with a jerk, you're more likely to pull the fly upstream away from the fish, even out of its mouth, than you are to hook it. If the trout has turned and is already powering away, you'll break it off if it has any weight, in other words if it's just the sort of trout you'd most like to catch. The best way to set the hook to a soft take with a wet fly fished on the swing is to hold on, do nothing. Let the hook find its seat, and let the trout hook itself. If it doesn't, let the fly continue its swing. You'll be surprised how often a trout will follow and take again, or come back on the next cast.

This is especially true with plucking takes. You feel a tap. That's a miss. If you set the hook, that's the end of it. If you let the fly continue its swing, about one-third of the time the trout will take again. If it doesn't, lift the line at the end of the swing and make the same cast, without lengthening it, without taking a step. Repeat the swing through the same water, and about one-third of the time the trout will take on the second or third cast.

The thrill of the soft take is half the fun of wet-fly fishing. It's precisely the same take a summer steelhead makes to a damp fly fished on the swing. Sometimes you feel a thud, and the hook is set before you can react. More often you feel a slow uptake of pressure, and either the hook slips home in the corner of the steelhead's jaw or it does not. Either way, that fish's lie is marked and can often be caught on subsequent casts. It's the same with trout. I love that suspended moment in which I know a trout is out there, has the fly, is going to be either on or off, and there's little I can do but wait for that moment when the trout—or summer steelhead—finally reacts to the bite of the hook and makes its first dash and dance.

This type of soft take often occurs at the end of the swing, when the fly slows and dangles straight below you. This is certainly true when your cast puts the fly across a current that is fast but you stand in slower water. Trout hold along the inside of the seam between fast water and slow. When the fly crosses that seam and coasts to a stop straight below you, trout can't resist it. Sometimes they'll whack it. More often they'll merely accept it. You'll feel an increase in pressure. You can use this type of take to make yourself look good, if you'd like.

When you feel a trout pluck at your wet fly, or feel no more than a slight uptake of pressure out there at the end of the line, then it's best, though sometimes very difficult, to discipline yourself to do nothing. Wait until the trout has set the hook itself. The force of the current against line and leader will slide the fly to the corner of the trout's mouth, even as it tries to eject it. A fish hooked in this way will almost always have the hook seated in the hinge of its jaw. That's a sign that you did it right . . . though if it's hooked somewhere else and you catch it, that's not an indication that you did something wrong.

I did this just yesterday, as I'm writing this, on a float down Oregon's Willamette River. Richard Bunse stood in his anchored boat, in slow water off to the side of a brisk riffle. He cast to trout that rose at random in the slow water downstream from the boat. Occasional March Brown mayfly duns sailed off the water and into the air. Bunse cast a dry fly to match them. Fishing was slow, but Bunse is as near to a dry-fly purist and as much of an expert with them as you're ever going to discover, so he was catching a few.

I hiked upstream 50 feet from Bunse's boat, waded in, and cast a March Brown flymph into the riffle, letting it swing down and around. It swam out of the fast water and into slow water just a couple of rod lengths upstream from Bunse's bow. I lifted and cast again. A trout rose at the edge of the current seam a few feet below the first swing, so I fed a little line into the drift. Then I just followed the fly with the tip of the rod held low over the water. Bunse and I were talking about something, so my attention was elsewhere, when the fly swam out of the riffle and into the slow water close to his boat.

Tension began to gather on the line while Bunse and I talked. I let it build, didn't do anything to set the hook or to pull the fly away from the fish. The hook finally found its seat, and the trout bolted. I didn't react to that, either, since not reacting is one of the best ways to keep a trout in play during the first moments of any engagement.

Long, choppy riffles are excellent for fishing with the traditional downstream wet-fly swing. Trout might be anywhere out there. A wet fly, or pair of them, fished on a fairly long cast and broad swing, can scout them out for you. Wets will also take trout when a few fish are feeding, but their rises are so scattered that it's impossible to cover them individually with dry flies. Just work your way downstream through the water with wets on the swing. Trout will see them and almost always accept them if they look like anything in nature.

I kept on talking to Bunse. While I did, the trout put a deep bend into my rod, goosed my reel and made it squawk, then tumbled into the air right alongside Bunse's boat. He stopped talking and looked down at the frolicking trout for awhile, from his elevated position in the boat. Then he said, "If I'd known you were going to fish wet flies today, I wouldn't have rowed you in my boat." He cast his dry to another rise, but this time the trout ignored it.

Chuck-and-chance-it can catch trout for you even if you do no more than cast out and fish your wet flies down and around without any more thought about it. But you can improve on the method in a couple of simple ways and fool a lot more fish with it. The first is to calculate the angle at which you cast across the current. This will determine the speed at which your flies swing. The second is to mend line, usually upstream but sometimes down, to slow or—rarely—to speed the swinging fly.

If you cast straight across any current, the thicker fly line behind the tapered point will catch the current, cause it to belly quickly, speed the wet fly downstream and across faster than a natural insect would ever be able to swim. If the current creeps along very slowly, a downstream belly can be beneficial, because it can animate a wet fly that would otherwise essentially be sitting still. If the current is moderate to fast, however, that belly can be bad, because it races a wet fly unnaturally.

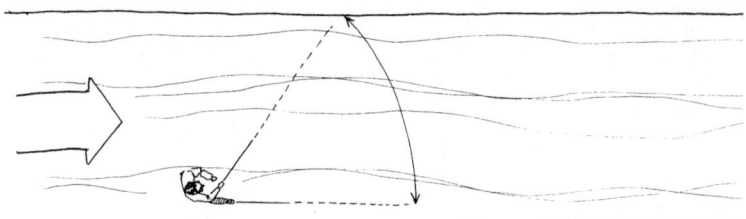

When casting across a slow to moderate current, angle the cast higher into the current for the right speed in the fly swing.

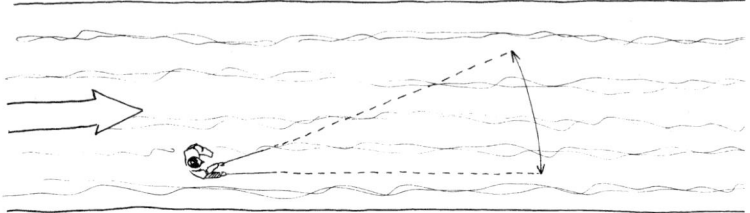

If the current is swift, cast at an angle farther downstream. You'll get a shorter swing, but it will be at the right speed, not too fast to fool fish.

As an experiment sometime when you're out on water, armed with a wet fly, try casting at an angle just a bit out into the current from straight downstream, cutting across just a few feet of flow. The line will have little chance to belly as the fly swings through its short arc. If the current is very slow the fly will hang almost without movement. If the current is very fast, the fly will still swim slowly across it because there is so little line to belly and speed it. As the second part of the experiment, cast almost straight across the same current. If it's fast, the line will soon belly, and the fly will race. If it's slow, the line might slowly belly, but the fly might fish on the swing at just the right speed, perhaps even too slowly.

Now you can begin to put the picture together. If the current you're fishing is slow, cast higher up into it, sometimes nearly straight across it, so that the line will belly slightly and give the fly some animation. If the current is fast, cast at an angle farther downstream, to keep the line from bellying and speeding the fly too fast.

To complete the picture, imagine yourself standing in front of a riffle, with the current flowing from your left to your right. If you cast straight across, that is 90 degrees. If you cast straight downstream to your right, that is 0 degrees. In slow to moderate currents, a cast between 45 and 60 degrees will give you the best swing. In fast currents, a cast between 30 and 45 degrees will swing the fly at the correct speed. In an average current, a 45-degree cast will be about right. You'll quickly learn to gauge the correct angle to cast across any current. The faster it is, the farther downstream you cast. The slower it is, the farther upstream.

Choosing the correct casting angle for the traditional wet-fly swing is a matter of experience. The faster the flow, the farther downstream the cast should be made, so the current has less chance to form a belly in the line. In modest flows such as this, the normal 45 degree angle is about right. Place your cast tight to the grass on the far side. Don't lift the line for the next cast until the fly, or pair of them, has passed out of the main current flow. Trout might follow all the way across before taking, or they might be holding in the quiet water around those boulders, waiting to take what drifts by on the main currents.

To get wet flies to fish at the right speed, all of your decisions must be based on observation, backed up by experience. You gain experience by going fishing, casting across currents of different speeds at various angles, watching the way your line bellies, and what your fly is doing when you get strikes from trout. It will not take long for you to achieve some feeling for those moments when the fly is coaxing trout, because you'll get almost all of your takes when the fly is fishing at the right speed. When it's going too fast, you'll begin to feel it, and you'll make your next cast farther downstream. When it's creeping along too slowly, you'll also begin to feel that, and you'll make your next cast farther upstream.

After some time spent fishing wet flies, and enjoying a lot of takes from approving trout, you'll be able to walk up to any piece of flowing water and quickly calculate the angle at which you should cast across it for the best wet-fly swing. You won't even think about it. Before long you'll forget the times when you used to wade into any riffle or run, cast 50 to 60 feet straight across it, hold on, and think you were fishing it right, no matter the speed of its current. That is one reason wet flies got so far out of favor: They were so often fished wrong. Natural insects don't race. Your wet flies should not swim any faster than the current would move them, or trout will ignore them.

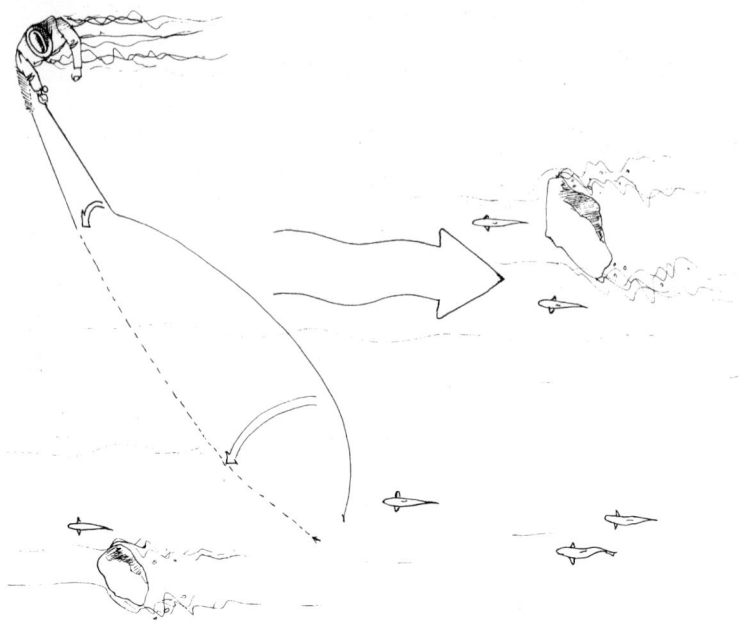

When current pushes a downstream belly into your line, causing the fly to swim too fast, an upstream mend will slow it to a pace trout prefer.

The second major step toward improving your catch over simple chuck-and-chance-it, after working out the correct casting angle, is learning when and how to mend and tend the drift and swing of your wet fly.

Mending line is the most important maneuver to speed or slow the drift or swing of any fly: dry, nymph, wet, or streamer. You'll use mends often, sometimes almost constantly, when fishing wet flies on downstream swings. Again, you want to sense when the fly is fishing at the right speed, coaxing fish. If it's fishing too fast, the problem is nearly always a downstream line belly accelerating the fly. If it's fishing too slow, then an intentional downstream belly will always speed the drift.

An upstream mend removes a downstream belly from the line and creates an upstream belly. A downstream mend removes an upstream belly and converts it to a downstream belly. You'll use both types, but about 90 percent of the time you'll use upstream mends to eliminate a downstream belly that causes the fly to fish too fast.

A long rod and double-taper floating line aid in making mends. Your line should be clean, so that it floats well. It's difficult to mend with a line that is even slightly submerged. Clean your line at the beginning of every fishing day, and whenever during the day that it begins to sink. Modern high-floating fly lines are excellent, but they get dirty and should be cleaned more often than most folks think. It's possible to mend with an intermediate line the

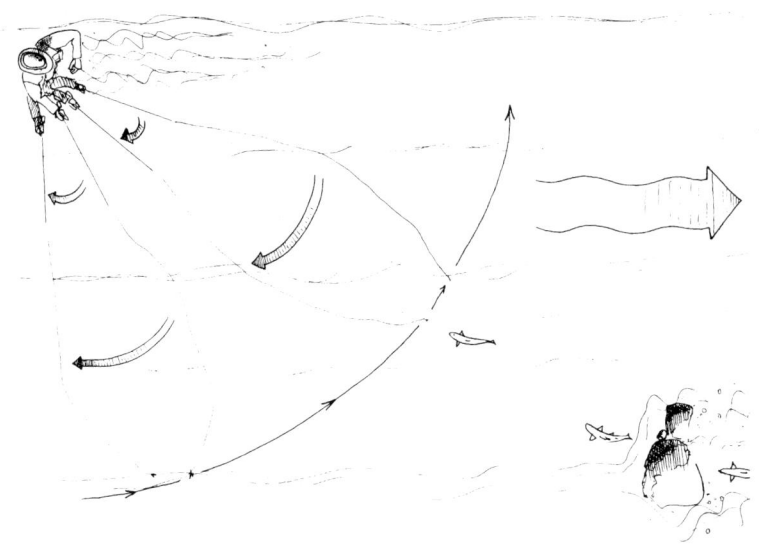

You can improve your chances on any downstream swing of a wet fly by mending whenever the speed of the swing becomes faster than a natural insect might drift and swim.

instant the line lands on the water. After that, it's not. It's possible to mend the floating portion of any sink-tip or sinking-belly line, though the mend will never get very close to your fly.

When we think about mending, we're generally thinking about floating fly lines. Weight-forward lines can be mended, but only on short to moderate casts, especially if the heavy casting portion of the line is 30 feet or less. If the cast is long, the running line behind the casting head lies on the water, and it's very difficult to get that thin part of the line to lift and turn the thicker forward section. Double-taper lines mend best, weight-forwards with 40-foot and longer casting portions almost as well.

A mend is made by lifting the line up and off the water with a rolling motion of the rod that lays the line back onto the water in the opposite position from which it started. It should be a quick, full motion. On a long cast, when the belly is 20 to 30 feet from the rod, you'll have to make a long sweep with the rod, up and over. When the cast is shorter, and the belly lies closer to the rod, the mend can be a brisk, flicking roll that lifts just a little line and repositions it. The goal is to lift and reposition the line without moving the fly, though it's not a major problem if you cause a wet fly to make a short swim forward each time you make a mend.

On an average downstream wet-fly swing, an experienced angler might mend half a dozen or more times. It becomes an automatic movement, the line lifted and flicked over every few feet, in response to the line's curve on the water. Similar to calculating the angle to cast across the current, you soon

If you're trying to reach a trout or a lie that is out of casting range, you can wiggle slack onto the water after the cast and feed it into the current to extend the downstream drift and swing of the fly. Such creative solutions to specific problems will become automatic when you've fished wet flies long enough, had enough success that you can feel when your fly is fishing right, and sense what to do about it when it's fishing wrong.

get a feel for when the fly is fishing right, and what to do about it when the fly fishes wrong.

Tending the drift and swing can also be accomplished by feeding line into the drift of the fly. This is done simply by carrying a little extra slack in the line hand, behind the stripping guide. If your fly starts to race so fast across a current that you can't slow it enough with mends, then it's best to correct the problem by casting at an angle farther downstream on subsequent casts. But you'll find times when you want to reach good-looking water so far across stream that the correct amount of downstream angle won't let you get your flies over there. So you're forced to cast almost straight across currents that are certain to cause an instant downstream belly and race your fly. Or you might already be into a swing, and your fly is approaching a good-looking lie or the position of a recent rise, but is moving too fast. You don't want to kill the lie by lifting the line and fly off the water right on top of it so you can make another cast at the correct angle.

If you release a few feet of slack line and let it slip through the rod guides, it will instantly slow the swing of a wet fly. On a long cast, when the line belly is too far from the rod to reach with a mend, let some line slip and the fly will slow long enough to fish a few feet of water at the right speed. On a cast where the fly races toward a lie, let some line slip and the fly will suddenly slow down, swim through that lie at just the right speed.

Once in a rare while, you'll run into a lie too far downstream to reach with a cast, or see a rise that you'd like to cover with a wet fly, but it's beyond the

When fishing out any traditional wet-fly cast, be patient enough to let the fly or flies swing across the current seam between the faster and deeper water, outboard, and the slower and shallower water, inboard. Trout will often hold along that seam, and take a wet when it arrives. Other trout will follow a fly through the main currents, then take only when it appears to be getting away into the lesser currents. Either way, if you lift your wets too soon, you'll cost yourself chances at some trout.

farthest point you can reach while wading safely. You can make a shorter cast, then feed line into the drift to cover water 100 feet, or even farther, down-stream from your position. If it's possible to change your position, get closer. Feeding line might be a mistake, because you won't get the hook set in many trout that take a long way from the rod. If feeding line is the only possible way to cover a lie, however, then do it. Simply make your cast, strip line off the reel, and wiggle the rod tip back and forth to pull the slack through the guides and onto the water. All that slack will make it almost impossible to set the hook. You can only hope that any trout sets the hook itself.

Experienced cross-stream fishermen constantly juggle things on almost every traditional wet-fly swing. They change the casting angle to experiment with the speed of the swing, getting it just right. They mend this way and that to slow or speed the swing, after the line has landed on the water. They feed line or draw it in as the fly swings across the currents, speeding it for this bit of water and slowing it for that. They make sure their fly crosses the seam between fast water and slow at the end of its swing.

One or another of these movements is made on nearly every cast. That is what separates a thoughtful traditional wet-fly swing from chuck-and-chance-it. When you get it worked out, your wet flies will look and move like lots of the things that trout make a living eating. When your flies spend most of their time coaxing trout, your catch will suddenly take a jump upward.

Chapter Twelve

The Greased-Line Method and Crosfield Draw

The greased-line tactic was devised by A. H. E. Wood to apply against Atlantic salmon in Scotland's River Tweed. Wood's thorough notes were recorded in Jock Scott's 1935 book *Greased Line Fishing for Atlantic Salmon*. The essentials of the method were translated for trout fishermen in Sylvester Nemes's 1975 book *The Soft-Hackled Fly*. The goal of greased-line fishing for trout is to present a wet fly drifting downstream as free as a leaf adrift on the current, as if it were not attached to the line or leader.

Line control is a primary component of the greased-line method. A fairly long rod, at least $8^1/2$ to 9 feet, and a double taper floating line will help you apply it. When employed with wet flies against trout, the greased-line method is one where a $9^1/2$- to 11-foot rod would be beneficial. Light Spey rods and newer switch rods would be excellent, if they carry lines that float and can therefore be mended. However, it's always my assumption that you go to a stream or river armed to fish a variety of methods, and that you'll be carrying a rod suitable for more than wet-fly fishing. Your typical 9-foot, 4- or 5-weight rod will be fine for greased-line trout fishing, and it will do a lot of other things as well.

The leader should be the length of the rod or a couple of feet longer. The method is most useful on broad runs and riffles, with moderate to brisk currents. The water must be wide enough to let you cast directly cross-stream, so you'll usually fish greased line on streams a cast across or larger, or on rivers with broad runs and riffles. You won't often find places to use the method on small streams because their narrowness forces you to fish them either upstream or down. The greased-line tactic works best where the water

234

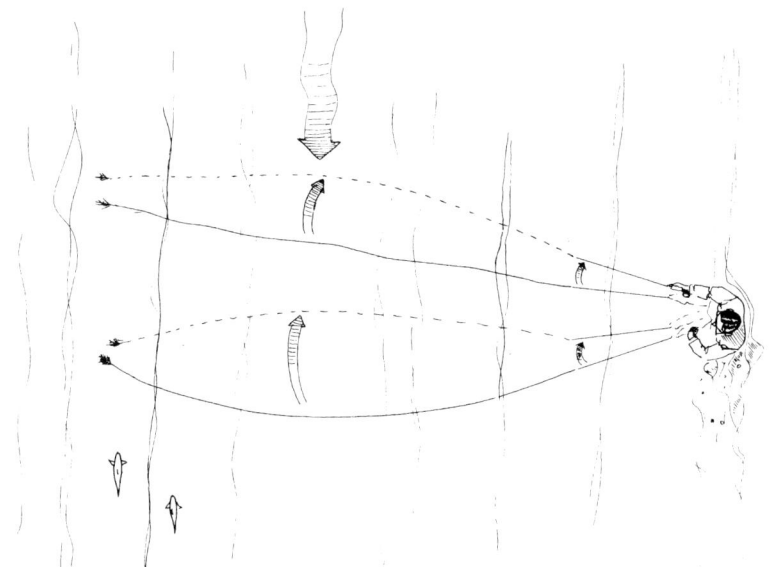

In the greased-line method, you use constant mends to keep the fly drifting freely straight downstream.

is 2 to 4 feet deep and well featured, if not broken by boulders that protrude through the surface, then marked with choppy waves and boils that reflect lots of rocks and boulders on the bottom.

Take your casting position to the side of the main current, the holding water where you expect to find trout, and at the upstream end of the riffle or run to be fished. Don't wade out into water that might hold trout. That is the most common mistake beginners make. Such shallow holding water often has a seam along the inside edge where slow water meets the faster water just outside of it. Wading is easy right up to that edge. Many people plunge right out to the seam and begin casting farther out to where they think the big ones are. Don't make that mistake. The big ones and little ones and lots of in-between ones hang right along that seam between fast water and slow, because living is easy there. They can rest under the seam and dash into fast water to nip at whatever food drifts by. You want your wet fly, or pair of them, to be part of what drifts by.

Wade shallow at first, and make your casts short. Cast at an angle from just upstream from straight across to about a 45-degree angle upstream. Because the currents are a fairly even sheet between your position and the fly, the fly will begin drifting downstream immediately, a few inches deep, but without drag, just like a dry fly might if drowned. The line, being bulkier than the leader but riding in currents of the same speed, will form a down-stream belly, pick up speed, and begin to tug at the fly after a few feet of drift. You don't want this to happen in the greased-line method, because your goal is to have the wet fly drifting freely, just as a natural mayfly dun, adult caddis, or winged stonefly might do when drowned.

To slow the drift of the fly, toss upstream mends. Make each mend by lifting the floating line up and off the water with an upstream rolling motion of the rod. The rod turns an arc; the line follows. The downstream belly lifts off the water, flops over in the air, lands on the water in an upstream belly: an upstream curve across the currents between the rod and the fly. The fly will drift freely again until the current pushes at the fly line, forms a downstream belly again, and tugs at the fly. The greased-line method, then, consists of an up-and-across stream cast followed by a series of mends while the wet fly drifts freely and straight downstream, usually well past your casting position.

If the water is fast, or if currents under the rod are faster than currents out by the fly, your mends must be made quickly and often. You might make five to fifteen mends on a single drift. If the water is slow, or if currents under the rod are slower than currents out by the fly, one or two mends might accomplish a long drift.

You must learn to gauge the fly's drift speed and its attitude in the current. It should drift at the same speed as the current, and broadside as it moves downstream. This gives trout the best view of it. Whenever the fly seems to be drawn into a rush by the line and leader, make a mend.

You should also know about a slow-water method called the Crosfield Draw, also based on Atlantic salmon fishing, this time for pools with very little current to activate the sunk fly. I use the draw whenever I'm fishing a wet, or a pair or even three of them, in water so slow that the wet fly, if left to proceed at its own pace, would simply subside toward the bottom.

The Crosfield Draw is perfect for fishing long, slow pools with water 3 to 6 feet deep. I use it most often in low-gradient streams, where the pools might be 100 to 300 feet long, slow, marked by occasional boulders or slight boils. If an occasional trout rises lazily down the length of the pool, then I

For the greased-line method, the cast is made across stream, with some slack in the line, especially if the line will be draped over conflicting currents, as it is here.

It's overdramatized in this photo, but a downstream belly will form in the line as the wet fly drifts downstream.

An upstream mend is made by lifting the rod and turning it over. The line will follow.

After the mend, the line will lie on the water with an upstream belly in place of the downstream belly that was causing the fly to begin racing. When that upstream belly straightens and then forms downstream again, it's time for a following mend. Some casts will require one or two; others will need ten or more.

As the greased-line cast is fished out, with mends as needed, the wet fly, or pair of them, drifts downstream freely, broadside to the current, as if not attached to the line and leader.

It's often wise to fish out the remains of a greased-line drift by using a traditional wet-fly swing to swim the fly across and downstream, as long as the wet fly remains in promising water.

Takes with the greased-line method, or in the traditional swing that follows it, will rarely be violent. Usually you'll feel a tug, and will be best served by letting the trout hook itself. An early set from your end will often pull the fly away from the trout. The fight that follows, however, might contain some violence.

Results of the greased-line technique, properly applied, can be pleasant to hold in your hand.

know that the Crosfield Draw used with a soft-hackle, a flymph, or an all-fur wet fly, or some combination of them, will coax a trout or two. In this type of water, it's likely they'll be big ones.

I used this method once on Oregon's Powder River, out in the desert. The water was low. It galloped here and there through short boulder-studded riffles and runs. These held the most fish, and they were the most tempting places to spend time, because of the abundant 10- to 12-inch-long rainbow residing there.

These runs were punctuated by long, lazy pools. They were about a cast across, their surfaces smooth. Current tongues fed in at the top of each pool; tailouts gathered the slow flows and rushed them out at the bottom. But the current just ambled through centers that were 100 to 200 feet long. Rare rises welled up, one here, one a little later over there, another five minutes later far out of casting range down the pool. They were too scattered to cover effectively with dry flies. But they spoke of actively feeding trout too big to be ignored.

I left my rigging the same as I'd been using to fish dry flies in the shallow riffles and runs, a 10-foot leader tapered to a 4X point, since the water was not enormously clear and the trout were far from leader-shy. I nipped off the dry fly I'd been using and tied on a size 12 March Brown Spider soft-hackle, one I often reach for when nothing specific is going on. My rod that day was the Leonard bamboo, $7^1/_2$ feet long, carrying a double-taper 5-weight floating line. I waded in at the head of the first pool but didn't go in over my knees, because I wanted to fish each cast all the way around, and wading out too far would not let me do that.

The bank behind was clear. Casting was easy. I placed each cast straight across the stream, almost to the willows that lined the far bank, then instantly tossed a downstream mend into the line to install an intentional downstream

In very slow currents, the Crosfield Draw, in which you use a mend to put an intentional downstream belly into the line, can be used to speed up the creeping swing of the fly.

belly. This caused the slight current to pick up the line and coax the fly into the slightest movement. Each cast swung around with agonizing slowness. It was tempting to speed things up by retrieving the soft-hackle. But that wasn't what I wanted because I suspected the trout were picking occasionally at something subsurface and drifting at the speed of the current, not swimming across it. I based my suspicion on the knowledge that most of the time, in such water types, that is what trout see. I would have expected more aggressive feeding if the trout were chasing something swimming.

It took a long time to fish out each cast. I took a long step before making each following cast, just as one would do in summer steelhead or Atlantic

In the Crosfield Draw, you make a downstream mend as soon as the line lands on the water. In slow water, the resulting downstream belly gives the current something to brace against. The drift speeds up, and the wet fly is animated. The method is designed for Atlantic salmon fishing in long, slow pools. It suits this situation perfectly, where Jim Schollmeyer fishes a river that has its broad but slow beginnings in the outflow from a big Canadian lake.

salmon fishing. I made two or three downstream mends during each drift, to increase the line belly on the slow water, and therefore to pick up the patient pace of the wet fly. The soft-hackle must have looked like an insect drifting broadside downstream, aiming toward shore but not getting there very fast, because a broad-shouldered trout intercepted it about halfway through the third drift.

It's hard to describe the take of a big fish to a shallow and creeping wet fly in water that just ambles along. No arrow is drawn to the fly. The water just suddenly wells up, is shoved aside, goes out from the fly in concentric waves. Sometimes you feel nothing and must set the hook gently to the visible take. More often you feel a powerful surge, not sudden but instead sullen. Don't react with a firm strike; even 4X tippet won't hold such a trout when it has taken the fly and already turned away with it. If you pull one way at the instant the trout pulls the other, you're going to break it off unless it's tiny. Just lift the rod, let go of the line, and let the trout perform the hook set itself when it feels the hook point.

I took three trout down the length of that pool. The smallest was 15 inches long, shaped like a football, probably weighed 2 pounds. The others were a few inches longer, might have weighed a pound or two more—not giants, but not the small ones the faster water I'd been fishing upstream and down from those pools was producing, either.

Two young fellows passed behind me while I fished, politely leaving me the pool, but paused to watch when I hooked a trout, played it out, then landed and released it. I didn't notice them back there until I heard one of them quietly say to the other, "That guy looks like he knows what he's doing." It was pleasant to hear. It's one of the few times in my fly-fishing life that I've felt an overheard comment was correct. I did feel like I knew what I was doing, which was no more than what was needed to make my wet fly swim as if it were alive in that slow water. I suspect the main reason I impressed the fellows was not that I caught that big trout, nor that I played it well enough to bring it to hand, but that I was fishing a bamboo rod.

In that distant day, anybody carrying bamboo was thought to be an expert. Adding in the trout was just small confirmation.

The Crosfield Draw is a method to remember any time you feel your wet fly, or cast of two or three of them, is not fishing fast enough. That will be a rather rare occurrence. Most of the time your wet fly will fish too fast. You'll want to mend upstream to slow it, not downstream to speed it. Nevertheless, you'll find a few places where mending downstream with the Crosfield Draw works. If you learn to recognize them, knowing how to use it will increase your odds on the very water where trout are often largest.

Chapter Thirteen

Ray Bergman's Natural Drift

Ray Bergman's 1938 book *Trout* is well worth reading to this day, as much for its fine, quiet voice as for the broad range of tactics it reveals so gracefully. Many of these tactics work as well today as they did in his day. Bergman was fishing editor of *Outdoor Life* magazine for twenty-six years, from 1934 until 1960. He wrote as often with anecdote as direct instruction, so it's educational to extract fishing information out of his stories. But he was brief and direct about his main method for fishing wet flies, which he referred to as the *Natural Drift*. He covered it in just three total pages, of which one is a full-page illustration. I've never seen such a useful method defined so succinctly, and yet so precisely.

Tackle was in transition in Bergman's day. His favorite rod for wet-fly fishing was an 8-foot bamboo with a moderate action, though he noted that steel rods were getting better all the time and might replace split cane, while *glass fibre* rods "have come into the picture . . . they are being steadily improved . . . now giving steel and bamboo some stiff competition."

Wet-fly leaders of Bergman's day were usually 6 feet long, though he preferred $7^1/2$ feet for most fishing, and 9 feet for clear water. The latter is about standard today. Flies were usually *snelled*—the fly purchased already attached to the tippet, which was either gut or nylon, again in transition. Tippets were 2X or 3X, heavier than the standard for wet-fly fishing today.

In his descriptions of wet-fly fishing, Bergman always referred to his *flies*, never his *fly*. It's easy to assume he used two-fly casts most of the time, though he describes three-fly casts for fishing pocket water. His wet flies were typically sizes 6 to 12, rarely smaller, and there is little evidence that he related wets to natural insects. The study of trout-stream entomology was also beginning its transition in that day

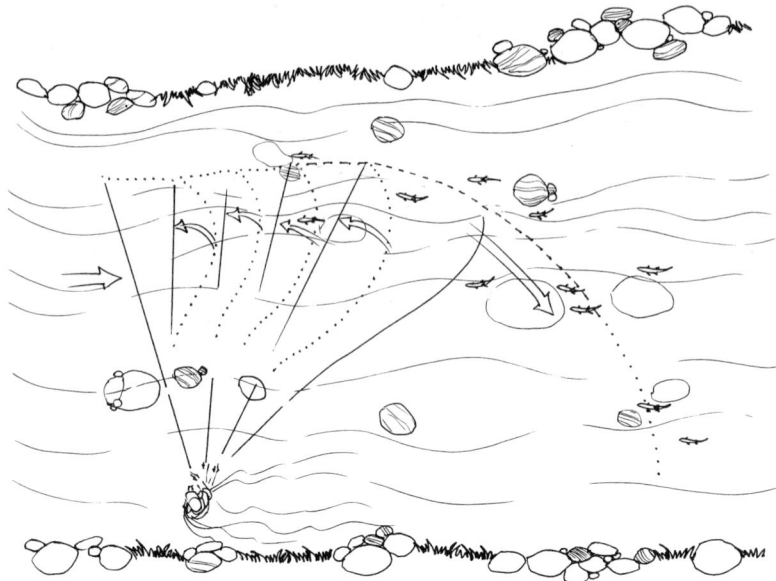

Ray Bergman's *Natural Drift* method calls for a cast at a 45-degree angle upstream, a free drift, as in the greased-line method, until the flies are at a 45-degree angle downstream. Then they are fished around, as in the traditional downstream swing, until they come to a stop directly below the angler's position. If the water is shaped right for the long drift and wide sweep across the currents, the Natural Drift is a way to combine two effective methods into one.

Strangely, in his short notes on wet-fly tackle, Bergman did not mention lines. He started with silk, and by the time his book was written would have been trying out their eventual nylon replacements. In his notes on lines for dry-fly fishing, he pointed out that manufacturers were just beginning to experiment with coatings for nylon lines. They were not perfected for many more years. I've seen and fished a few lines from that early experimental era of coated fly lines. There was little pleasant to write about them. It's easy to assume, and probably correct, that the lines Bergman used, whether silk or nylon, were about the equivalent of intermediate lines we might use today.

Bergman's Natural Drift wet-fly method could be considered a melding of the greased-line tactic and the traditional downstream swing. Jock Scott's book *Greased Line Fishing for Atlantic Salmon* was published only three years before Bergman's *Trout*, so it's possible but unlikely that Bergman would have been able to read it, translate it to his own trout fishing, and report on it in such short time. If so, he didn't mention the greased-line method in his wet-fly writings in *Trout*.

Ideal water for the Natural Drift would be a modest-sized trout stream or small river, about a cast across. Bergman's drawing and his notes depict the angler wading close to one bank and casting to the far bank. Because the method calls for long drifts, followed by cross-stream swings, it would be most suitable on pools with substantial length, at least 75 to 100 feet, with even current flows for most of that distance. That's a perfect description of many New England trout waters where Bergman did most, though far from all, of his fishing. The method could be used as well on large rivers, with broad riffles and runs, though you might be wading farther from the near bank and would rarely be casting close to the far bank.

In Bergman's method, the initial cast in the Natural Drift method is made upstream, at a 45-degree angle across the current, or close to that angle. Lower the rod slightly, and let the line follow, as the flies sink. The line should be "slack and yet just on the verge of being taut." Anticipate takes as the line approaches a 90-degree angle across from you, almost straight across the stream. You might mend during this upper part of the drift to keep the line pointing directly at the flies. The flies should drift freely, just as they would in this portion of a greased-line presentation.

As the flies pass the point where they're directly opposite you, begin to release line into the drift. This allows the flies to continue drifting straight downstream, again freely as in the greased-line method. If the line were to be drawn tight at this point, the flies would enter into a swing down and around below your position. Instead, feed out the line until the flies reach an angle 45 degrees downstream. This is the "hot spot" where you can expect a lot of strikes, according to Bergman.

From this 45-degree point, allow the flies, using Bergman's word, to "drag" across the current in what amounts to a traditional downstream swing. Bergman describes this part of fishing out the cast in a sentence or two, without comment about its potential to hook trout. In my own experience, it's the part of the Natural Drift method where I hook most of my own trout.

When the flies have finished their swing and hang directly below you, patiently retrieve them upstream a few feet, let them drop back, and possibly repeat the movement one or two times. I've never had the patience to do that for as long as Bergman recommends, but it's a wise idea to let the drift complete itself before the flies are lifted and lofted into the next cast.

Before departing from Bergman's method, it's important to point out that his illustration, and his description, are of a single cast. It's made from the near bank, the flies placed so that they drift freely along the far bank. This would be the final cast reaching out over a riffle, run, or pool, to cover the most distant water. Though it's not mentioned, Bergman would have started with short casts, to the near water, with the same 45-degree angles and same sweep across a small arc of water. Then he'd have extended each cast out a foot or two, and thereby covered all of the water between his initial position and that last illustrated cast that fishes the flies along the far bank.

If the reach of water to be covered was longer than could be covered with one long cast, drift, and swing, then Bergman presumably would do the same thing you or I would, though he did not mention it in his brief notes on the

The initial cast in Bergman's Natural Drift is made at a 45-degree angle upstream into the current.

In the upper part of the Natural Drift, wet flies move freely downstream with the current, much as they might in the greased-line method.

Make mends throughout the drift, to ensure the flies do not begin to race during this upstream portion of the presentation, when they should still be moving without influence from the line.

When the flies are straight across from the angler, they should continue to move freely with the current, like leaves unattached to line or leader might. This is a "hot spot" in Bergman's eyes, where a strike might be most likely.

When the flies are downstream, and come into loose contact with the line and rod, tug them into the beginnings of a downstream swing. At this point and through the rest of the swing, you should use mends to slow the flies, if they're needed.

method: He would take his initial position at the head of the holding water and work his casts from short to long until his flies fished water near the far bank. Then he would have worked his way down the riffle, run, or pool, a step at a time, covering all of the water the length of whatever type of water he deemed might hold trout.

Bergman did demand each cast be fished out thoroughly, writing that "a desire to make casts rapidly tends to make the angler slight the actual fishing of the flies, which, after all, is the thing that catches the trout."

I can't say that I use the Bergman Natural Drift as a specific method very often. However, it's composed of a couple of parts—the greased-line method and traditional downstream swing—both of which I use almost all of the time. If the water is shaped right for a cast placing the flies upstream, fishing them for some distance on a free greased-line drift, then bringing them

Ray Bergman, in his excellent book *Trout*, wrote about fishing three wet flies downstream through pocket water, dangling and dancing and even dragging them around, so trout got lots of chances to see and take them. It's not a method that I've used extensively, but it can be an effective way to explore fast and broken water, to fish it quickly, and to extract some trout. Short casts, a high rod, and flies that fish shallow, sometimes the top fly even bouncing around on top, keep you out of trouble with all the rocks that would hang you up on a more traditional swing in small and shallow water. The method allows you to guide your flies into and through all the most likely holding water. When you get hits fishing wet flies this way, they always lead to bursts of sudden and splashy excitement.

around on a traditional wet-fly swing until they're straight downstream, then that's what I do.

As I've already mentioned, it's critical to allow the flies time to swim all the way out of the faster water, across the seam that usually separates fast from slow currents downstream from your casting position. At times I'll let the flies hang there, and at rare times trout will take them when I do. I wish I had the patience to retrieve them upstream a few feet and let them drift back downstream, as Bergman recommended, even repeating this a time or two, but I don't. I'm sure I'm missing out on some trout that Ray Bergman would have caught. But I'm restless; I need more of my own movement than that.

It's a fault. The more patient you are in your wet-fly fishing, the more success you'll enjoy. Some of the extra trout you catch should have been mine.

Chapter Fourteen

Fishing the Surface and Just Beneath It

I just read a brilliant book by Larry Tullis, *Small Fly Techniques*, in Lefty Kreh's *Little Library* series. For fishing purposes, Larry breaks the surface of the water into three layers: on top of it, in it, and just beneath it. That's an excellent way to look at the surface when you're fishing the full spectrum of fly types—drys, emergers, wets, and nymphs—which you should be. But it's not a concept to forget when you're thinking only about wet flies, as we are here. Wets can also be fished in each of the three surface layers.

Even a single wet-fly pattern can be fished in any of those surface layers, depending on whether or not you treat it with floatant and fish it on top, leave it undressed and fish it awash, or give it a tug and fish it just subsurface. For example, take the Little Olive Flymph dressed for Blue-Winged Olive (*Baetis*) mayfly duns. The naturals are tiny, size 16 at the largest, more often matched with size 18 and 20 flies. Such small insects find the surface film a barrier to emergence because they lack the mass to break through it swiftly. They might be taken by trout as crippled duns on top, struggling emergers in the film itself, or failed duns that have subsided just beneath the surface.

The Little Olive Flymph is dressed roughly. Its fibrous body and half-palmered hackle trap so much air that the fly floats until you give it a tug to pop it under. I often take advantage of this ability of the fly to float, even without floatant, and fish it on top on purpose.

Richard Bunse, illustrator of this book, recently anchored his 12-foot Santiam Drifter in a back eddy on the broad Willamette River. It was early spring, and we'd been out exploring, hoping for the first feeble hatch of

Big trout often rise to take small insects in eddies, such as this one on Oregon's Deschutes River. Crippled naturals get trapped there, and are swirled around as if on a smorgasbord. But water with so many conflicting currents makes it difficult to get any more than a brief free float with a dry fly. Then you've got drag. Switching to a wet fly can solve that problem. Trout turn away from drag on a dry, but are often attracted to it in a fly fished wet.

March Brown mayflies. We'd seen some, but trout ignored them. A few trout poked vigorous noses in and out of the surface film in the eddy where we anchored, but we saw no large brown mayflies there for the trout to take. It took a while to notice what the trout were so eager about. A few BWO duns had gotten stranded on the surface. A fraction of them escaped into the cold spring air. More disappeared in bold swirls.

Bunse is an excellent and diligent fly tier, close to a dry-fly purist. He quickly tied a size 18 Olive Compara-dun to his leader and sailed it out to the rising trout, while I still pondered my fly boxes, trying to decide what to tie on. A trout took his dry, and he had his first fish of the season dancing toward the boat.

I settled on a size 16 Little Olive Flymph, dressed the rough fly with floatant, then blew on it to fluff its fibers. That's a standard trick among dry-fly fishermen, fluff the fly up to make it look good and float well. I cast out and let the flymph sit on the surface of the eddy. It wasn't easy to see, but the water was smooth, and I had no trouble following the arrow of my line and leader pointing toward a slight speck on the water. About the same time Bunse had his second strike, a nose arose and that speck that I thought might be my floating flymph sank from sight.

A small flymph that is allowed to sink a bit can be far more effective than a dry fly in eddies and other situations with conflicting currents, because drag is a problem with the dry, but serves to animate the wet, make it look alive. A Little Olive Flymph can be more effective than the best dry-fly imitation in eddies and on other difficult waters.

When you fish an eddy over rising trout, and you see duns such as this tiny Blue-Winged Olive, it's easy to assume the trout are feeding on perfect insects, afloat on top. The normal tendency is to fish a dry-fly imitation. That's not a bad place to start. If trout take the dry, stick with it. If they refuse it, however, try switching to a flymph or soft-hackle rather than to another dry.

I lifted the rod slowly, merely questioning, "Are you out there?" It's the best way to set the hook whenever you use small flies and fragile tippets. If the answer is no, you don't rip the fly off the water, blow it over your shoulder, and frighten the trout you're casting among. If the answer is yes, that gentle lift doesn't hit the trout too hard and snap the tippet. Trout that you lose with a hard hook set are usually the very ones you'd most like to catch, since they're the ones with enough weight to break a tippet.

The answer to my query by way of the gently lifted rod was *yes*. A trout was out there, and it began dancing around with the one Bunse already had on. Neither was large, but the first few fish of the year are always nice ones, no matter how big or small. We landed and released the two trout at the same time, made a few more casts over the eddy, and hooked a few more fish each. I dried and dressed the flymph after each fish, cast it back among the rises, let it float until it either enticed another nose or drifted well away from the rises. Sometimes the fly drifted a short time, then drag set in and the fly sank, then almost always got taken by a trout. I began letting it sink intentionally, and hooked more trout than I did when I dressed it with floatant. Their takes were sometimes marked by visible rises, but more often by the merest dart of the line tip.

After half an hour, we'd stunned enough of those noses to put the rest of the trout down. I was reluctant to leave the eddy, though, because we'd been scouting all day for rising trout, and those were the first we'd seen. So I kept on for a few more casts while Bunse sat at the oars and fidgeted. I cast to where the rises had been, tugged the wet fly under the surface, let it settle a bit, then retrieved it back to the boat with tiny twitches of the line hand. It shouldn't have worked. No trout has ever seen a drowned mayfly dun act with that much agility. The nymph of the BWO, however, is a swimmer. It emerges precisely like that, darting up toward the surface and sometimes back down, in short, sharp bursts.

The flymph must have reminded trout of those nymphs, because a couple more came out of nowhere and whacked it. Then everything was over and I was ready to move on downriver, too.

Most of the time flymphs and soft-hackled wets are fished flush in the surface film only on fairly flat water, to rising trout. The reasons are simple. First, the surface film is a barrier to emerging insects only where the water is smooth. Where it's wrinkled, no barrier forms, and even small insects escape through it with little hesitation. Second, trout in the rough water of riffles and runs rarely become so selective that you need to dress a wet fly with floatant to represent the emerger. They'll accept a high-floating dry fly, which is much easier to see. That's what you should fish when you want to fish on the surface in rough water: a dry fly.

The wet fly dressed with floatant and fished on top is a method generally restricted to flats, pools, eddies, and the tailouts of pools. You should rarely cast straight upstream to feeding trout on such water types. If you do, your line, leader, and fly will all fly over the fish in the air. Then your cast will land on the water on top of the trout. The line, then the leader, and finally the fly will float over the fish, each in its turn. Any trout that has been fished over a few times will recognize this arrival of line, leader, and later fly as a danger signal. If the trout does not dash down to the depths and wrap its fins around its head in fright, it's at least forewarned into wariness, and will almost surely refuse the fly trailing along at the end of its tether.

Always get into position to cast upstream and across, not straight upstream, whether you're fishing dry flies or wets dressed to float in the film. It's a common courtesy you can pay to yourself. You'll catch lots more trout when you do.

When fishing wet flies, whether on top, in the surface film, or just beneath it, treat them as you would dry flies. Present them to trout on drag-free drifts, and watch for rises to them. Even subsurface takes will be so near the top that you'll often be able to see them happen.

Once you've gotten into a position off to one side of the trout or the water you want to fish, so you can cast upstream without lining the trout, you can present a surface wet fly in a couple of ways. The first is to dress the fly with floatant and fish it exactly as if it were a dry fly. This imitates the emerging stage of many insects, especially midges and smaller mayflies— the types of tiny insects that find the surface film a formidable barrier. It's a method that will often take trout for you when your best efforts with dry flies fail. The problem is not your tackle or casting, though it always seems so. The problem is that trout are feeding on injured insects, cripples, and still-borns, not on perfect adults.

If you're already rigged to fish dry, you need do no more than nip off the fly you're using and tie on the wet you want to use. If you're not already fishing dry, then your leader should be fine-tuned to the kind of water you'll be fishing with this method. It should be 10 to 14 feet long, tapered down to a 5X or 6X tippet. Be sure that the tippet section is 2 to 4 feet long, to give the fly a drag-free float. I tend to go through a half-panicked series of fly changes in such a situation and wind up with a tippet about a foot long. That's too short. The tippet itself becomes the problem. Always lengthen your tippet before switching flies, if it's been clipped short. You'll often discover that the fly you've been using works fine once you've fixed that tippet.

Tackle for fishing a wet fly dressed and afloat on or in the surface should not be a single bit separate from the tackle you'd use to fish a dry fly on the

Feeding trout might appear to be taking on top, but when their rise-rings are without bubbles, it means they've taken something just subsurface, and you should fish a wet fly inches deep rather than a floating dry fly or a wet fly fished dry.

same water. It's a rule you can follow on any water type: Rig for the wet fly the same way you'd rig for a dry in the same situation.

It's often better to fish just beneath the surface, rather than on top of it or in it, with an upstream winged wet fly, soft-hackle, flymph, or all-fur wet. This method is exceptionally effective when trout rise so close to the top that they send visible swirls to the surface. It also works over trout holding high in the water column, feeding just subsurface with winks and turns that don't show nearly so boldly on the surface itself.

The typical signal telling you that you should fish upstream but subsurface is the absence of bubbles in riseforms when trout take naturals. Bubbles indicate that a trout has broken the surface plane in the take. When you see those bubbles, you should use a dry fly, an emerger fished flush in the film, or a wet fly dressed with floatant and fished floating, not submerged.

When bubbles are missing, the trout has fed slightly beneath the surface, not broken through. You want your fly inches deep. The best way to make this happen is to dress your line and leader with floatant down to the tippet knot, but don't dress the tippet or fly. This suspends a wet fly a few inches deep. At times it's best to dress the leader to within 6 or 8 inches of the fly, to hold it nearer to the surface.

When fishing wet flies just subsurface to working trout, your casts should be made upstream and across, just as you'd do with a dry fly or a wet fly fished dry. You can detect takes by a visible swirl out where you know your fly to be. Watch where your line tip points. If you see anything at all suspicious near it, lift your rod, asking that question, "Are you out there?" If a trout has taken the fly, the mere lift will draw the hook into the fish.

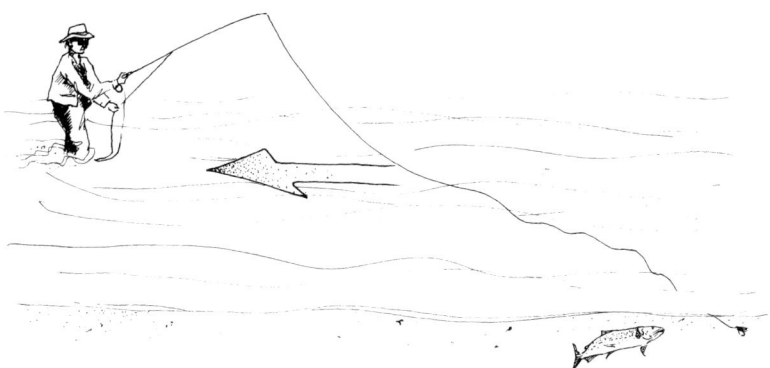

When fishing wet flies upstream to feeding fish, present them precisely as you would dry flies: upstream and across to the trout, or to the lie that you suspect holds them, rather than straight upstream, which would line them.

This subsurface method is effective on smooth flats, pools, and tailouts. Unlike the wet fished dry, it's also effective in runs and riffles, where trout often feed on ascending nymphs and pupae, or crippled duns and adults. It's not uncommon to fish fast water with a dry fly, get half-hearted takes or outright refusals, then switch to the upstream wet fished just beneath the surface, and suddenly receive solid takes.

Refusals to a dry fly are a signal that you should at least change flies, at most switch to a wet fly with a dressed leader. Refusals can be difficult to read, especially if you're casting long, over rough water. On smooth water, whenever you see a rise to your fly and set the hook softly but the trout is not on, it indicates a refusal. A trout looked at the fly but changed its mind. Don't suffer more than two or three such refusal rises without changing something: your position, tippet, fly, or your fly type—from surface to submerged.

In rough water it's more difficult to notice refusals. Get right up on top of your fish. Cast just 15 to 30 feet. Then you might notice winks beneath your fly. These are trout that rose and about-faced. Some of them change their minds so late that they send boils up to the surface. Whenever you see signs that something is happening around your fly, gently but quickly set the hook. If the hook set results in a miss, assume the fly has been rejected. If you're fishing dry, change flies or switch to a wet fly. If you're already fishing wet, try a different fly. It should usually be smaller and closer to the color of the insect over which you're fishing.

If you get frustrated fishing wet flies upstream, it will nearly always be because you're getting takes but aren't able to see them. Or you might just lack confidence that you'll ever notice it if a trout does take the sunk fly. Here's a heresy, but it's what I do when I'm unable to detect takes when fishing sunk flies upstream, and it's what guides have their clients do all the way from the East Coast of North America to the South Island of New Zealand: Tie a tiny strike indicator to the leader just above the tippet knot.

My favorite indicator for such situations is a small tuft of yellow or white yarn, or New Zealand lambswool. Capture it in a slip knot 2 to 4 feet up the leader from the fly. Trim it tiny, dress it with floatant, tease it into a fan. Make your casts upstream and across, the same as you would without it. Set the hook any time the indicator acts contrary to the way the current would tug it. Because you're fishing with wet flies just beneath the surface, a movement of the indicator never reflects a hangup on the bottom, as it might in deep nymph fishing. If your indicator moves, it's a trout. Set the hook.

A cross-stream cast, as opposed to an upstream presentation, can be as useful when you fish floating and submerged wet flies as it is with drys. It sets you off to the side of feeding trout, so your line and leader never sail over their heads.

Doug Swisher and Carl Richards wrote about the *reach cast* in their excellent 1975 book, *Fly Fishing Strategy*, which to this day is hard to beat on basic and advanced trout fishing tactics. The reach cast is designed to present imitative dry flies to fussy trout feeding in currents that appear to be an even sheet, but on closer look are full of conflicting micro-currents that drag dry flies around, causing refusals. You can apply the cast to your wet-fly fishing to get a relatively drag-free drift just subsurface. The goal is not to get a completely drag-free drift, but to get a long downstream drift rather than a short one before the line and leader come tight, and the fly begins to swing across the currents. Drag is usually fatal on dry-fly drifts. With wet flies, it can serve as a bit of a benefit.

The reach cast is an extension of the basic overhand cast. You take up your position across the currents from a feeding fish, prospective lie, or promising drift line that you'd like to ply. Make forecasts in the normal fashion, in the direction of the target but not directly over it, except that you'll want to extend 5 to 10 feet of extra line. When you're ready to make the delivery stroke, aim the rod right where you want the fly to land. Once the line has been propelled on its way by the forward stroke of the rod tip, lay the rod over to the upstream side. The rod should end up almost parallel with the water. Reach out as far as you can with the casting arm, again upstream.

The result of the reach cast, in essence, is what you've tried to achieve with upstream mends in the greased-line method: a line that lies on the water upstream from the fly. The current pushing downstream against the line must erase the entire upstream belly before it can cause the fly to race. You can defeat this by following the drift of the fly with the rod tip. As it moves down with the current, follow along at the same pace. Soon your rod points straight at the fly.

As the fly continues its drift down the current line past your position, continue to follow it with the rod, reaching downstream. Follow it until you

The reach cast begins with an upstream lean of the rod while the line is still in the air. After it lands, follow the drift of the fly, ending by reaching as far as you can downstream to extend the drift.

can reach no farther, and a belly forms in the line, tugging the fly out of its drift line. You can fish the cast out with a traditional wet-fly swing to complete the presentation, or lift the fly and cast again as soon as it has passed through the water you want to cover. The wet fly will drift free of drag as far as 20 to 30 feet. This method, designed to fish a dry fly, allows you to cover water with a free-drifting wet fly.

You can also fish wets dressed with floatant on top with the reach cast. You can just as easily dress most of your leader and fish a fly or pair of wet flies just inches deep. These are both effective uses of the reach cast with wet flies.

Another cast that can look somewhat magical will let you fish a cross-stream wet fly on a fairly free subsurface drift. The *aerial mend* can make you look like an expert and help you land more trout at the same time. That makes it an important trick to learn, if not to impress some extra trout, at least to impress your friends.

The aerial mend is simply a way to create an upstream belly in the line *before* it lands on the water. The current must push the belly out of the line before it can tug at the fly. You can delay that moment, and lengthen your free drift, by following the cast with normal mends. Or you can pick up and cast again. It's most useful when casting over a somewhat fast current to trout working in slightly slower currents on the other side.

To execute an aerial mend, aim a basic cast right where you want your fly to land on the water. While the line loop unfurls in the air, delivering the fly, tip your rod over upstream, wait a beat, then bring it back up. The line will follow, curving out upstream, then straightening again. It will land on the water in an upstream curve. If you tip the rod over as soon as the power stroke ends, then bring it upright quickly, the curve will land out toward the fly. If you wait a bit, then tip the rod over and back, the curve will land nearer to you, closer to the rod.

If you get into an opposite situation, where the current close to you is slow and you want to cast over it to trout working in faster water on the far side, then you'll want to use a downstream aerial mend. Simply tip the rod over downstream while the line lays out in the air, wait that beat, bring it back up, and the line will land on the water with a downstream belly. The line tip, leader, and fly in the faster water out at the distant end of things will drift faster than the line. Eventually they'll pass the line, tighten, and cause drag. Until then, you've had several feet of free drift. Aerial mends compensate for conflicting currents, and delay the moment when you need to make normal mends once the line is on the water. It's another dry-fly trick, but it can be used to extend your wet-fly drifts.

When your free drift ends after an upstream-and-across cast, cross-stream reach cast, or aerial mend, you can stop the rod and let the line lead the fly around in a traditional downstream swing. If the water below you looks at all promising, that's a pretty smart thing to do.

Chapter Fifteen

Four Men
and Their Methods

It was early May. A bitter wind snorted through Paradise Valley of the Yellowstone River. It felt more like winter than spring. Mother's Day Caddis hatched in vast numbers at midday, though, and it was good to bundle up and be out where trout were rising.

Brown trout and Yellowstone cutts worked on the small, dark caddis along the edges of the big river. They fed with sipping rises, moving up and down the bouldered banks in pods of a dozen or more. Noses arose in one spot for a while, then moved upstream a few feet and plucked a few more of the many struggling naturals that speckled the surface. I had no difficulty matching the adult with a dry fly. A size 18 Deerhair Caddis or Quill-Wing Caddis was close enough to satisfy the trout. But it was not easy to get the trout to notice a dry fly floating among all those naturals. It was even more difficult to pick out my own fly and follow its drift, especially if it was a fair imitation of the insects surrounding it, because it got lost in the fleet. So dry-fly fishing, amid dozens of rising trout, was not much more than fair.

Sylvester Nemes, fishing just upstream from me, dealt with no such problems. He had fished this hatch for years, had worked out his own Mother's Day Caddis soft-hackle to match it. He fished it a few inches deep, on the swing, where it was not necessary to follow the fly with his eyes in order to detect takes. His trout hit with *whaps*. He felt their arrival as thuds. Consequently, Sylvester prodded lots more trout into the air than I was able to entice with dry flies. I switched.

Fishing suddenly became easy. Sylvester and I turned our backs to the downstream wind, stood onshore or waded just a few feet out, and made short casts that angled slightly down and across the current. I watched Sylvester fish, as I'd done other times, in other places. He held his rod upstream from the cast while the line unfurled in the air, so that the line

The natural Mother's Day Caddis (*Brachycentrus occidentalis*) is small at size 16, and dark. Its body, not visible in the photo, is an olive that is almost black, making it suitable for imitation with peacock herl, a material that trout always seem eager to take.

Sylvester Nemes's Mother's Day Caddis soft-hackle is a lot easier to fish than a dry fly during a heavy hatch of naturals, because it's easier to feel a take than it is to see one. This fly, tied by its originator, is a bit tattered from catching trout on the Yellowstone River.

landed on the water in a bit of an upstream reach. As soon as the current pushed the belly out of his line, he began mending to slow the fly. His mending was almost constant through the entire drift of the soft-hackle.

The fly swung downstream and across the current, part of the time at about the speed a drowned caddis adult might drift along, and part of the time at about the speed a caddis pupa might swim toward the surface. I'm not sure which stage the trout mistook Sylvester's imitation to be. But they took it often.

The beauty of this wet-fly method goes far beyond its effectiveness. It lies also in the ease with which you can present the flies to feeding trout and the accuracy with which you can detect takes. You don't have to see the fly; you follow its drift by watching the line tip. You don't have to see the take; you feel the thump. Most often the hook is set before you have time to raise the rod. All you've got to do to fish the fly right is make the correct cast and toss those constant mends.

Sylvester Nemes leading a Yellowstone trout to hand. It took his Mother's Day Caddis soft-hackle on the swing, in the gentle water on the inside of the riffle, the sort of water where the naturals hatch.

I call the method the Nemes Mended Swing, because Sylvester was the first I saw do it, and because he employed it so often to the surprise of so many trout. He used it just a few days later to fool lots more trout on the Madison River, in a snowstorm, on a size 18 Syl's Midge. Tiny black naturals came off right at the shoreline, drifted on the currents in clusters. Sylvester waded a few feet out in shallow flows, turned and cast short back toward shore. He fished across and slightly downstream, just as he'd done with the Mother's Day Caddis. As soon as his line landed, he began those soft mends that kept the midge imitation drifting along at the correct slow pace.

Sylvester selected his fly pattern in accordance with what insect was on or in the water. Most of the time he matched the adult insect, but always with a soft-hackle imitation. He tied his soft-hackles to capture the features of the natural, but recognized that those insects are in different shape when they're submerged and tossed by currents than they are when sitting primly on the surface. Like W. C. Stewart on his Scottish hill streams, Sylvester captured the main features of the natural, tied his flies sparsely, choosing materials that worked well and reflected every movement of the stream.

Sylvester varied the length of his casts to suit the size of the water he fished. If it was wide, he cast long. If it was narrow, he cast just 30 to 40 feet. He chose the angle of the cast according to the speed of the current. If it was swift, he cast at an acute angle, almost straight downstream. If it was slow,

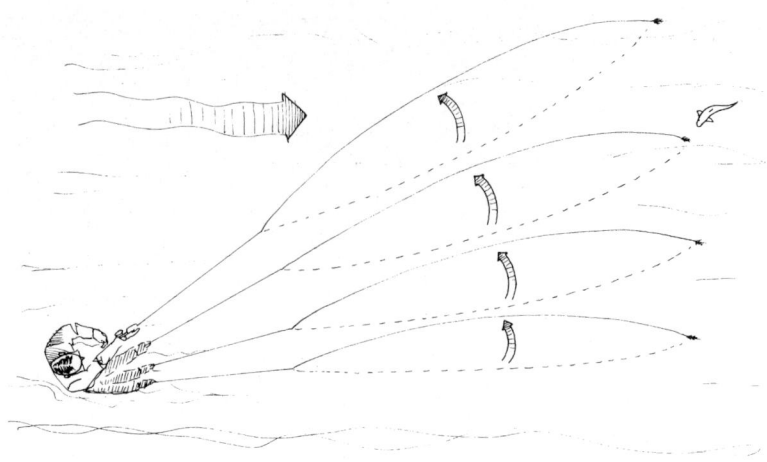

Sylvester Nemes used constant mends to keep his soft-hackles swimming through their drift at the right pace.

he angled the cast farther up into the current. He made his mends more or less often depending on the speed at which the fly moved through its swing.

At every moment, he was aware of where his fly was drifting and its speed in relation to the current. He controlled his line unconsciously to speed up or retard the drift. In all the waters I watched him fish, Sylvester made his soft-hackled flies look alive.

Though I associate Sylvester with his Mended Swing, it would be a mistake to think it's the only method he fished. In his book *The Soft-Hackled Fly*, he described the greased-line method as applied to trout fishing with soft-hackled wets. In later books, *The Soft-Hackled Fly Addict* and *Soft-Hackled Fly Imitations*, he described other methods, including the upstream cast to feeding trout. But most of the time, in fishing situations that I shared with him and observed while he fished, he used his Mended Swing and fooled lots of trout doing it.

I met Pete Hidy at his home in Boise, Idaho, and had long conversations with him there. He was already weakened with emphysema, and I had no chance to fish with him before he passed away. He told me about the book that he and James Leisenring intended to write about wet-fly methods, as a follow-up to *The Art of Tying the Wet Fly*. He lamented that everybody came to associate both of them with the single method they covered in the first book, the Leisenring Lift. He said it was just one of many methods that Leisenring used, and that it was far from the most important.

Pete described his own favorite method to me. Later I was able to reconstruct it from research in the chapters he added to *The Art of Tying the Wet Fly & Fishing the Flymph*, plus a few lines of advice in a little book titled

Pete Hidy, co-author of *The Art of Tying the Wet Fly*, and author of the valuable addition to that book in the 1971 edition, *The Art of Tying the Wet Fly & Fishing the Flymph*. Pete's Subsurface Swing method might find a place in your wet-fly fishing more often than the more famous Leisenring Lift.

COURTESY GUNNAR JOHNSON

Book of Wet-Fly Fishing that Pete wrote for *Sports Illustrated*. Without the personal conversation, however, I doubt I could have drawn the method together from the various writings, because he didn't describe it in its entirety in any one place. So I'll describe it here as Pete told it to me.

Pete did not name the method. I dubbed it the Hidy Subsurface Swing in an article I wrote for *Fly Fisherman* magazine. The Subsurface Swing calls for fishing with a flymph designed to entrap bubbles of air in its body and hackle, and to take the air underwater. The method is specific to casting over trout feeding on insects just beneath the surface, in a lie where it's possible to wade into position upstream and at an angle across the currents from the trout. The ideal angle is somewhere between 45 and 60 degrees, as always depending on the speed of those currents.

If you're like me, you'll use the Hidy Subsurface Swing most often on a smooth flat or in the sweeping tailout of a pool. You'll already have tried the trout with drys and failed. But there are a few indications that a flymph will work better than a dry fly in the first place, if you cease fire and take a bit of time to observe the situation. The first thing to notice is if there are any rises, and the second thing is if bubbles are absent from those rises.

When adult caddis dance around in the air over the water, it's likely they're also diving down to deposit their eggs on the bottom. Trout might appear to be rising to the surface to take floating adults, but at least as often they're actually taking swimming adults just beneath it. If mayfly duns are hatching, or have hatched in the last couple of hours, then lots of drowned cripples might still be drifting along. Trout often feed on them inches deep, so close to the surface that they look like they're taking on top, but no bubbles are left behind in their riseforms. When mayfly spinners are in the air, falling to the water, laying their eggs, a sparse flymph fished just beneath the film will usually take more trout than a spent dry fly fished up top.

These are all indications to fish a flymph rather than a dry fly. In my own fishing experience, any trout that appears to be rising at the surface but refuses dry flies becomes a candidate for a flymph and the Hidy Subsurface Swing.

Be very careful when wading into position to use the method. You'll be entering the water upstream from a single spotted trout, or an active pod of them, and you'll almost always be fishing relatively smooth water. Any wading waves you push up will wash downstream over the trout. If you let that happen, you've either got to give up on that trout or that pod and find another, or wait like a heron as long as it takes for the trout to begin rising again. That's usually at least ten to twenty minutes. Don't risk it. Wade carefully.

If you're working over a single rising trout, take up a position upstream and off to one side, within 40 to 50 feet of it. If you're moving in on a pod of them, choose one nearest you, at the upstream edge of the pod, and approach it as you would a single. You don't need to get as close to the trout as you do when fishing drys. Once you're ready for the cast, make your measuring forecasts and backcasts off to one side or the other. Don't line trout on this kind of water, or they're gone. Measure a few feet of extra line in the cast; you'll be presenting the fly just beyond the trout's feeding lane. Once the cast is measured, change the direction of the delivery stroke to place the flymph softly onto the water 4 to 5 feet beyond the trout and 4 to 5 feet upstream from it.

Now the critical part of the presentation: Lift the rod tip slightly to straighten the line and give the fly the slightest tug. Until you do this, the flymph will float. When you do it, the fly will pop underwater, taking a few bubbles of air under with it. If you fail to give this tug, the flymph will remain on top and cut an unnatural dragging wake right in front of the trout. You know what happens then.

After you've given that slight tug, drop the rod point again, but not enough to let the line go entirely slack. Instead, you want the line to draw the flymph in a slow arc right across the bow of the rising trout. Most of the time the water will bulge up, and you'll feel a pull. If you can resist yanking on the rod, the trout will set the hook on the take without your assistance, and the fight will be on.

If the trout fails to take, let the flymph swing well away from it before lifting the fly to cast again. Keep trying. Vary the entry point of the flymph

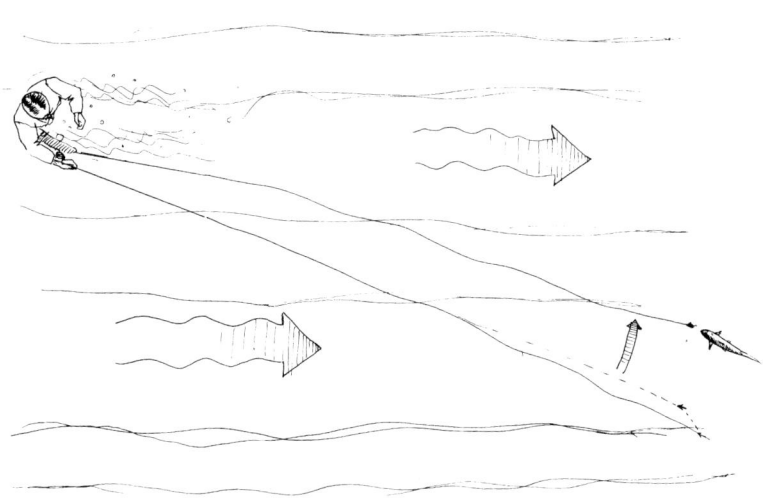

To execute the Hidy Subsurface Swing, cast a few feet upstream and beyond the lie of a feeding fish. Give the flymph a slight tug to pull it through the surface film, then let it swing in front of the nose of the trout.

in relation to the trout, farther or nearer, upstream or down. Remember that the trout might be backing down from its lie on each take, so that the rises you see are a few feet below the actual holding position of the fish. Try casting higher into the current. It's often best to make your first cast 10 feet or so upstream, working the swing closer to the trout with each subsequent cast. You'll get a feeling for the particular cast that is going to deliver the flymph into the trout's vision. You'll be braced for the take just before you feel it. I hope you can manage to let the fish set the hook itself. I sometimes jerk, and far too often break a fragile tippet.

If you're fishing the Hidy Subsurface Swing to a pod of trout, begin by casting to a trout in the upper portion of the pod. Present the flymph to it, then simply let the fly continue its swing through the pod. Don't lift the fly to cast again in the middle of the pod, after it's past the first trout, or you'll scatter the rest of them, and they'll take the first one with them.

I use this method often during caddis hatches. But my freshest experience with it came last year during a March Brown mayfly hatch. Trout fed across the width of a tailout in the broad Willamette River. It was nearly impossible to get a good dry-fly drift on the slick and fast current. But it was easy to tie on a size 12 March Brown Flymph and sweep it across the entire tailout. The casts were at a 45-degree angle downstream. The tugs to submerge the flymph were brief and far beyond the working trout. The fly entered their vision swimming slowly across the tailout, but drifting downstream with the current, not swimming upstream against it.

It was a rare cast that didn't draw at least a subtle pluck, or else that slowly increasing weight that reveals a trout holding onto the flymph, unable to get it out of the corner of its mouth because the current had it pinned there. A slow lift of the rod usually sent a trout into the air. It happened a dozen times before the rest of the trout went down. Those were a dozen trout I could not have taken with any other method on that particular piece of the accelerating tailout.

The Hidy Subsurface Swing has become my favorite method for fishing flymphs. I use it far more often than the more famous Leisenring Lift, because it's not nearly so restricted in the kind of water where it will work.

The Leisenring Lift has been written about more than any other wet-fly method with the exception of the traditional downstream swing. It's effective, and it deserves such notice. In water shaped right for the Lift, it will work better than almost any other method you can fish, short of strike indicators and split shot and weighted nymphs. In an ideal situation for the method, it might work even better than such a depth-charge nymph. But it's wise to understand that situations in which the Leisenring Lift works well are limited.

It works best in water 2 to 3 feet deep, not more than 4 feet, where you can pinpoint a trout or the prospective lie of a trout. The water leading into the lie must flow in a single sheet of current for 15 to 20 feet, with few conflicts to tug your line out of alignment, causing drag. You must be able to cast your wet fly several feet upstream from the trout or suspected lie, to give the fly time to sink slowly to the level of the fish. You also must be able to follow the progress of the fly, so you know when it arrives at the right point, inches from the eyes of the trout, to animate it.

It's commonly overlooked that the Leisenring Lift was designed to fish an unweighted wet fly right on the bottom. In *The Art of Tying the Wet Fly*, Leisenring and Hidy wrote, "The fly comes straight down to him bumpety-bump over the gravel and stones along the bottom with the current." The method is restricted to water where you can reach the bottom without added weight on the fly or the leader, which is far from everywhere. Given a set of conditions where you can make that happen, no fly type is more apt to interest a trout than a wet fly that looks like a bit of drifting detritus, then suddenly springs to life right before the trout's eyes and begins to swim toward the surface as if for emergence.

I fish all manner of mountain creeks, freestone and meadow streams, and large rivers, mostly in the West. It's pretty rare that I find a holding lie ideally suited to the Leisenring Lift. When such a lie is encountered, however, it's likely to be a prime one and to hold a large trout. Such a lie delivers lots of bottom-drifting food to a trout. If you find a lie like that, the Lift is an excellent way to present your wet fly as if it were one of those living bits of food.

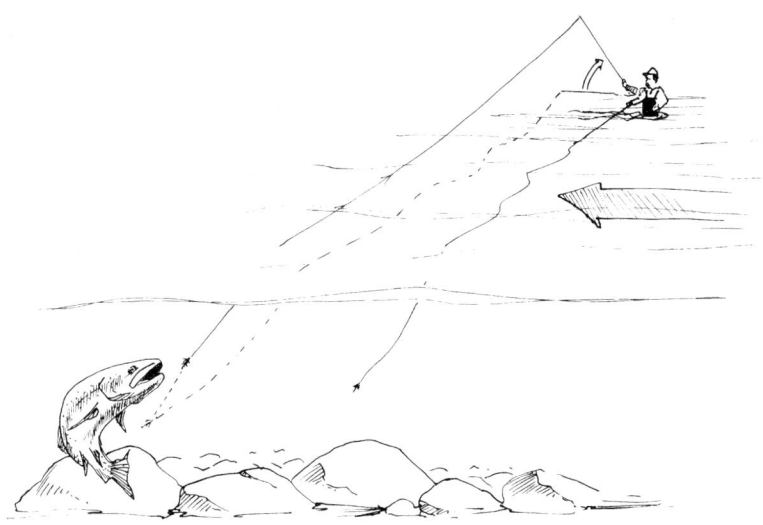

In the Leisenring Lift, let the fly sink to the level of the trout. When it reaches the trout's position, stop the rod, and the fly will become animated and begin swimming toward the surface at precisely the right point.

Leisenring's method calls for a fly tied sparsely on a heavy-wire wet-fly hook. He did not believe in adding weight, feeling that it killed the action of the fly. He used a floating line, though in his day that might have amounted to what we'd now call an intermediate, sinking better than it floated most of the time. Now that we have nylon leaders rather than the gut Leisenring used, we can sink flies faster by using a long leader and a fine tippet. If you use fluorocarbon on streams—I don't because it degrades so slowly and is worse for the environment than regular tippet—this would be the place for it. It sinks more quickly. The method is restricted to lies 2 to 4 feet deep, in moderate to slow currents, because that's about as far as you can get a fly down to the bottom without weight.

Once you've found the rare ideal lie, or the even rarer visible trout suspended in water 2 to 4 feet deep, move into position at an angle just upstream and across from the lie or the visible trout. A 30-degree angle is about right. If you move much higher in the current, above the lie, you won't be in position to execute the Lift. Place your fly 5 to 20 feet upstream from the lie, depending on the speed of the current, the depth of the water, and the sink rate of your fly. Mend line in order to give the fly a free drift while it sinks. Follow the drift of the fly with your rod tip, but do not tighten the line between the rod and the fly.

Leisenring wrote, "I always fish my fly so that it becomes deadly at the point where the trout is most likely to take his food." He had the trout, or its

This is the sort of lie where the Leisenring Lift might be applied successfully, on Stoney Creek in Pennsylvania. The water is 2 to 3 feet deep, with an obvious lie right in front of the massive root wad, and several feet of even currents leading downstream to it. Though all of the water should be fished down to that most likely lie, a wet fly ought to be brought to life within just a foot of that root system.

most likely lie, envisioned precisely in his mind. When the fly reaches the bottom and then bumps along to the point where the trout can see it, Leisenring advised merely stopping the rod. This tightens the line, with the result that the fly lifts off the bottom and swims upward, all in sight of the trout.

Few trout can resist when you bring this off correctly. The problem is that the ideal setup—one in which you can see the trout or its lie and get the drift and sink rate timed precisely—is so rare that you don't often get a chance to bring it off just right.

If you can't see the trout but do know its likely lie, you can fish the water with a series of Leisenring Lifts, plucking the fly from the bottom every 2 feet down the length of a lie, say a narrow trench in the bottom. That's a way to explore a very small reach of water. But by its essence, the Leisenring Lift is not a method for searching out trout. It's a method for taking trout that you've already found holding along the bottom in relatively shallow water or to fish pinpoint lies that you suspect will hold trout. It's a useful tactic to know, but it's not one you're likely to use often.

Polly Rosborough also called for tying his fuzzy nymphs without weight. However, he often fished with a wet-tip line. His theory was that the largest trout feed during a hatch of insects, but the big trout stay down near the bottom and continue to take nymphs beneath the hatch, rather than following the insects up and feeding at the surface on adults. The surface is for the small ones, according to Polly's book, *Tying and Fishing the Fuzzy Nymphs*. He fished in southern Oregon and northern California, where the streams and rivers are low gradient, with deep runs and lots of ledgerock trenches and

A fuzzy nymph, the Near Enough, tied by the master, Polly Rosborough. Though it's clearly a nymph, not a wet fly, it's unweighted, and Polly fished his nymphs much as wet flies should be fished on his favorite low-gradient rivers.

pools. The trout in these waters, especially his home Williamson River, are large. Polly was right: Trout the size he was after rarely poke their noses through the surface until after they've felt the sting of a hook.

I've watched Polly fish his big nymphs, which average size 10 and up. He cast quartering down and across the stream, much as Sylvester Nemes did. But Polly cast long, with a stout rod. He placed the fly line at a more modest angle downstream, in line with the current, eliminating the need to mend for the right speed in the swing. He gave his sinking-tip line plenty of time to tug the fly toward the bottom. Then he began a pulsing movement of the rod tip: up and down, up and down, a few inches to a foot at a time. He leaned forward, concentrated not on the rod movement, but on the point in the water out where the fly swam. Watching him, you could see that he almost listened for a take.

It was fascinating to watch Polly fish. The posture of his body, the movement of his rod, and the way he teased his fly were all designed to entice trout. By watching Polly fish, I learned that when a wet fly, or in his case a fuzzy nymph, is fishing just right, you can feel it enticing the trout. This feeling soon gets based on positive experience: You remember how your fly was fishing at the instant when most of your strikes occurred, and you learn to repeat that feeling. It becomes intuitive. With Polly, it became sensual. You could see him coaxing the trout, seducing them.

I fished with Polly a few years before he passed away, when he was entering his eighties, near his home on his favorite Williamson River. When he sat on a streamside log to take a rest, I asked if I could borrow his rod and make a few casts with it. He handed it to me. The rod was bamboo, a Fred Thomas, 9 feet long and armed with a weight-forward 8-weight line. It lofted

I borrowed Polly Rosborough's rod once, and almost immediately caught a nice Williamson River rainbow with it, using Polly's fuzzy nymph method that holds a lot of lessons for fishing wet flies. I always say that this photo is of my wife trying to take my fish away from me, and Polly trying to take my wife away from me. JIM SCHOLLMEYER

a large fly, his own cross between a wet fly, nymph, and streamer, and propelled it far out over the broad river.

I cast down and across the current, just as I'd watched Polly doing it. I gave the big fly some time to sink at the end of the wet-tip line. Then I began swinging it across the current, above a bottom pitted with ledgerock trenches, just as I'd seen Polly pulsing it. I didn't see the precise moment when the fly entered the window over a trench, but I felt a great thud and instinctively reared back to set the hook. Polly's stout tippet held. The biggest trout I would catch that year tumbled into the air.

When I finally brought the trout to hand, it weighed at least 6 pounds. I was quite proud to have caught a rainbow like that on the great man's rod. But Polly had fished the river for many years, and knew the size of its fish, because he'd held so many of them in his own hands.

He looked at mine and said, "That's a nice little fish."

I released the trout and handed back his rod.

Though it was not exactly a wet-fly method, there was a lot to learn about fishing wet flies from the way Polly fished his fuzzy nymphs. He rigged to get them deep. He made his casts according to the speed of the currents and the depth of the water where he wanted his flies to swim. He fished them on a teasing swing. Like Sylvester Nemes, Pete Hidy, and James Leisenring, Polly Rosborough made his flies look alive.

Chapter Sixteen

Keeper of the Flame: Lessons from Davy Wotton

I recently fished with Davy Wotton on the White River near Cotter, Arkansas, and received a set of lessons that gave the effectiveness of wets a leap for me. I was invited to present a workshop for the North Arkansas Fly Fishers, in Mountain Home, and did two smart things: accepted the invitation, and booked a day to fish with Davy while I was there. I'd met him at fly-fishing conclaves, discussed writing with him, studied his videos *Wet Fly Ways* and *Wet Fly Tying*, but had never fished with him, and had not gotten around to incorporating his concepts into my own wet-fly fishing. When I finally got that chance, I was astounded at the breadth and depth of his knowledge about fly fishing.

Davy grew up in Wales, worked as a gamekeeper, and seems to have been plugged directly into nature. He is more aware of the intricate relationships among flowing water, natural insects, trout flies, and trout themselves than anybody I've ever met. As an example, as he rigged my rod his way at riverside, leaning against the gunwale of his parked White River boat, he explained how his selection of flies depended on the quality of light, pushiness of current, his estimation of the ambition of the trout, and what was likely going on in the underwater world of the insects and crustaceans on which those trout might be feeding at the moment. All those accumulations of knowledge are based on three things that Davy Wotton has in abundance: wisdom, study, and experience.

Davy studied the literature and history of fly fishing early. He fished England, Scotland, Ireland, and on the continent. He became a member of the British competition fly-fishing team, which propelled him out to fish for trout all around the world. Then he started a successful fly-tying materials business, perhaps best known for his SLF dubbings. His travels took him from his native Wales to Arkansas to fish with his friend Dave Whitlock. Davy subsequently transplanted himself there to guide, write, and run a fly-fishing school. He lives on twenty acres with his companion, professional fly tier Theresa "T-Bird" Van Winkle, and a vast sea of dogs, cats, chickens, game birds and exotic birds for their fly-tying feathers, and wild whitetail deer.

The day we fished together, the water ran low and steady, though a surge related to daily power production was reported to be coming down from Bull Shoals Dam right behind us. Davy upped anchor and moved us downstream from time to time to keep ahead of it. On the dammed White River, an acute awareness of fluctuating water levels is essential to any successful fishing day, and also to safety. Davy started the day by motoring his long and slender White River boat far upstream to a broad and well-defined shoal—a riffle in any other trout river—beached the boat, got out and began the process of rigging our rods and at the same time explaining what he was doing, and perhaps more important, why he was doing it. T-Bird, not needing the instruction, hopped out, splashed off, and immediately began applying the method against trout.

The shoal was 2 to at most 4 feet deep, somewhat brisk, rippled on top: perfect wet-fly water. The weather was mild, the sun out; prospects that trout would be interested in feeding were increased slightly by the presence of scattered caddis and mayflies, though they constituted no hatch, and no trout worked the surface.

Since the devil is in the details, and success usually resides in them as well, I'll explain that for his own fishing Davy used a modest-action 11-foot, 5-weight rod and double-taper Snowbee 5-weight floating line, and he rigged a three-fly cast of wet flies, a couple of them standard British patterns from the 1800s. He helped design TFO's 10- and 11-foot, 5-weight rods specifically for his method. Casting with a three-fly rig requires an open loop, so you don't want to try this method with a fast rod. If that's all you own, slow it down with a line at least one weight heavy, maybe two full weights, to open up your loops. Davy recommends British Snowbee lines, in both floating and intermediate, in particular for their suppleness and lack of memory. Davy doesn't like a fly line that keeps its coils.

I'd like to emphasize that Davy built his leader and mine while observing the water we were about to fish. Though he varies his leaders from 12 to 18 feet in length, for that water, on that day, he rigged 6 feet of Sunset Amnesia 12-pound-test as a base, then 20 to 24 inches of P-Line Halo 6-pound fluorocarbon to the top dropper, the same length of Halo 4-pound-test to the middle dropper, and a similar section of the same material to the point fly. That added up to a 12-foot leader. He used surgeon's knots to join sections, leaving 6 inches of the heavy end of each knot for the droppers. His flies were

Davy Wotton holds three types of wet flies (from left to right): an attractor, large and bright, designed to push water and to be seen by trout; a deceiver, designed to roughly resemble food that a trout might be willing to eat; and an imitator, designed to represent some specific food form such as a diving caddis adult. These are only approximate examples, from one of the rigs Davy used as he changed flies throughout the day. I didn't learn the names of these precise patterns, but their size and brightness give you an indication of how you might select flies that show trout distinct choices, from large and brash to smaller and more imitative.

fastened with the figure-eight Davy Fly Knot, which is small, strong, and elegantly simple. Google it, and you'll get instructions on how to tie it.

Davy divides wet flies into three types. His *attractors* are bright, brash, somewhat large (size 8 to 12), and often designed so they push water, create a disturbance. They go on the top dropper, and are there to attract the attention of trout, though as I have found out by fishing the method, they also often catch the trout. His *deceivers* are tied in more lifelike colors and the mid-range of sizes (12 to 16) but are not tied to represent specific insects. They are generally fished as the central droppers in three-fly rigs. His *imitators* are usually tied for the pupal and emerger stages of particular hatches on his waters, and are the appropriate sizes for those naturals, though he's not always fishing over those exact hatches when he fishes them. These go on the point.

Davy's presentation with this three-fly rig, as I observed him fishing it on the White River, also has three parts. His casts were made slightly upstream from straight across, and the initial part of each drift was somewhat free, close to the greased-line method described in Chapter 12. During this part of the presentation, however, Davy lofted his rod and drew in enough slack line to put him in touch with his flies, to respond to any interest expressed by trout. Because that first shoal over which he fished was broad, with even currents, mending wasn't needed, though in more brisk and conflicted water, it would be.

In the second part of Davy's presentation, he teased the three flies through a down-and-across swing, the closest part of the cast to the traditional wet-fly swing. However, he kept that long rod lifted high, and gathered line in his left hand, using the figure-eights of a hand-twist retrieve, in order

The keys to Davy Wotton's wet-fly method are the long, lofted rod, and the curve of line from the rod tip down to the water. The two give you total control over the drift and swing of your team of wet flies. When anything about that curve changes, you've probably got a trout out there, attached to one of your flies.

to keep perfect control over the drift of the flies, and also to keep in touch with them in case any got attacked by a trout. As often as he brought line in, he also let it out, at the whims of the present tendencies of current speed. With his rod held high, Davy's bright white line descended toward its contact point at the water in a gentle curve, creating a strike indicator of sorts. When that curve changed, action with a fish was afoot.

Two things stood out to me as I watched Davy fish this central swinging part of each cast. First, he had constant and total contact with and control of his flies, imparted by the loft of that long rod and the give and take with his line hand. Most of the time he let the flies swing freely. At times he took command and animated the top attractor fly. When needed, he tossed twitching mends down that curve of line to speed the flies or slow them. His posture was relaxed but his focus intense. I recall watching only one other angler, Polly Rosborough, fish with such a connection to what his flies were doing out there in the water.

The third part of Davy's presentation was a variation on the standard advice, rooted in Ray Bergman's book *Trout* and his Natural Drift (see Chapter 13), to let your fly reach the end of its swing, then retrieve it upstream a few feet, let it fall back, and retrieve it again. This gives any trout that has followed the flies through their down-and-across-stream swing plenty of chances to whack one of them when the flies come to rest at the end of the swing. With Davy's long rod and three-fly rig, it's possible to bring the top

Wet-fly expert Davy Wotton releasing a small rainbow that took one of his traditional flies on his home White River. By the time the trout got larger, later in the day, your unfortunate author had made a slight slip and doused his camera lens in the river.

fly to the surface, dance and dap it upstream a bit if desired, then let them all go, to drift freely back downstream. In my brief experience, this all seemed to goad trout into action and incited a lot more strikes than I've ever had by merely drawing wets upstream and letting them drift downstream again. But I still lack the patience to fiddle with my wet flies in this last part of any swinging presentation. It's a fault that I know costs me chances at trout.

During my day on the White River with Davy, I learned that his method—that devil in the details again!—is by far most effective when fished with the right long rod and supple fly line; with the appropriate attractor, deceiver, and imitator flies tied to leaders of proper construction; and with the right tippet materials, brought together with the listed knots. Following Davy through his shoals, watching him work magic with his gang of flies, observing wistfully as he brought trout after trout to his hands, made me realize that there are a myriad of intricate parts to what he was doing and how he was doing it. In writing about his method so briefly, I've written an oversimplification of it. On water different from the tailwater we fished that day, no doubt he would rig and fish differently. But the basics were there, and I've recorded them here, so you can work your own changes on them to suit the water wherever you're fishing.

I also learned that it's possible to employ Davy's method, if a little less effectively, with the rods, lines, and leaders you would normally be armed with when astream on streams or rivers of various sizes. I followed Davy down through those shoals with an $8^{1}/_{2}$-foot rod, the only one I'd brought with me on the trip, the less-than-supple floating line I always have on the reel, and the leader Davy rigged for me. That gear was far from his gear, but I wasn't inactive. Trout didn't ignore me. Some flapped into my hands, too. I didn't catch as many as Davy and T-Bird did. But I was able to catch sufficient trout to make me happy, and I now use Davy's methods with the normal range of gear I'm carrying when I suddenly decide to rig his way and I'm already on the water, armed with rods suitable to dry-fly fishing, nymphing, or whatever else I might decide to do on that water.

I did realize the need to outfit myself to employ Davy's method properly. When I got home, I bought a replica of Davy's exact outfit and have now had a few trips to try the method in my own fishing, without the benefit of instruction. I've found that it works best on riffles and runs of modest to large size, with active and fairly even currents, just the way Davy taught me to employ it on the White River. I've tried one wrinkle that Davy didn't mention, probably because we didn't get into any hatches the single day I fished with him. I whimsically call the wrinkle *downsizing Davy*. If I'm in a boat, and can carry extra rods, then I use it with the gear Davy used. If I'm afoot, I use whatever rod I already have in my hand.

Downsizing calls for rigging two or three small wet flies that resemble an active natural insect in its various stages, and fishing the flies as somewhat of a *gang*, just as Davy might fish his larger attractors, deceivers, and imitators. As an example of downsizing, I might use size 18 dark pupa and drowned adult patterns during an American Grannom caddis hatch (*Brachycentrus americanus*), or rig with similar size 20 wet flies for the smaller long-horned sedges (Glossosomatidae). When Blue-Winged Olive mayflies (*Baetis*) hatch, size 16 nymph, emerger, and drowned adult dressings that resemble the naturals might all be tried as a team. Exact pattern doesn't seem to matter as much as approximate size and color.

I suspect it's the action of the wet flies, fished near the surface as if they might be about to escape through it, that incites trout more than the nearness of the wet flies to the naturals. I also believe that the sudden appearance of more than one wet fly swimming into view acts as a stimulus to take at least one of them, perhaps out of desire to beat brethren to it. Whatever the reasons, trout seem to get goosed into action by a gang of small wet flies when they're feeding on small emerging or drowned naturals. I'll confess that at times one or even two of the flies are not wet flies, but nymphs, when I do this. But I fish them as I would wet flies.

I've employed the downsizing method on broad runs and riffles of the Bighorn River in Montana, in the period before a BWO hatch. It has added a lot of interest to those hours. I've also used it on the Deschutes River in Oregon, when great gatherings of tiny dark caddisflies gather in grasses

When you suspect trout might be seeing and eating quite a few of any given aquatic insect, such as this dark and small American Grannom caddis, you can often do well by showing those trout a gang of three imitations, each roughly resembling one stage of the natural, for example the pupa, adult, and diving adult of the caddis.

A trio of wets, any of which might look like an American Grannom pupa or adult in the eyes of a feeding trout: a Yamsi Special, with its wire body for weight as the point fly, a Dark Mole & Herl as the middle dropper, and a winged Leadwing Coachman as the top dropper.

along the banks, beginning in early spring. You don't see them on the water much, though you see occasional trout rising whenever these insects are busy in streamside vegetation. Fishing a dark size 20 dry fly on the rough water of that brawling river is not only difficult, but also rarely draws any interest from trout. A gang of small wet flies sometimes motivates them.

I've tried the downsized Davy method on several smaller streams, with lighter gear, and always seem to interest a few trout in wet flies when nothing else moves them. The next time you get into a hatch of any insect and dry flies fail, try rigging two or three wet flies that roughly resemble the naturals in their various stages. Follow Davy Wotton's prescription: Cast them with

This is a perfect setting for employing Davy Wotton's wet-fly method on smaller water, using the tackle you're already carrying for the size stream you're fishing. In this case it's on the border between a small- and medium-sized stream, and I'm armed with the old Leonard bamboo, $7^1/_2$ feet long for a 5-weight line, that I use in so much of my wet-fly fishing. I rig more often with two wet flies than three for such situations, just to reduce the chances for tangles.

Note that the main current in this runout from a small riffle is pushed against the far bank. You want your wets to fish through all of that water. It's critical when fishing wet flies with any of the swinging methods discussed in this book that the flies cross out of that faster flow into the slightly slower flow inside currents on the near side. Many trout will hang under the main current and follow the wets across, and take one of them when it slows down. Others will wait in the softer flows, dashing out to feed on what comes down the faster currents. You'll miss out on both the followers and the patient waiters if you pick your flies up for the next cast before they have crossed that seam between fast and slow water.

open loops, lift your rod high, and keep contact and control as they swing through a riffle, run, or even across a flat. Watch the downward curve of your line between rod tip and water for any signs of movement contrary to the way the water might move it. If that curve straightens a bit, or the line tip at the entry point takes a slight dart in any direction, you've got business with a fish.

I've come to think of Davy Wotton as the keeper of the flame, bringing traditional British and European wet flies and wet-fly methods to our continent alive and well and catching lots of trout. I'll confess that since fishing with Davy, I've not had time to tie his flies, so I've not incorporated them into this book. I use his method with the wet flies I've already got in my

A dozen wet flies that Davy Wotton tied for me, including many of his favorite dressings (from top): Alder, Invicta, Hare's Ear, Iron Blue Dun, Peter Ross, Alexandra, March Brown, Whickham's Fancy, Silver Invicta, BWO, Greenwell, and Muddler Daddy. The Muddler Daddy on the right is one I fished on Davy's home White River; it has been roughed up by a few trout.

It's interesting to note that the preponderance of these flies are small, averaging size 14, and more drab than bright. They are in perfect keeping with the move from big and bright wet flies, used by our fishing forefathers to fool native brook trout, toward smaller and more natural wet flies, to better con what we think of as "smarter" brown trout. One species of fish is not smarter than the other, but you would be smart to take lessons in both fly-pattern selection and wet-fly presentation from Davy Wotton.

boxes, and at times when I'm imitating a specific insect, with nymphs that I tie to fish for that hatch.

If you'd like to try tying and fishing traditional British wet flies, and some new variations worked on them, I'd advise studying Davy Wotton's videos, and also Roger Fogg's 2009 book, *Wet-Fly Tying and Fishing*. The latter is a repository of information on British wet flies. It's certain that you'll find a few patterns that are fun to tie, that are outside America's own much more recent wet-fly traditions, and that will catch some extra trout for you. As an exercise in that direction, I've listed the materials and steps for tying one of Davy's favorites, the Silver Invicta. The original dressing calls for a throat of blue gee—kingfisher—for which blue jay is often substituted. I'm not sure either would be legal. I know I don't desire to deplete the supply of such beautiful birds, so I substitute the iridescent blue feather from the collar of a rooster pheasant, which already resides among my tying supplies.

SILVER INVICTA

Hook:	#12-14 standard wet fly, 2X stout
Thread:	Black 8/0 or 10/0
Tail:	Golden pheasant crest
Rib:	Silver wire
Body:	Medium silver Mylar tinsel
Hackle:	Red-brown rooster, palmered
Throat:	Blue kingfisher (substitute ringneck collar)
Wing:	Hen pheasant

1. Measure the tips of a golden pheasant crest feather the length of the hook shank, and tie in with a soft loop and two tight turns of thread. Take a third turn of thread under the tail to prop it up. Secure with another turn forward of the first two. Clip the excess tail butts just behind the hook eye; they'll be part of an even underbody. Tie in a 3- to 5-inch section of medium silver wire, overwrap with thread to just behind the hook eye, and clip or bend to break off the excess wire.

2. Tie in a 4- to 5-inch section of medium Mylar tinsel, with the gold side down. Always, when tying a wet fly such as this with quite a few materials, use just the number of thread turns needed to secure it—in this case three to four. Wrap the tinsel in even turns to the base of the tail, then reverse it and wrap forward to just behind the hook eye. Clip the excess.

3. Select a rooster hackle with fibers sized to the hook and tie it in at the end of the tinsel body, by the stem, and clip the excess stem. Take three turns of hackle at the tie-in point, each behind the one in front of it. Wrap three to five turns back over the body to a point one turn short of the base of the tail. Leave a bit of a gap there. Capture the tip of the hackle with one or two turns of the ribbing wire.

4. Take four to six evenly spaced turns of ribbing forward through the hackle. Tie it off and break or cut the excess. Break off the hackle tip by yanking it forward. Hold back the forward hackles and use a thread layer to tidy up the head area and lay an even base for the wings.

5. If you're tying rotary, this is the place to use it. Turn the hook upside down. If you're using kingfisher, strip enough fibers to make a throat, measure them just past the hook point, and tie them in with the same soft loop you use for the tail. If you substitute blue ringneck collar fibers, peel the fibers from one side of the feather. It's a tiny feather, so the fibers usually won't be long enough for a fly larger than size 12. Measure these fibers past the hook point, tie them in, and clip the excess. (*Note:* This can be done without the rotary vise, but it's more awkward to place a soft loop on the underside of the hook.)

6. Return the rotary to its normal position. From paired hen pheasant wings, select matching feathers, and cut matching sections from each wing approximately the width of the hook gap. Meld these sections back-to-back, with their tips pointing upward if you prefer, or downward if you'd like. Measure them to the midpoint of the tail. Tie them in with a soft loop, take four to five turns of thread forward to capture the feather sections firmly, and clip the excess. Form a neat head, whip-finish, and apply head cement if you'd like this to have a nice, traditional appearance, which I traditionally neglect so I can go fishing with it faster.

I use Davy Wotton's wet-fly methods about half the time with the long rod and supple line that I bought after my day fishing with him on the White River. Those are times when I'm wading into trout water specifically to fish his method, and they're almost always when I'm boating a river, and therefore have room to keep an extra rod strung. The other half of the time I'm already on a stream or river, usually far from the boat or vehicle, armed with a rod appropriate for the size water I'm on: a 7- to 8-foot rod on a small stream, an $8^1/_2$- to 9-foot rod for a medium-sized stream on up to a large river. When a situation arises that makes me want to try a brace or trio of wets, whether large, medium, or downsized—or as often a combination of the sizes—then I sit down at streamside and re-rig the outfit I've got in my hands. I don't trot back to the rig to get that long rod. I'll probably do fine with the shorter one.

You'll probably do fine fishing two- and three-fly setups with the rod that you already own as well. But you'll find it's a lot of fun, and on the sorts of broad riffles and runs that are shaped perfectly for Davy Wotton's methods, you'll catch some trout that might have eluded you before, if you rig with the long rod and fish with it held high.

Chapter Seventeen

Czech Wetting

While fishing with Davy Wotton on the White River in Arkansas, I developed a liking for one of the top droppers he rigged me with, an attractor called the Muddler Daddy. It's based on the Muddler Minnow, a streamer with which I've had a lot of luck in my past. As a streamer, the Muddler style has no place in this book about wet flies and wet-fly fishing. But Davy rigs his Muddler Daddy, with its long pheasant tail legs, as the top dropper in a wet-fly rig. In that sense it's an *attractor* wet, excellent at pushing water, making a disturbance, getting the attention of trout. It's also great when fished as a *dangler*, lifted and lowered so that it fishes just subsurface, then in the surface itself, and finally dances a bit in the air just above the water.

I fished it this way on the White, and caught as many trout on the Muddler Daddy as I did on the deceivers and imitators fished on the same leader out beyond it. A couple of times I hooked trout on one of the other flies and got second hookups on the Daddy as it got tugged around enticingly by the trout already attached. You've seen those following fish when you're playing a hooked trout; sometimes they're bigger than the one with which you're already engaged. It's nice to have a second fly in the water that gives you a chance at those followers, though it can get pandemonious when that second trout strikes and takes off in a different direction than the first.

I never did successfully solve the definition problem—whether the Muddler Daddy is a streamer or wet fly—but I like to go by my own rule that if I fish a fly as a wet, then it's a wet fly. So I now use the Muddler Daddy often and get a lot of enjoyment out of it, and I don't care much what it's called.

When I got home to Oregon from Arkansas and took the Muddler Daddy out to one of my favorite medium-sized mountain trout streams, I first fished it as a streamer, just as I would a standard Muddler Minnow, and considered it such. I fished it downstream on the swing across fairly wide riffles and boulder garden runs. It worked well. Trout chased it down and killed it, much as they would a sculpin, which the original Muddler was tied to imitate. I

Muddler Daddies might be streamers, not wet flies. When dressed with floatant, they can be fished as dry flies. The original purpose of the gangly fly is to serve as an imitation of a long-legged cranefly adult. I first fished the fly on the White River in Arkansas, with wet-fly guru Davy Wotton. He rigged it as the top dropper in a three-fly rig, as an *attractor*, for the way it pushes water, and obviously for the way it catches trout. It worked for me on the White, sometimes causing engagements with doubles. It has continued to work as well for me ever since, mostly on boisterous mountain streams in the West, and most often as part of a two-fly setup with an anchor wet fly against which to brace it, so it can be given some action, if desired, on an upstream cast and downstream drift.

also popped it into boulder and bank lies, and sometimes under root wads and in beneath fallen tree trunks, casting either a bit downstream or, if the situation called for it, straight across stream, retrieving it out of danger from snags. I caught lots of trout in such places, and still considered myself to be streamer fishing when I did.

One bright afternoon, I fished a floating hopper pattern upstream over bois-terous water. Though the stream flows through a sparse ponderosa pine forest, its banks are heavily grassed, and an excellent supply of big, gray grasshoppers take to the air as you walk alongside it in summer sunshine. Trout rise to take the hoppers that land on water, but do so with surprisingly gentle sips, consid-ering that the naturals are about size 4. That day trout rose to an appropriate dry-fly imitation, one that had always worked, but consistently turned away from it at the last second. I tried a downsized version of the same floating hop-per, on a size 10 hook, but the trout were still bashful about it.

I rigged a Muddler Daddy to fish upstream damp—awash or just submerged—to see if that might satisfy the trout. But I realized I'd need

What I've come to call an *anchor wet* is nothing more than a standard wet fly tied on the stoutest nymph hook I can find. It should be tied sparsely, with water-absorbing materials, and at least slightly undersized for the hook, which should be size 6 or 8. Its purpose is to serve somewhat the function of a Czech Nymph: to help sink smaller wet flies to deeper depths.

Though I originally tied these anchor wets to serve as escorts for flies that I expected trout to be more likely to accept, it turned out that many more trout than expected took the bigger flies and ignored the smaller ones. For simplification in rigging, and fewer tangles when casting, I now normally fish them with just one other fly, which at this point is usually the Muddler Daddy.

There are no secrets to tying anchor wets. Just tie them as you would winged wets in standard fashion, except sparsely and on oversized heavy hooks. The one in this photo is the first that I tied and tried. Note the lack of tail, and the heavy oval tinsel ribbing. I tie it with a more slender body now, and sometimes smaller on the same size hook, approaching what Atlantic salmon and summer steelhead tiers would call *low-water style*.

something to anchor it against if I desired to dandle it near the surface, as I'd been taught to fish it on the White River, but on an upstream rather than downstream cast. On an earlier trip to the big and brutal Lochsa River in Idaho, I'd tied a few experimental wet flies—the traditional Hare's Ear Wet and the Leadwing Coachman—on the heaviest size 6 curved-shank nymph hooks I could find. I used them on that trip to get deep, in theory on the point of the tippet to tug a couple of more realistic soft-hackles and flymphs deeper, without adding weight to the flies or the leader, which would have violated my own set of descriptions about what constitutes wet-fly fishing. The anchor wets worked perfectly except for one thing: Trout took the big, deep, oversized point flies far more often than they took the smaller ones that I thought they ought to take.

I noticed those same heavy anchor wets in my fly box while standing there in the smaller mountain stream, with a Muddler Daddy already tied on, looking for something to brace it against. I spooled off 4 feet of 4X tippet, tied one end to the hook bend of the Muddler Daddy, tied a heavy size 6 Hare's Ear to the other end. I began casting the two flies upstream to the same water where I'd earlier caught nothing but refusals on floating hopper patterns. The results were more than modestly enjoyable.

Most trout took the Muddler Daddy awash or just beneath the surface. Because the takes were almost all subtle sips, just as they were to drys when trout would take them at all, I was rarely able to see the take as you would one to a dry fly: a small splash and the sudden disappearance of a fly floating along visibly. Instead, most often, I'd merely notice the sudden absence of the submerged fly that I was doing my best to keep in sight. Fortunately the water was clear, and the size 8 Muddler Daddy could be seen as often as not, and also the trout that tipped up and sipped it.

By a slow and somewhat osmotic process, I shifted the way I fished the brace of wets—by then I'd subconsciously promoted the Muddler Daddy to a wet fly—from the way I would fish a dry fly in the same water to the way I might fish nymphs with the Czech Nymphing method, as if I knew much about that. I haven't done much of it, but have seen enough videos and read enough articles to know that, reduced to an oversimplification, you cast short in Czech Nymphing, give your nymphs a bit of time to achieve the right depth, then lift the rod and lead the flies as they drift downstream toward you, and finally set the hook at the end of each drift just in case a trout has attached itself but hasn't sent you any signal about it.

That's what I began to do with that heavy anchor wet and much lighter Muddler Daddy. I cast them at most about four rod lengths—I was armed with my wet-fly favorite, the $7\frac{1}{2}$-foot Leonard—and more often just about half that. At times I kept the cast to no more than a rod length of line plus the length of the leader. The shorter the cast, the better I was able to observe the top fly. Keeping visual contact with the submerged Muddler Daddy eventually became the key to catching trout, of which I began to catch many.

After each short cast, and a pause long enough to let the heavy point fly sink a foot or so in water that was no more than 2 or 3 feet deep, I would lift the rod tip, not coincidentally establishing the same curve of line from rod to entry point in the water that Davy Wotton taught me to use when fishing wet flies on the White River. That curve served as a backup strike indicator when I was not able to establish eye contact with the Muddler Daddy itself. Most of the time, I was able to lift the dropper close enough to the surface to be able to follow its drift. Then I fished the drift out, usually without any action, though sometimes it was fun to dance the top fly a bit, get trout to chase it.

The initial cast in what I've come to call Czech Wetting is made short. The anchor wet on the point is given at least a few seconds to achieve some depth. In water as shallow as this, just 2 or 3 feet deep, a foot or so of depth is all you need out of your heavy fly. Trout will lift off the bottom and intercept it if they want it. Its larger purpose is to serve as something to brace the Muddler Daddy dropper on its downstream drift.

Small ones did. Big ones took it only when it was just beneath the surface and drifting without any added movement, exactly as a drowned grasshopper might move with the flow. Those takes were visible, the signs of them anything from the mere disappearance of the slightly sunk fly to the rare sudden appearance of a dashing form in the act of a slashing take. But even those caused no disturbance of the surface. The most beautiful takes were those in which a trout manifested in the current, as if a bit of the bottom had detached itself and slowly lifted up and as it did took the shape of a trout, the white of an opening mouth appearing and disappearing, and then the fly gone from sight and that bit of bottom beginning to descend. I could almost see the look of surprise on these visible trout when I raised the rod to bring the hook point home.

Those slow and gentle risers were usually the largest of the trout that I caught that first day in that small stream, 16 to 18 inches long. They were wild redside rainbows, native to the water, never near a hatchery, which made them all the more satisfying.

The completion of each drift became a matter of leading the two flies downstream, keeping constant touch with them, but not swimming them

After the anchor wet fly sinks a foot or so, lift the rod and lead the two wet flies downstream with the line, without speeding them faster than the current. The purpose is to lift the top fly, in this case a Muddler Daddy, high enough so you can see it, though the water won't always be as clear as this, and keeping the dropper in sight won't always be possible. When it's not, then the entry point of the line where it meets the water, and the curve of the fly line as it descends from the rod tip to the water, will become your indicator. If anything changes—the line tip darts or the curve flattens—set the hook.

any faster than the current might move them. The rod remained high. Slack line got gathered as it formed. If the Muddler Daddy got out of sight due to turbulence, bad light, or by sinking too deep, then the curve of line, and its entry point into the water, became the indicator. If the line tip took a dart, or the curve changed, then the hook got set. Most times a trout was out there.

If the holding water was shaped right for it, the cast was fished all the way to the end of its drift by turning and following with the rod still held high and leading the flies. Usually this worked where a run or bench gathered to plunge over a boulder lie, into the next run or bench downstream. Trout always seem to hold around those boulders at the lower end of any bit of holding water. If you lead a pair of wet flies right up to that point, then lift in a quick hook set, it's surprising how often you'll discover a trout to be already on, even in the absence of any indication that you might have had a take to one of the flies. It's almost always the deep fly at that point; if a trout had taken the dropper you'd probably have seen it happen.

When the brace of wet flies reaches the lowest point of its drift, just before it hangs up on the rocks that form the plunge out of the run of holding water, lift the rod sharply to raise the flies for the next cast. Often a trout will be attached without any signs that one of your flies has been taken. Usually it's the anchor wet that produces a trout in such a situation, and it happens far more often than you would ever suspect.

In this drift, I would give the flies about two more feet before executing that final hook set. Trout will find favorable lies in front of all those boulders, and they'll usually dash to take a drifting wet fly at the last second. Give them every chance before you set the hook on suspicion, then yank your flies out of danger of snagging the rocks.

The first day that I worked my way into what I've come to call Czech Wetting, I hooked about half of my trout on the dropper, half on the point fly. Half were visible takes, the other half signaled by some movement of the line. That proportion will change dramatically depending on shape of the water, air and water temperatures, activity of insects, and willingness of trout to rush up and take something shallow. The purpose of the heavy anchor wet, when I tied it for the much larger Lochsa, was to deliver more normal wet flies deeper. On smaller water I consider the heavy flies braces for droppers, and that's why I've come to call them anchor wets.

I fish the same Czech Wetting rig a lot now, almost always on small water, or in shallow water in larger streams and rivers. So far I've stuck with my original brace of flies, the Muddler Daddy and Hare's Ear anchor wet, though I'll admit I've experimented with weighted nymphs in place of the heavy wet. In truth they work, but then I don't know what kind of fishing I'm doing. I'm rigged with what might be described as a streamer as the dropper, and what is clearly a nymph on the point. I know it's no longer

This trout took an anchor wet fished a foot or two deep in fast and clear water, in a small mountain trout stream. Though originally tied to the tippet to brace a Muddler Daddy on an upstream cast, so the dropper could be lifted and fished just subsurface, it turned out that the deeper fly fooled about half of the fish. The only sign of a take to it was a slight change in the curve of the line between the rod tip and water.

Whenever the upper fly is in sight, it's wise to watch it closely, just as you would a dry fly in the same situation. Sometimes you'll see takes to it that are surprisingly subtle. Just as often the dropper will take a sudden upstream dart against the current. That's a sure sign a fish has taken the trailing anchor wet. Set the hook quickly; the trout will get rid of that fake bit of fur, feathers, and steel as quickly as it can.

wet-fly fishing, so I'll drop the subject here, and you can continue those experiments on your own.

TYING THE MUDDLER DADDY

I haven't tried the Muddler Daddy for its original purpose, as an adult crane-fly imitation, though I suspect it will be excellent the next time I get that chance. Perhaps the trout I think are taking it as a hopper are actually mistaking it for a cranefly. Since I've had excellent success with the fly when neither insect is around, I suspect they're interested in it because it acts alive and looks like food.

I have two versions of the Muddler Daddy stuck in a sheet of a dozen sample flies that Davy Wotton tied and gave me. Both are relatively simple, though one has a palmered hackle over its fur body, held firmly in place by a copper wire rib. The other has the wire rib but lacks the hackle. Each has six sets of pheasant tail legs, each set knotted twice, and spun deer-hair heads that are tightly compacted and neatly trimmed. These things distress me. I have enough trouble knotting pheasant tail legs once, and I'm not very good at compacting and shaping neat Muddler heads.

Polly Rosborough once told me, "Don't worry about how many tail fibers you put on a fly; trout can't count." I'm going to trust trout not to count the number of legs I put on my Muddler Daddy, or the number of knots I tie in each leg. Four legs seems enough, each of them knotted once. I'm terrible at spinning tight heads; I'm not the one you'd want to be your barber. I've come to prefer my Muddler Daddies with sparse and poorly trimmed heads, because that way I have time to tie about twice as many of them, and they seem to fish fine.

I'm going to recommend that you tie your Muddler Daddies with six pairs of twice-knotted legs, and that you finish them with compact and tidy heads. Add palmered hackles and wire ribs if you desire. But you're not going to learn those things from me. I like to spend more time fishing, less time tying, and I haven't had any trout complain about my Muddler Daddies recently.

MUDDLER DADDY

Hook:	#10-12 3X long
Thread:	White 3/0 or 6/0
Body:	Hare's mask fur and orange Sparkle Yarn, mixed
Legs:	Four to six sets of two or three pheasant tail fibers, knotted once or twice
Collar:	Tips of spun deer hair
Head:	Spun deer hair
Note:	The original calls for hare's mask fur for the body, and that is what you should use. But I live in Oregon and do most of my trout fishing in the Northwest, which includes Idaho and Montana: all states where October Caddis populations are heavy. The Muddler Daddy, when dressed with floatant, or when fished damp as described in this chapter, makes an excellent imitation for that insect. Some cranefly adults also have an orange tinge to their bodies. So I include orange in my own dubbing. If you've never tied with spun deer hair, expect this to take some practice.

1. Dub a cigar-shaped body of fur and Sparkle Yarn mixed. Stop about $1/4$ hook-shank length behind the eye.

2. Knot a set of pheasant tail legs. Tie it in on the far side of the hook. Length should be equal to 1- to $1^1/2$ hook shanks. Use just a couple of turns of thread so you can tug and tweak it into position either on the upper far side, or the lower far side. Repeat with three more sets, each positioned as well as possible to surround the body. Don't worry about their exact placement; the currents will change it all anyway. Trim the butts only after all sets are tied in and positioned.

3. Clip a patch of deer hair from the hide. I've read everything from a pencil thickness of hair to a specific count of hairs. I'm going to say start with half a pencil thickness, and adjust up or down from there as it suits what you want from the finished fly. Clean fuzz from the butts, and stack to align the tips. Measure the tips to reach the bend of the hook, then leave $^1/_2$ shank length more for the spun head, and trim the hair straight across, with even butts.

4. Place the hair in position so that the tips will reach the bend of the hook when flared. Work the hair between your off-hand finger and thumb tips so that it surrounds the hook. Take two loose turns of thread around the hair. Draw the turns tight at the same time as you release your grip with the off-hand. The hair should flare and end up somewhat equally spaced around the shank. Take thread turns forward through the hair butts to bare shank, flaring the rest of the hair. Use the thumb- and fingernails of your tying hand to compact the hair back against the body. This should leave enough bare shank for another clump of spun hair.

5. Clip a second patch of hair equal to the first. Clean the butts, and clip them straight across. Clip the tips of the hair, leaving a clump a $^1/_2$ inch or so long.

6. Hold the second clump of hair on top of the hook. Take two loose turns of thread around the center of it. Draw the turns tight and release the hair at the same time. It will spin around the shank, distributing itself evenly. Take several thread turns through the hair to the hook eye. Use thumb- and fingernails to work the hair back from the eye, just enough to clear it. Whip-finish and clip the thread.

7. Give the spun head its haircut. Begin by separating the short butt hairs from the long collar tips. Trim the bottom flat. Taper the sides from narrow at the front to wider at the back, forming a bullet-shaped head. If the hair collar is thicker than you'd like, or out of balance, nip at it here and there to tidy it up. Try not to cut off any legs.

If your finished Muddler Daddy pleases you, it will almost certainly please the trout. There are many ways it can do that: floating on the surface, dancing in and out of it, submerged just beneath it, or on the swing. It won't always be a wet fly when you fish it, but it can be fished as a wet fly. The Muddler Daddy will add a lot of fun to your wet-fly fishing when you use it in wet-fly ways.

Chapter Eighteen

Fishing Small Streams with Wet Flies

The old standard method for fishing small streams with wet flies is the downstream dapped pair of flies, or sometimes a trio. The flies are usually winged and large, size 6 down to about size 10. They are fished more as swimming, darting minnows than they are as natural insects. There's nothing wrong with that; trout in small streams eat lots of small fish, including their own fry.

Setting up for this type of fishing is simple. The rod should be around 8 feet long, the line a floater, either double-taper or weight-forward: It doesn't matter because casts will be short. The leader should be about the length of the rod or a little longer. The point fly should be your favorite wet, the one you take trout on most often and therefore the one in which you have the most confidence. The first dropper, 2 feet up the leader, should be different from the point fly in color. If the point is drab, make the dropper bright. Sometimes it helps to use one large, the other small. The important thing is to offer the trout a choice and see what they prefer.

If you use a second dropper, another 2 feet up the leader, consider making it a Muddler Daddy dressed with floatant, or even a dry fly. It then serves as a marker, telling you precisely how the flies below it are fishing as well as a strike indicator, disappearing suddenly whenever one of the other flies is taken by a trout. And don't overlook the fact that it also serves as enticement. Trout will often take it. Though dry-fly fishing is not the subject of this book, catching trout is never a bad idea, and a dry fly as top dropper is one way to do it on a small stream.

You want to dap and dangle these ganged flies downstream far more than you want to attempt to cast them. Casting in tight confines with two or three flies on the leader is going to present you with some tangles. The few times I've used the method, I've found it best to settle the flies into a current tongue and feed line to let them wash down into a pool. I watch the line tip or the top dropper carefully for any sign of a take. To me, this free drift is the most productive part of the cast, because the flies are at the whims of the current, just as natural insects would be.

When they've gotten as far downstream as I want to fish them, I lift the rod and tease the wet flies back upstream. It's possible to cover lots of water in some small pools by sweeping the rod slowly one way and then the other, which leads the flies back and forth, makes them swim from side to side. I tease the flies upstream in short darts, usually dancing the top dropper on the surface. After bringing the flies up a few feet, I lower the rod and feed some slack to settle them back into the current. This lets them sink a few inches and also lets them drift downstream so that I can tease them upstream again.

This method is most effective in pockets, plunge pools, and swift riffles studded here and there with boulders. Since that describes many small mountain waters almost precisely, it's a method that I should use a lot. But I don't. I use it rarely. I prefer fishing upstream on small waters. I rarely risk dealing with more than one fly on my leader in the confines of the forested streams I fish most often. You should try it, though. When you do, you'll be in touch with the type of fishing Charles Cotton did on his Devonshire streams 250 years ago, and also with what our fishing forefathers did when they first arrived on this continent not long after. Ray Bergman covers this downstream wet-fly method in detail in his 1938 book *Trout*.

Possibly the most logical wet-fly setup for small streams is a pair of flies—three of them if you dare—fished upstream. These can be winged wets, soft-hackles, flymphs, or the combination of Muddler Daddy and anchor wet that I covered in the last chapter. It's best to combine a couple of fly types. With the point fly tied on a heavy-wire hook, you can fish it near the bottom, assuming the water is shallow, and a middle dropper in the mid-depths. You can add an attractor, a large fly that pushes water and fishes just subsurface, and fish it as both indicator and enticement on the top dropper. But you're likely to get more than occasional tangles if you fish three flies on confined small streams.

This method—the three-fly setup cast upstream—was used by Stewart on his British border streams. But picture his waters, with their open grassy banks. It's easy to cast a high, open loop there. Stewart's *short* rod was 10 feet long, and in all likelihood had an action that by today's standards would be considered slower than slow. Now picture a closed-in stream, with alder and huckleberry and laurel all crowding around its pools. On that type of water, a lazy backcast with three wet flies is an invitation to constantly drop back and untangle yourself from your surroundings. I sometimes use

When fishing wet flies in the pools of a small stream, take up your position upstream and dance the flies downstream. Let the current take them. Watch for any wink in the water, or dart of your leader or line tip. If you use a Muddler Daddy or dry fly as your top dropper, it will serve as a strike indicator, but it also has a hook in it, and will catch a high proportion of your trout for you.

If the small water you're fishing has sufficient openings overhead, allowing casts with open loops, then a two- or three-fly rig might serve you well. Cast upstream and short. Watch your flies if you can see them, your line tip if you can't. If anything moves out there that looks unusual, set the hook. Most likely the movement will be a trout taking one of your wet flies.

something close to this method, with a dry fly on the dropper and a single wet fly at the point. The wet is usually a soft-hackle, and it's the fly that takes the most fish for me when I fish this setup. The dry, fished upstream and dead drift, marks takes when trout hit the wet, but it also gets hit quite often itself. I'm not sure this is a legitimate wet-fly method. It's used more often as a dry-and-dropper with a nymph on the tippet. But it's a way to fish a wet fly and catch lots of small-stream trout.

I don't go to small streams carrying rods to fish wet flies. I do more dry-fly fishing on small water, and use quick 7-foot rods to punch out short casts with tight loops. That's about the only way I can hit the tiny targets on my Coastal Mountain home streams. I suspect you would be well served by the same kind of casts on your own home streams. Those tight loops are not compatible with two- and three-fly rigs, because the flies often get tangled. If you fish small waters that are more open, however, try multiple flies fished upstream. You've got to creep in close, cast short, and watch carefully for any swirl or dart of the line tip that means a take.

This kind of fishing will make you a more observant fisherman. It's an excellent way to hone your skills. I always recommend beginning on a small stream, whether you're dry-fly fishing, casting nymphs, or fishing wet flies. What you learn on your small home waters will go with you wherever you cast flies, all over the world, on all sorts and sizes of trout water.

Another method that takes trout from tricky lies was shown to me by Richard Bunse. We were on tiny Teal Creek, near his home in Oregon, trying to draw trout out of a submerged boulder lie 20 feet downstream from a bridge, under an overhanging alder tree, beneath a cable strung across the stream with a No Trespassing sign dangling from it. This was a challenging lie.

Bunse approached it from the only direction that sign would permit: upstream, crouched beneath the bridge. The stream was too narrow to cast across, and he couldn't get a backcast strung out behind him anyway, for all the brush back there. So he flipped about 15 feet of line downstream and across. The fly nearly lit on the far shore, several feet upstream from the lie. As soon as the fly landed Bunse began feeding line into its drift. The fly and line all ambled down, lying across the stream, the fly near the bank, the line in the middle, the leader between.

When the line pointed at the submerged boulder, Bunse stopped feeding slack. The curve of line and leader across the current started to straighten out. Bunse's wet and white-winged Royal Trude swam out from the bank toward the upstream side of that boulder. A trout pounced it, a nice fish for a stream that tiny.

After releasing the first trout, Bunse made the same short drop cast, let his line escort the fly downstream, but didn't draw tight until the line began to ride up on the bulge of water going over the boulder. The fly swam straight at the boulder. Then the line was swept over the boulder and the fly darted

The Royal Trude, a bright wet-fly adaptation of the more famous Royal Coachman and Royal Wulff, is an example of an effective small-stream wet fly that looks like nothing in nature. Like the best dressings, it has a long history of taking trout and is worth a try when you fish small streams, or any other.

into the eddy behind it. A boil welled up, and Bunse drew a trout upstream that was fully 11 inches long, a monster that had caused many fatalities among the insects and small fishes living in that tiny creek. Bunse released it, so it could cause some more.

Feeding line into a downstream drift works whenever you're forced to approach a pool or other holding lie from upstream. It's an excellent way to deliver a wet fly to a bit of water you couldn't reach otherwise. It has the advantage of showing the fly to the fish ahead of the line and leader. The fly appears suddenly, swimming into the trout's vision. It must be hard to resist, because the downstream feed works lots of times for me, and not just on small water. I'm usually forced to use it by constraints of low-hanging trees overhead and brush along the banks, not by bridges and cables with No Trespassing signs hung on them.

My favorite wet-fly method for small streams has become the one I described in the introduction: the upstream soft-hackle fished with very short casts. It works best on mountain creeks with steep gradients. The faster they plunge down, the more stair-step pools they form. These sharp drops make it easier to approach a pool from downstream, crouching low, staying out of sight. It's critical not to show your silhouette to the trout, and not to show your rod or line to them on anything but the delivery stroke.

Recall the description of Stewart's fishing: "Twenty-four hours of creeping and crawling." That's nearly what I do when I fish soft-hackles upstream, a tactic rooted in Stewart's book *The Practical Angler*, written more than 150

When fishing a wet fly or soft-hackle upstream, use the cover of boulders to get as close to the holding water as you can. You want to be able to see the fly, and even the trout that rush to it, if possible, but you don't want the trout to see you.

years ago. He fished two or three of his spiders on a cast, over his open waters. I cast one over mine, to avoid tangles. His rod was 10 feet long; mine is 7 feet, either a blond 5-strip bamboo built for me by Dean Jones, or a black graphite built for me by author Skip Morris. They're both brilliant rods for small streams: light, bossy, quick, balanced to 4-weight lines. I wrote about them in my book *Trout from Small Streams*.

My favorite streams are broken by tumbled boulders, some the size of living room furniture, some larger, some smaller. They form beautiful dark pools. They also form ideal shelters to creep up behind. It's like casting from a blind, and it allows what I enjoy most about this kind of fishing: getting up so close that I can follow the drift of the fly in the water and watch everything that happens to it.

The cast is upstream, the merest flick, 15 to 25 feet. I fish the lower part of each pool first, because trout often hang out there, especially later in summer when terrestrials plop in from streamside trees. Then I probe the edges with a cast or two. Finally, my last casts are made up toward the current tongue, which is where I expect most trout. Failing to fish the other water first, however, means any trout holding downstream from the main current will be frightened by your initial casts over their heads, and dash up to alarm trout at the upper end of the pool.

The fly I like best for this kind of fishing is the Partridge & Yellow, tied on a light-wire hook in size 10 or 12, with speckled gray hackles. It's the

When you fish a small trout stream that has little overhead cover to obstruct your casts, then all of your options are open. You can approach a pool from the side, lower your profile, and present your wet fly—or even better, a pair of them—sliding down the currents just as fallen insects might be delivered to trout. It's easy to read the most likely lie in this case: right where the depth and shade coincide.

brightest soft-hackle I carry. I'm usually able to keep it in sight and follow its drift in the clear water, while a drab wet fly would disappear against the background. Trout don't seem shy about the bright fly. If they did, I'd be forced to use a darker fly.

All casts, whether at the foot of the pool, along its edges, or up toward the current tongue entering the head of the pool, are made straight upstream. As soon as the fly hits the water and begins drifting downstream, I begin gathering slack line at the same pace. This is precisely the way a dry fly is fished, gathering line to remove slack so the hook can be set, without taking line in so fast that the free drift of the fly is influenced.

The key to this kind of fishing is the ability to detect subtle takes. If you can't see the fly itself, but see a boil in the area, set the hook. If you see a slight flash, set the hook. That is the flank of a trout catching light as it turns to take the fly. The surest sign of a take is any dart made by the line tip or the leader. Rarely this will be an abrupt movement of a few inches or more. Most of the time the line tip or leader will merely twitch upstream an inch or two. At first you'll set the hook only to the most obvious takes. In time you'll find yourself setting the hook when you're not even aware of what prompted you to set it. A trout will be there, though you'll not be certain exactly which sixth sense let you know that something had happened.

The sequence for fishing a soft-hackled wet fly upstream to a small pool is simple: Take a position at the foot of the pool, using any cover you can find; make the cast short and upstream; gather line as the wet fly drifts toward you; watch for the slightest sign of a take; and make your pickup and delivery for the next cast only after the fly has drifted downstream and out of water where you might expect a fish to take it.

Fishing this method is best when the sun is out and bright, slanting down through the water to illuminate everything in a pool. In these kinds of light conditions, trout seem to be bashful about taking anything on top. They'll splash at drys but fail to take them. If you switch to a wet fly, fishing it upstream, submerged but shallow, you'll be amazed at the clouds of trout that suddenly flock to your fly. Because your casts are so short, you'll see it all happen, especially in the clear water of a clean stream. It's a lot more exciting than dry-fly fishing in the same set of conditions, on the same small water.

Trout seem surprised by the sudden advent of the wet fly in their water. The antics they pull—swirling around the fly, taking it, spitting it out, rushing back to take it again—will astonish you as much as its sudden arrival astonishes them. But I won't describe all the surprises you'll get fishing soft-hackled wet flies close in on small waters. Certain thrills you need to experience for yourself.

If you slip a pair of wet flies into such a promising lie as that bit of depth and darkness along the overhanging willows, you might get surprised by more than one trout. It's a rarity, and it's not the reason you fish two wet flies, sometimes even three, on a cast. But it's fun when it happens . . . unless the trout are of about equal size and large, and they choose to go in opposite directions. Then you're lucky if you land either one of them. In this case the little flapper that took the dropper caused no such troubles.

PART IV

THE WET FLY
AS IMITATION

Chapter Nineteen

Stages of the Mayfly

Rick Hafele was generous with his water. He'd floated the same big river a week earlier, anchored at the head of the same riffle, and caught lots of trout during the Western March Brown hatch. His son Graham, about six years old at the time, floated with us the following week. We hoped lightning might strike twice in the same place. After dropping the anchor, Rick waved me downstream toward the best-looking water, where the riffle smoothed out a bit and could be called a run. That's where most of the mayfly duns ended up adrift, and where trout would rise up and take them.

"You fish down there, Dave," he told me. "I'll stay up here and talk to Graham." I got out of the drift boat and trotted downstream a hundred feet or so, under the assumption that Rick, having fished the water so short a time ago and so successfully, was sending me down to where the fishing would be better. I began casting, catching nothing. A few duns boated the water, but trout hadn't gotten around to rising to them yet.

Rick leaped over the gunwale of his anchored drift boat, leaned casually against its up-tipped bow, and chatted with Graham. While he did, he flipped a size 12 March Brown Flymph of his own recent devising a few feet out into the choppy water at the head of the riffle. He mended a bit while the fly washed down and around into the soft corner pocket just downstream from the boat. But the fly never did get very far into that calmer water. Rick got a hit on nearly every cast.

Experience on the water pays. But so does some knowledge of the way an insect emerges.

The March Brown, *Rhithrogena morrisoni*, belongs to the clinger group of mayflies. Its nymphs live on bottom rocks in the fastest riffles and runs, but migrate to the nearest calm water when it's time to emerge. The migration dislodges lots of them. They swim feebly with the currents. Those that

The presence of Western March Brown duns is often an indication of some of the season's earliest and finest dry-fly fishing. If you're careful in your observations, however, you might also find that wet flies extend that good fishing for an hour or two both before and after each hatch. There are also times when wets fish better than drys right through the middle of a March Brown hatch.

The same thing is true of wet flies during most mayfly hatches: You can usually extend the best fishing by using wet flies, and you can also catch more trout on wets than drys during many mayfly hatches.

make it to the edges of fast water, whether by crawling or swimming, must then make it to the top for emergence. Most do, and they split the nymphal skin in the surface to escape as duns. But many exit the nymphal shuck beneath the surface. These are forced to finish the last few inches of the trip to the surface as duns, with their wings beginning to unfurl in the current.

All of the above adds up to a lot of nymphs and emerging duns drifting and swimming and struggling on the current, but beneath the surface, during any March Brown mayfly hatch. The farther upstream you go, toward the fast water at the head of a riffle, run, flat, or pool, the more naturals trout see in the drift. Rick knew that, which is why he anchored at the riffle corner, pretending it was to chat with Graham, and caught trout after trout on his flymph while I exercised my casting arm with dry flies downstream in water that looked better, but wasn't.

Mayflies have four basic stages: nymph, emerger, dun, and spinner. Most of the average annual life cycle is spent as a nymph, eating and growing on the bottom or in rooted vegetation. When water temperature and the cycle of light tell the nymph it's time to hatch, it makes its way to the top, becomes an emerger either in the surface film or just beneath it. The winged dun stage

The life cycle of the mayfly exposes it to possible subsurface feeding at several more points than it would appear at first glance. The nymphs must rise to the surface; many duns drown at emergence; many spinners are drowned after laying their eggs. Trout enjoy them all, and wet flies fish for them all.

arrives on the surface after escaping from the nymphal shuck. It flies to nearby vegetation, where it casts a final thin skin and becomes the reproductive spinner. It mates in this final stage. If it's a male, it finds a mate in the air, then usually returns to vegetation to expire. If it's a female, it returns to the water to lay its eggs and to die where trout can get at it.

The nymph stage of the mayfly is not an excellent candidate for imitation with wet flies. When lots of them either drift or swim around during a hatch, a wet can work. But a nymph usually works better, and I would lead you astray to tell you it's a good time to fish wet flies, though in a few cases it's a good time to fish nymphs with the same methods you would use to fish wets.

One mayfly nymph that can be imitated with winged wet flies is the still-water Speckle-Wing Quill, in the genus *Callibaetis*. It doesn't make sense, because it's a swimmer nymph that bolts to the surface for emergence as a nymph, not a dun, with its wings still in wing cases, not trailing free. But the best fly I've found to fish this hatch is the standard Hare's Ear Wet in sizes 12 and 14. It's a traditional tie with fiber tails, a hare's mask fur body, and slim wings. It can be tied without hackle, the dubbing picked out to serve as legs (see page 139 in Chapter 7).

When speckle-wing duns hatch on lakes and ponds, these winged wets work well fished just under the hatch. Cast them out on a floating line and long leader. Give them a bit of time to sink. Retrieve them with several short

When mayflies emerge and trout feed right along the shoreline, in quiet water of rivers and streams, you can often do well by wading out, then casting a wet fly back to the shallows. Most often the insects will be Pale Evening Duns, and as their name implies, this happens most often at dusk.

strips of line. Let them rest a few moments, then goose them along again. It shouldn't work, because the nymphs rarely move that way, parallel to the surface, and the duns never do. But trout often take the wet fly, even when duns are afloat all over the water, while ignoring a dry imitation.

Some moving water mayfly species emerge from their nymphal skins on or near the bottom, and escape to the top as duns, not nymphs. These are perfect for imitation with soft-hackles and winged wets. The most prominent group in this category includes Eastern and Western Pale Evening Duns, in the mayfly clinger family Heptageniidae. The nymphs live in fast water, but crawl toward quiet water along stream and river edges before emergence. The nymph takes a grip on a bottom rock, splits its skin, and the dun emerges there. Then the insect struggles to the surface with its wings beginning to unfold.

Trout nose into water 1 to 2 feet deep and feed on the swimming emergers during these Pale Evening Dun hatches. When you see trout working right next to shore, especially in the evening, suspect that's what they're taking. Rather than tying on a dry fly, try a Partridge & Yellow soft-hackle, Pale Watery Dun Flymph, or Light Cahill winged wet, all in size 12 to 14.

You can fish from the streambank, casting a few feet out and downstream, letting the fly swing back in toward the edge. But it's usually best to wade out 20 feet or so, if you can, and make the cast across stream and right to the edge. Let the fly drift downstream and sink slowly, without any action added. Often trout work these hatches with their dorsal fins out of water, or they take with their noses tipped down and their tails breaking the surface. When you see this happening, it's usually when light is almost gone, and it's easy to mistake for surface feeding. It's usually not. Present a wet fly to an individual trout, just as you would a dry. Since the trout are looking down, it's possible to float a dry right over their backs without getting any takes.

Many other mayfly types emerge in open water, but are prone to getting stuck either in their shucks or in the surface film. I've pointed out earlier that this happens primarily among smaller species. The surface film becomes a major barrier to them because they lack the mass to bust through it in a hurry. It also happens most of the time on relatively smooth water, because surface tension is a factor there. In bumpy water the surface is broken, and insects are less hindered by it. Mayfly emerger fishing is something you'll do most often with small flies, on flats and the tailouts of pools.

Little Olives (*Baetis*) and Pale Morning Duns (*Ephemerella*) are the most common candidates for emerger fishing. Their populations are heaviest in the micro-niches abundant in spring creeks and tailwaters. Such waters prompt intense hatches. Trout become selective, even if fishing pressure is light, which on such favorable waters, it's often not. You've got to key in on the right fly that matches the correct stage of the emerging mayfly in order to fool many trout. It's surprising how often the emerger stage, not the perfect dun, turns out to be the right stage to match on smooth water.

It's also surprising how often a wet fly fished just beneath the surface, or dressed and fished in the film itself, turns out to be the right fly to match the emerger. The rule for choosing between a submerged wet fly and a floating wet is familiar: Look for bubbles left behind in rises. If they're there, the trout took something floating, and you should dress your fly with floatant. If bubbles are absent, the trout took subsurface, and you should dress your leader to a foot or so from the fly, but leave the fly untreated.

It's easier to describe this on paper than it is to work it out on water. A better rule might be this: If you get into rising trout and can't take them on dry flies, first try a wet dressed with floatant; if that doesn't work, try dressing your leader with floatant, but fish the fly a few inches deep. If all else fails, try a wet or soft-hackle on the swing beneath the rises. You'll be surprised how often that works when everything else fails. If you're like me, you'll feel like you're cheating when you catch rising trout this way. It seems that when trout rise, they ought to be caught on dry flies. But they often appear to be taking on the surface, and instead are taking so near the top they send apparent rise-rings to the surface. Never let catching fish on wet flies rather than drys subtract from the pleasure of having trout dancing around at the end of your line and leader. Solving such a difficult situation, no matter the type of fly with which you do it, is a satisfaction in itself.

The setup for fishing wet flies to working trout is precisely what you would use to fish dry flies on the same water. It's easy to make the mistake of not respecting the trout because you're fishing wet, not dry, and to therefore use a tippet that's too short or too heavy. My rule for this kind of fishing, over rising but refusing trout, is simple on paper and on the water: Whenever I switch flies, I check to make sure my tippet is at least 3 feet long and 5X or 6X, depending on the size fly I'm fishing. If the tippet has become shorter, then I add a new one before tying on that new fly—this applies to drys and emergers as well as wets. That new tippet alone might solve many of these situations for you, no matter what type of fly you try.

Try to match your wet fly to the prevailing dun, which you should capture and examine in your hand, not at 15 feet. Such close examination will often reveal that you've missed the color completely, and that you're using a fly one or two hook sizes larger than the real thing. Usually you'll want to be fishing a Little Olive flymph or a Partridge & Green soft-hackle in size 18 or 20, or else a Pale Watery Dun flymph or Partridge & Yellow in size 16 or 18. One of those on a long 6X tippet will usually take at least a few trout for you when they're fussy about emerging mayflies. Trying two of them on the same cast will up the odds that you solve the problem faster, which can be a big benefit, especially when light is failing.

When you're fishing wet flies during mayfly hatches, you'll always increase your chances by collecting whatever natural might be around and matching it as nearly as you can in size and color with your wet fly. This Pale Evening Dun will hatch so close to nightfall that you might never notice it, or the trout feed on it so close to the surface that it appears a dry would be better than a wet. That's usually not true.

Presentation should be exactly what you would use to fish a dry fly to rising trout on the same water. Cast upstream and across to the feeding trout if they're in water that is at all rough: a riffle or fast run. Use the reach cast or even the downstream wiggle cast if the shape of the currents demands it, usually on flats and pools. Strive for drag-free floats, though some tension will not kill your chances with a wet as it would with a dry. Trout will take a wet

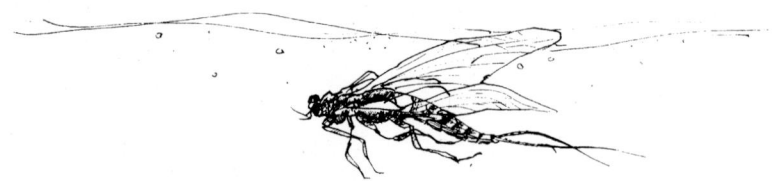

Mayfly duns are normally imitated with dry flies, but so many drown during an emergence that trout often feed selectively on the tangled duns just beneath the top. Wet flies are more effective when that happens.

fly with some movement; they'll rarely accept a dry fly or surface film emerger that drags even minutely. Presentation, in this type of fishing, is at least as important as pattern.

Duns that drown during an emergence become perfect candidates for imitation with all sorts of wet flies. The insects lose their composure. Their wings are free and trailing in the currents. Legs and tails tremble with every movement of the water. You want a fly that is similarly disorganized and that responds to the same currents. Soft-hackles do it best, which is probably one reason they're so effective even when no particular insect activity is happening. Trout are accustomed to seeing a wide variety of drowned insects drifting their way. They'll often take a sunk imitation whenever they're not feeding selectively. You can use a soft-hackle effectively between hatches, or as an imitation during a hatch.

The rule is easy to emphasize: If a hatch is going on, or if one has just ended, or if it's scheduled to happen an hour or so later in the day, try a soft-hackle roughly the size and color of the dun. Fish it down and across the currents, on a traditional wet-fly presentation, but use mends to slow its drift and give it all the freedom you can. That's about all. Be sure that you fish the fly slowly enough that you feel it coaxing the trout. When you accomplish that, you'll begin to get hits. If you like, try two wet flies, or cheat and fish a wet fly that imitates the dun and a nymph that resembles the natural nymph. If you fish nymphs like wets, it's easy to pretend they're wets.

Mayfly spinners are mysteries to me. I've rarely gotten into the kinds of spinner falls that prompt trout to feed greedily. When I do, it's usually on a midsummer evening, just before dark, over the flat parts of the stream. Even mayflies that are about to die are smart enough to settle their eggs onto the smooth water upstream from a riffle rather than right into the midst of the maelstrom. It increases the next generation's chances for survival.

In my limited experience with spinners, a sparse wet-fly dressing, whether soft-hackle, flymph, or winged wet, is more effective than a spent dry fly. I fish these wets on slow swings, usually on flats and tailouts, right through rises. I try to collect a natural from the water or out of the air and match it as closely as I can in terms of size and color.

Mayfly spinners are elegant, and they fall to the water often. When they do, trout take them with subtle sipping rises. It's often better to fish a sparse wet fly roughly the size and color of the natural, rather than a spent spinner dry. Because such falls happen so often in failing light, it's easier to detect felt takes to a wet than it is to notice it when a trout takes a dry fly that you have trouble keeping in sight.

You should do the same, because I'm not going to be very instructive here. I'd rather give you guidelines on the steps to take during your own spinner falls: Collect a natural, select a sparse wet fly that looks a little like the insect might when drowned, fish the fly as the natural might drift on the currents when drowned. That's all.

Let me know how it works for you.

Chapter Twenty

Emerging and Egg-Laying Caddis

When I first met Randy Stetzer, who is now well known for his gorgeous book *Flies: The Best One Thousand*, he was still a youngster sneaking along the banks of the brawling Deschutes River, plucking trout from its troubled waters. He sat behind me and watched me fish for half an hour one evening, without letting me know he was there until the fishing was over. I don't know where Randy got all his discipline.

It was an accident, but I was catching trout like crazy.

I had arrived at a brisk riffle corner just before dark and beheld the strangest sight. Big trout ghosted into the air, hung there, then tipped over to arrow back in without even making a disturbance. They were simply big, black forms up in the air over the riffle, visible for an instant and then gone. A lot of caddis adults were in the air with them, but I knew trout that size weren't flying around trying to catch caddisflies. Tiddlers leap for flying caddis, but big trout don't.

The caddis were tan, size 16 or so. I'd already tried dry flies earlier, and they'd failed me. I didn't know what to do, but I knew I had to try something subsurface. The only fly I saw in my fly boxes that was tan and size 16 was a roughly tied and slightly weighted Gold-Ribbed Hare's Ear Nymph. I tied it on for lack of any other idea. I was fishing my $7^1/_2$-foot Leonard rod—it was new back then—and at the time was deep into reading Sylvester Nemes's *The Soft-Hackled Fly* for the first time. I hadn't gotten around to tying any of his soft-hackled flies at that early moment, but I'd paid attention to the greased-line method he described.

I flipped that nymph out all of 20 feet into the riffle, slightly upstream, and mended the line while it drifted downstream into the area where those occasional trout lofted out of the water to hang briefly in the air. It worked, though I didn't know why at the time. Several trout intercepted the fly with

When you're on the water and caddis adults are in the air, but trout are not interested in dry flies, it's a good time to check your assumptions about the level at which they're feeding. Those adult caddis might be a sign that egg-laying activity is taking place and that trout are feeding on diving and swimming adults a few inches down rather than on top. They might also be an indication that a hatch is happening, and trout are taking more rising pupae than they are floating adults. In either case, switching to a wet fly—or if you prefer and it's legal, two or three of them—might provide you some surprising action.

solid, sullen tugs. When they felt the bite of the hook, they squirted back into the air, then dashed down with the powerful Deschutes River current. I babied them on that rod and a 5X tippet; it took a long time to land each one of them. I released about ten before it got too dark to stay there and keep casting. The trout averaged a couple of pounds; the largest weighed at least 3.

When I reeled up and quit, I turned to find Randy sitting quietly behind me, watching. We talked for a while and have been friends ever since. He knows now that I don't always know what I'm doing when it comes to fishing. Back then he made the mistake of believing that because I fished a bamboo rod and hooked all those trout on a tiny fly fished a few inches deep, I knew what I was doing and had the situation solved. It wasn't entirely true, though I didn't tell Randy that.

I'm still not sure whether those trout were taking caddis pupae on their way up for emergence, or gravid female adults diving down to deposit their eggs. The trout hanging in air make me suspect, in retrospect, that they were chasing caddis pupae on their way toward the top. Sometimes a trout intercepts a pupa just beneath the surface, and its momentum carries it right into the air, where it hangs until it runs out of thrust, then falls back in. This is still speculation on my part. Those Deschutes trout might have mistaken that scruffy Hare's Ear for a pupa; they might have mistaken it for an adult swimming toward the bottom. Whichever mistake they made, they made it so pleasantly and so often that I was able to impress a young man who would later become famous.

That's a worthwhile accomplishment even if I don't know which stage of the insect caused it.

I've done it often since—not impress Randy, but catch trout on sunk flies, usually wets, when caddis are in the air. It usually happens just at evening, with a small wet fly, fished in or near rough water on a very slow swing. It usually happens with a fly that I've selected based on the size and color of the adults in the air, not on any speculation I might make about the elusive pupae in the water.

The caddis pupa is a transitional stage, hard to collect. Sometimes you'll see them crawling up your waders, using you as a launching pad for emergence into aerial life. But most often, you'll never see them unless you kill a trout and examine its stomach, which I rarely do, or use a throat pump, which I don't often do. In truth, the single best way to observe caddis pupae is to let trout do the collecting, and by using a throat pump during a hatch. Some of the pupae you'll be able to observe will still be alive.

Caddis come in four fishable stages: larva, pupa, emerging adult, and egg-laying adult. In the larval stage they live on the bottom, some in cases constructed of sand and tiny pebbles, others in crude shelters, some without any armor at all. They could be imitated with wets tied on heavy hooks and fished on or near the bottom, especially in water just 2 to 3 feet deep. But caddis larvae are almost always in the province of strike indicator and split-shot nymphing.

Caddis pupae are the ultimate insect for imitation with soft-hackled flies. The naturals rise from the bottom with their legs kicking and antennae quivering. Their wing cases slant back. Their bodies, shaped like stubby cigars, are often bright. The fibers of a soft-hackle, collapsed around a silk or floss body and working with every tendril of current, must look almost exactly like one of them.

The difficulty with caddis pupae is getting a look at one in order to select an imitation. They leave the bottom, kick and drift to the top, escape as adults. That's it; it's a quick transition. Trout see it happen, but you don't. Unless you're aware of this stage of the caddis, it's easy to entirely miss the opportunity it represents. Once you're aware of it, however, it's easy to capitalize on it.

Whenever you see caddis in the air but can't catch trout with dry flies, think soft-hackles or flymphs. That's the critical first step. Once you begin to do so, you'll start solving situations that puzzled you before. The second step is to capture a natural adult, if you can, and select a wet fly about the same

In the caddis life cycle, trout feed more heavily on pupae rising to the surface and adults diving down to lay their eggs than they do on adults riding the surface itself. The pupa and diving adult stages are prime for imitation with wet flies.

size and approximate color. This often works because many adults arise from pupae about the same size and color they turn into later. It also works because the caddis in the air might be ovipositing. If they are, then a wet fly the same size and color works because that is precisely what the trout are taking beneath the surface.

Adult caddis are often a different color than the pupae from which they ascend. In that case, a wet fly the same color as the adult might fail you if trout are focused on pupae. That's why it's often wise to try a couple of flies on the same cast at caddis time. It lets you cut through to the right color combination in a shorter time. A good combination to try might be a March Brown Spider at the point and a Partridge & Orange or Partridge & Green on the dropper, both in the approximate size of the caddis you see in the air. If you don't mind the extra foolery, and it's legal where you're fishing, try all three at the same time, or add a flymph the same size and color as the adult. This reasoning is based on the most common trout-stream caddis. As a vague rule, gray adults come from green pupae, and tan and brown adults come from green, cream, or orange pupae.

Adults always come from pupae a half size or so larger, because they've got that final skin to shed. That's why a soft-hackle about the size of the adult, or even a size larger, will usually work.

When matching caddis pupae with wet flies, there are fewer variables than you might expect. Most of the time one of the partridge soft-hackle patterns in the right size will solve the situation, because the pupae run nearly the same size as the adults and in a narrow range of colors: olive, amber-brown, tan, and cream. You'll do well if you reach for a soft-hackle whenever caddis are in the air but you can't catch trout on dry flies.

Caddis pupae rise from the bottom with some vigor. They have hairy swimming paddles on their legs, and also extrude air under the pupal skin to buoy them up. As a consequence, they rise quickly to the top. You should fish your soft-hackle imitation on the swing, inches deep. Let it drift downstream and cut across the current. Never swim it upstream; naturals don't do that. They swim toward the surface, and aim into the current, but actually drift downstream while rising.

Adult caddis, at the moment of emergence, are of little value to the wet-fly fisher. Many pupae drift beneath the surface film for a while, and it can be worthwhile to fish your pupal imitations very shallow, even greasing your leader to fish them inches deep. But caddis don't often get stuck in the film the way mayfly emergers do. Caddis get right on with things once they've gotten a grip on the surface. They hatch, perhaps sit on the surface briefly, but usually fly off at once. Such abrupt emergence might be the reason trout so often take caddis with splashy rises.

Egg-laying adults are another matter. The two most important groups of stream caddis, Gray Sedges (*Rhyacophila*) and Spotted Sedges (*Hydropsyche*), both display the same behavior: diving into the water, swimming down to lay their eggs on the bottom. This interests trout. When it's going on, they feed subsurface a lot more than they do on top, though enough trout rise to the adults to make it look like that's where all the feeding is happening. The average fisherman, seeing adult caddis in the air and trout appearing to rise to take them, does the natural thing by selecting a dry-fly imitation. When it doesn't work, he runs through a long litany of changes in both pattern and presentation. He doesn't think to switch to a wet fly.

Once you've made that switch to a wet, you'll begin catching some trout even if your pattern and presentation are way off. It's no accident, when you see adult caddis in the air and see splashy rises, that you begin to take trout as soon as you tie on a wet fly or two, and fish them with the old-fashioned chuck-and-chance-it swing. Trout are feeding on the adults that you see, but they're taking them down where you can't see it happen.

This activity usually takes place in water that is fairly brisk but not broken on top. Runs and pools with some movement enjoy the most caddis egg-depositing flights. Slick tailouts, just upstream from the whitewater of a riffle or cascade, often get the heaviest flights. Female caddis deposit their eggs just upstream from the heavy water.

It's easy to select a wet-fly pattern when you suspect trout are taking adult caddis subsurface. Just capture a natural adult or observe one on a limb or blade of grass. I often sweep my hat through streamside vegetation in order to get a look at whatever caddis might be active. The hat will often end up crawling with caddis adults; they'll be stunned long enough by their sudden capture that you can get a brief look at them.

Most of the time they'll have either gray wings and olive bodies, or tan wings and cream to orange bodies. They'll be size 12 to 16. Many times your

Caddis pupae are plump, their bodies somewhat bulbous, with no tails. Their wing cases are held back along their sides. When loose in the currents, their legs and antennae work in the water, opening and closing around the body. They're prime insects on which to base selection of a soft-hackled wet fly, in this case a Partridge & Green.

Adult caddis are taken by trout much more often while swimming down to lay their eggs on the bottom than they are sitting primly atop the surface. Though their presence might be an indication to fish a dry fly, and you would always be smart to try one, it's more likely you'll do better by switching to a soft-hackle, flymph, or traditional winged wet fly about the size and color of the natural adult.

hat will contain a mix of species that cover nearly the entire spectrum of colors and sizes. You can use a Partridge & Green or Partridge & Orange softhackle to match them. It's often better, however, to resort to one of two traditional patterns, the Leadwing Coachman or the Hare's Ear. These have wings; so do the naturals. That's a good reason why these two dressings have worked so well in streams for so many years: One matches the Gray Sedge, the other the Spotted Sedge, among the most abundant trout-stream caddis.

Soft-hackles or winged wets can be fished on the traditional downstream swing for adult caddis: chuck-and-chance-it. You can improve your odds by selecting the correct casting angle based on the speed of the current. You can

By carefully choosing your casting angle in relation to the speed of the current, then by mending and tending your line to speed or slow the drift of the fly, you can greatly improve your odds over an old-fashioned chuck-and-chance-it presentation when caddis adults are in the air and on the water.

increase your take again by mending and tending line in order to slow the drift of the flies. When caddis adults are in the air, diving to the water, and inciting trout to feed with splashy takes, the main thing is to get a wet fly, or a brace of them, out there and slowly drifting around and down on the current. Once you've learned to do that, you'll be a long way toward solving caddis situations.

These ovipositing caddis situations nearly always happen in midsummer, and right at evening, when it's already dark enough to make it difficult to figure out what's going on. Approaching darkness drives you toward panic to find the right dry fly quickly. It never works. Switching to an appropriate wet is the true solution.

When female caddis dive into the water and trout feed on them without breaking the surface, I often find it better to use an appropriate flymph, selected to match the size and color of the natural in the air. Pattern is not nearly as important as presentation. The Hidy Subsurface Swing will usually trick the trout, if you can pinpoint a single trout or get into position to fish a pod. You can place the fly a few feet above and beyond an individual trout and give it that tug that pops it underwater before swinging it across in front of the fish. Or you can cast to the general area of a few rising fish, tug the fly under, then let it swing through them.

Either way you'll enjoy some action on the wet fly. If you stick to dry flies when adult caddis are out, it's discouraging how often you'll fail to take any trout at all. That's why my last simple caddis rule is this: Whenever caddis are out, I think wet flies, not drys. I might try dry flies first, but I won't fish them long if they fail to fool trout.

Chapter Twenty-One

Wet Flies and Stoneflies

The largest and most famous of the stoneflies are not the most important in wet-fly fishing. Giant Salmonflies, and the more beautiful and only slightly smaller Golden Stones, crawl to shore and leave the water as nymphs before the adults emerge from the nymphal skin. This usually happens after dark. Consequently, most effective fishing is done with heavily weighted nymphs tumbled right along the bottom, or later with big and brushy dry flies fished right along the river edges.

Many smaller stonefly groups, less famous to nymph and dry-fly fishermen, fall into the province of wet-fly fishing at times, though far from as often as either mayflies or caddis. Knowing about these stoneflies—when and how how to fish wet flies that imitate them—can extend your fishing season and increase your catch.

Smaller stoneflies fall into three rough groups. The first to emerge are the Little Brown Stones. Some hatch so early that they can be seen clambering about on snowbanks near streams. Trout are aware of them and will sometimes feed on them in water that is still frigid. The more important hatches of Little Brown Stones take place in February, March, and April, after things have warmed up at least a bit. In American fly-fishing literature, the March Brown is a mayfly, East or West. In British literature, the March Brown is historically an early stonefly hatch.

The second stonefly group of importance is the Little Yellow Stones, more often called Yellow Sallies. These come off in late spring through midsummer, depending on the latitude and elevation of the stream that you fish. The earliest of them overlap with Little Brown Stones. Some of them trickle off far into fall.

The final group, and also the last to emerge, is the Little Green Stones, also called Olive Sallies. These prefer forested headwater streams. They are the pale sparks of light that catch the sun, gliding down toward runs and flats of tiny mountain waters to drop their eggs. They begin hatching in late summer and continue on into October. Much of their activity that interests trout takes place in late afternoon and evening.

Nymphs of these three groups migrate to shore to emerge, just like their larger relatives. And like those more famous groups, few of them are able to swim much more than feebly. But Yellow Sally nymphs are fair swimmers. When making underwater migrations, they stick close to the bottom, but do not necessarily crawl over it as Golden Stone and Salmonfly nymphs do. Instead, they often swim toward shore and gather there in great numbers, waiting for their moment to crawl out and emerge. Trout are aware of this. A wet fly in the appropriate size and color, such as a Light Cahill, fished very near shore, can take trout when you see adults of these smaller stoneflies active in streamside vegetation. The adults in the bushes are your indication that nymphs are gathered along the edges.

The key, as with so many other insect groups, is to see adults and make the association to their nymphs, and then to fish with shallow wet flies in approximately the same sizes and colors. If possible, wade out from shore and cast back in toward it, at an angle downstream. Give the fly a few moments to sink in the water right along the edge of the stream. Then begin to coax it out, alternating a smooth swing with some slight action imparted by twitching the rod tip. This method works particularly well in situations where you can make your cast up under tree limbs and bushes that overhang water with some brisk movement to it.

I've also used the method to fine effect on Oregon's Owyhee River tailwater, along willow-lined edges, or grassy banks with few trees in sight. Yellow Sallies hatch in abundance there in spring, April and May. When the hatch begins, and just a few adults are visible, it's an indication that nymphs have moved into shallow water along the banks, and trout have followed to feed on them. The Owyhee is broad and shallow in places, easy to wade, and there are no power-demand surges to make wading dangerous, as there might be on other tailwaters.

My favorite fly to imitate the Yellow Sally nymph has become Leisenring and Hidy's Tups Nymph, from their book *The Art of Tying the Wet Fly & Fishing the Flymph*. It's clearly a nymph dressing; that fine book includes a few of Leisenring's favorite nymphs. They're tied in a style close to, and perhaps based upon, G. E. M. Skues's *thorax nymphs*, which stride the border between wet flies and nymphs. Since I don't mind crossing that border when it's expedient, I often add a brass bead to a size 16 Tups, but I still consider it somewhat of a wet fly because of the way I fish it.

On the Owyhee, that way is to wade out well away from the bank I want to fish, then to cast back in toward it, placing the Tups as near to it as possible. The cast is usually a bit upstream, straight across, or slightly

Yellow Sally nymphs (Isoperlidae) are unique among stoneflies in that they're able to swim, at times fairly briskly. This ability makes them more useful as models for wet flies, rather than nymphs, because trout are accustomed to taking them at large and swimming rather than dead drift and right along the bottom.

Though Leisenring and Hidy's Tups is a nymph, it's from their book on wet flies, and if it's fished as a wet fly, it can be considered one, at least in my book. It's an excellent imitation for Yellow Sally nymphs, which are unique among stoneflies for their ability to swim. If you have something against nymphs, especially ones with beads at their heads, a Light Cahill is a traditional wet fly that works well for the same insect.

downstream. The big pools on the Owyhee are almost creepingly slow; that's the same pace I want my imitation to take as it sinks a bit and drifts slowly near the bank. Takes will be subtle. Most often the only sign that something is happening out there is a slight tightening of the line. Though the usual advice in such a situation is to wait it out and let the trout set the hook itself, in such slow water the trout will often eject the fly if you give it sufficient time. Instead, set the hook at the first sign a trout has taken the fly. By the time your line moves, the trout you have on is already trying to get off.

Trout in such placid water as this on Oregon's Owyhee River often hang out near the edges, taking whatever migrates to them from the water or falls to them from the terrestrial environment. When Yellow Sally nymphs are on the march for emergence, trout are susceptible to a wet fly or thorax-style nymph allowed to drift slowly right along the bank.

Small stonefly adults are just as important as their nymphs to the wet-fly fisherman. They hang out in vegetation near the edge of the stream; they make little sorties out over the water; and they often fall in. Trout appreciate this when it happens. They wait at the edges for all sorts of things that venture onto the water, arriving from either flights over the water or falls from the land. Little Brown Stones, Yellow Sallies, and Olive Sallies, in both their nymph and adult configurations, all arrive from both directions.

The accepted imitation for Little Brown Stones is what the British call a February Red, a soft-hackled wet tied with a claret silk body and grouse hackle. Use it in sizes 14 and 16. The Grouse & Orange is one of the oldest and most famous soft-hackles. In the same sizes, it's very effective for Little Brown Stones. You can fish these wets against the edges, the same as you would fish wet flies to imitate the nymphs. If adults are out and scooting over the water, as they often do in early spring, it can be better to cast soft-hackles upstream and across to working trout, fishing them just as you would dry flies, except submerged a few inches.

Midsummer Little Yellow Stones are a larger puzzle. Until recently it's always been supposed that all of them crawl out to emerge. Even the scientific literature agrees with this. But lately, professional aquatic entomologist Rick Hafele and I have noticed that some species seem to hatch out in the open water of big rivers. Rick tracked down some recent notes in scientific journals speculating about this behavior. Our findings on the water have backed it up. We've noticed it often in our own fishing. Yellow Sally adults appear on the surface of the water, but are not visible in the air. It has all the

Yellow Sally stonefly adults are as often good models for wet flies as they are for drys. It might be wise, as always, to try a dry fly when you see trout working them, but it's also smart to go straight to a wet fly if the dry fly fails. Trout seem to take more of them drowned than they do afloat.

appearance of a mid-water hatch, though most stonefly specialists call it egg-depositing behavior.

My most interesting moment with this activity took place a season ago on Oregon's Willamette River. The river is broad, placid, flowing slowly over a gravel bottom, braiding itself around cottonwood islands. It has excellent populations of Little Yellow Stones. One June day, I anchored my drift boat in the middle of a long but fairly shallow run, with trout rising all around. I expected a mayfly hatch but couldn't see any on the water. Still, I tried the standard dry flies that usually work for me on that stretch of river.

Nothing happened. I examined the surface, saw nothing on it. The only insects around were a few Little Yellow Stones on the water. They didn't add up to enough to interest the trout, or so I thought. I kept on trying various mayfly and caddis dressings for a while, finally approached that minor panic that is the result of anchoring in the middle of a bunch of rising trout, then not being able to catch any.

In a surprisingly calm moment amid my growing anxiety, I took another look at the scattered stoneflies, then peered into my fly boxes. Nothing there looked at all like them. The nearest thing was a row of Light Cahill wet flies in size 12. Since the steady current sweeping around the boat would make fishing a wet fly easy, I decided to fish one idly, on the swing, while trying to puzzle out what the trout were doing and what I ought to be doing about it.

What they did was climb all over that wet. They took it on the swing. They took it if I placed it softly above a rise and let it drift along like a floating leaf, free from any influence from the line or leader, greased-line style. A couple of apparently dumb ones took it after the end of its swing, when it dangled straight downstream from the boat, hanging against the current on a tight line.

It was obvious there was a link between the success of the Light Cahill and those scant Little Yellow Stones on the water. They were the same size and approximately the same color. Most nymphs tied to imitate Little Yellow Stone immatures would look exactly like a Light Cahill wet fly if you just nipped off the Cahill's wing. I stopped casting and let my fly hang straight downstream from the boat, the line tight in the current, long enough to watch one or two stoneflies in the air, and notice that they seemed to be going up and away from the river, not descending to it to lay any eggs. It had the appearance of an emergence, not an egg-laying flight. I'd have looked longer, but my gazing got interrupted by a whack.

That's when Rick Hafele and I got together and discussed the apparent open-water emergence of Yellow Sallies. Nothing is certain yet. We've got to get out and fish the hatch a few more times. We've got to stop fishing when it's going on, spend time watching into the water to try to see how the transformation from nymph to adult might take place, or how ovipositing females might appear suddenly coming out of the water with no evidence about how they got there. To date, all we know is that some of the insects appear to be emerging in open water rather than crawling to shore, and that a wet fly fishes far better than a dry when this kind of activity is happening.

Not surprisingly, the same two fly patterns that work for the nymph also work for the adult, and I've found no need to tie anything specific beyond them. The Tups Nymph and Light Cahill wet seem to be all that is needed, though I'm certain further inventions based more exactly upon the naturals would work even better.

Little Green Stones are among my favorite hatches. They begin drifting through the air over the plunge pools of my home coastal streams in late summer, when the water has dropped and trout are eager to feed on or near the surface. It seems that a dry fly would work best under these conditions, but it's rarely true. Trout get bashful about coming all the way to the top, perhaps because they've been harassed all summer by hungry kingfishers. If you cast a dry, trout will often come short. You get lots of splashes and think you're screwing up, failing to get the hook set. The truth is that the trout change their minds a few inches from the fly and fail to take it.

When this happens, I switch to a Partridge & Green or Partridge & Yellow, fish it just like the dry fly, and the results are vastly different. I described in the Introduction the first time I tried a soft-hackle on my home waters. It was one of the most exciting days I've spent on any small stream.

When small stoneflies are active, a Partridge & Yellow (from left), Partridge & Green, or Grouse & Orange soft-hackle should offer a suitable imitation, depending on the color of the natural insect.

The key to this kind of wet-fly fishing is to get up close, cast short, and follow the drift of your line tip, leader point, and fly as carefully as you can. Sometimes you'll see the take. Other times you'll just see the line tip dart forward an inch. When the take is truly subtle, you'll see no more than a change in the way the leader enters the water. It helps, when fishing soft-hackles on small water, to straighten your leader and dress the back half of it with floatant. This hangs the fly up higher in the water, and also gives you something to watch as the drift of the fly unfolds.

As with most of wet-fly fishing, an effective approach to stoneflies requires just a few flies, the majority of them carried and used for other reasons anyway. You should already have the Partridge series of soft-hackles and the Light Cahill wet fly in your boxes. Add the Tups Nymph, and you've got all that you'll ever need if trout suddenly insist on an imitation of this handsome order of insects.

Chapter Twenty-Two

Wet Flies for Midges, Alders, and Others

Ever since I fished with Sylvester Nemes on the Madison River below Bear Trap Canyon, and he caught so many trout with his Syl's Midge soft-hackle during a hatch of tiny black chironomids, I've been careful to carry a few of that fly. It doesn't pay off more than a few times each season. But when it does, it's always at times when nothing else will work. It's often difficult to match midges on the surface. As soon as you switch to a fly that steps under, however, you'll begin catching trout that are too snotty to take anything up top.

I tried Syl's Midge on a recent trip to a frigid February river in Oregon. It was too early to expect any insects to be hatching, or any fish to be feeding. But the weather had broken a bit from winter, and just getting out on a stream would make it a successful day. So I went. To my surprise, fish were feeding when I got there.

The water temperature was still 38 degrees, seemingly too cold for anything at all to be happening. But a few scattered trout poked their noses through the surface. It took a long time to tell what they were taking. I finally had to get my own nose down near the water, snoop right in the film, before I noticed tiny midges—smaller than size 20—emerging from their shucks, floating briefly on the current, buzzing off into the nippy air. Since nothing else was around, I knew the trout must be feeding on them, despite their tiny size.

I didn't have anything small enough to match them. But I did have half a dozen Syl's Midges, no more than peacock herl wound on the shanks of size 18 hooks, with a single turn of gray partridge hackle at the head of each.

Syl's Midge is far from imitative for midges, but it captures their essence, looks alive in the water, and is usually more effective during a midge hatch than the most accurate dry-fly imitation. Fish it on short casts, so you can either see or feel takes when they happen.

Midge adults are simple compositions of long bodies, short wings, and legs that are usually gangly. They're also small and are taken underwater by trout as often as they're taken on top.

The flies were wispy. When wet, they would size right down to tiny. I tied one on, waded to the edge of the riffle that fed into the pool where the scattered trout rose. I cast straight across into fairly fast water, but let the fly wash down into slower water, then angle across toward my side so slowly that it almost hung idly just under the surface.

It was easy to tell about the takes. The trout took the fly so near the surface that I could see their rises welling up right where my line tip pointed. With such a small fly, and the fragile 6X tippet required to fish it, I didn't

The ancient and effective Alder wet fly is still the most effective imitation, far better than any floating pattern I've ever tried for the natural alderfly adult.

An alderfly adult caught in the act of laying its eggs. They are deposited on leaves and reeds overhanging streams or stillwaters, so when the larvae emerge they fall directly into water. The adults are awkward flyers, and often fall to the water, usually just after the sun starts warming the air on spring and early summer days.

bother setting the hook. I just lifted the rod slowly, in that constant query that is so important to the fisher of wet flies: "Are you out there?"

Since the rises were visible, the answer was nearly a constant, "Yes, here I am leaping."

The trout were not large. But I was happy just to be out. I was enormously happy to be casting over rises and getting greedy acceptance of the closest fly I had to matching those midges.

I've run into dark midges often, especially when the weather is marginal for anything else. Syl's Midge works wonders whenever the naturals are black or dark olive. But it's commonly overlooked that midges arrive at times in a bright green. When you run into that situation, you'll have a hard time finding a pattern that works better than the standard Partridge & Green softhackle in the tiniest sizes. Sometimes a size 16 will do it. More often you'll need a size 18. That's about as small as you can tie them, since it's difficult

The sort of alder-lined pond where leaf packs are thick in the shallows, and alderfly larvae find lots of places to prowl and hunt midge larvae, mayfly nymphs, and crustaceans such as scuds. The larvae are not important to fly fishers, but alderfly adults fly clumsily out of the same trees, sink soon after they make the mistake of landing on water, and are taken greedily by cruising trout.

to find partridge feathers, up around the neck of the bird, any smaller than that. But you can always substitute snipe or starling feathers, depending on the color you want in your imitation.

Blood midges are bright red, and less common. They're normally found only in lakes and ponds. You'd be surprised how often a size 14 or 16 Partridge & Orange will take trout when they cruise and feed randomly on midges in stillwater. Fish the flies very slowly. Midge pupae are not dashing swimmers, though the largest of them can scoot right from the bottom to the top, usually without any hesitation along the way. If you fish your imitations on a fast swing in moving water, or with anything but a slow retrieve in lakes, you'll usually turn trout away rather than take them.

Alderflies look like caddis. They've got the same tent-shaped wings with bodies tucked beneath them. Their bodies and heads are blocky; they lack the delicateness and lightness that most caddisflies can brag about. When in the air, alderflies don't flit about like caddis adults. Instead they fly awkwardly, often in descending arcs out over streams, lakes, or ponds. When they land, they hit with a smack.

Most winged insects are so light and buoyant that they float, especially on the still surface of a lake or pond. Alderflies do not. They're so compact, have such a high density, that when they land on water, they usually *blub* right under. You'll see them in the air. You'll see them crawling around on floating logs. You'll see trout taking with swirls wherever you see alderflies touch down. Naturally, you'll try dry flies. But they seldom work. That's because trout feed on alderfly adults submerged, not floating.

Alderflies are perfect candidates for imitation with wet flies. Charles Kingsley tied the original Alder wet fly back in 1858, and fished it on his home River Itchen. Alderflies are less commonly important in moving water than they are in stillwater, but they can be found wherever the water is slow and currents are packed with leaf fall from streamside trees. In such conditions, they become very important. They hatch in late May, June, and early July, when the warm sun comes out to rev their motors. I've seen them from size 16 on the Hiwassee Tailwater in Tennessee to size 10 on tree-lined ponds in Oregon.

Alderflies take to the air only when it's sunny and warm. When they launch themselves from high in the trees and their heavy bodies cause them to spiral down, they land on the water as often as they do anywhere else. That is fatal.

Most trout that take an Alder subsurface are more satisfied if it is merely allowed to sink. I usually cast it to rises, getting the fly there as quickly as I can after the fish has shown itself. Chances are it has taken a natural alder that has just gone under. It will rarely be unhappy to be attracted by a slight splat, and turn back into its own rise to find another alderfly descending helplessly toward the bottom.

If you give that wet fly immediate action by beginning a retrieve as soon as it hits the water, the trout is suddenly seeing something it has never witnessed before: an athletic alderfly adult swimming away in a hurry. You might fool a few trout that way, but you'll fool a lot more by simply letting the fly sink.

Of course, you've got to get the fly back somehow, in order to cast it again, if the trout fails to notice and take it on the sink. In that case, I retrieve with slow strips from the line hand while watching the surface for other rises nearby. If I see one, I loft the fly and place it quickly into the new set of rise-rings, then let it sink. Once in awhile I'll hook a fish on the retrieve, often enough that it's worthwhile keeping the fly in the water, on a slow retrieve, while waiting for a rise to expose the location of the next trout.

My experience with fishing Alder wets on streams is thin. I know the natural adults don't swim there any better than they do in lakes. I've had my best luck fishing the wet Alder on a slow swing, right where a current tongue peters out into a deep pool. But I'm never sure when I do this whether I'm imitating a natural alderfly or just showing the trout a fly that looks like something good to eat, as likely to be mistaken for a dark caddisfly as for an alderfly.

I'm pretty sure that when winged black ants are out, trout respond well to a wet Black Gnat because it looks a lot like the real thing. When carpenter ants are in the air on their annual summer dispersal flights, trout see a lot of them on the water, but take most of them beneath the surface. This is especially true on tree-shrouded forest streams. Ants are in the air, on the leaves of trees, crawling all over streamside stones. You never see one on the water, but trout see lots of them submerged beneath the water.

Though the Black Gnat was not designed specifically as a winged ant imitation, it makes a fair impression of one on trout, or at least they take it readily enough when ants are in the air and on the water.

Winged carpenter ants make their dispersal flights in late spring and early summer. Many of them land on water, usually forested lakes and ponds or small streams. When they do, a wet fly can be far more effective than a dry.

Whenever I see terrestrials such as winged ants and big black beetles out and crawling about, I think of the Black Gnat wet fly in size 10 and 12. That's large, but trout never seem to mind. They're used to seeing the occasional dark bit of food delivered to them on the current. They'll usually take on any sort of presentation unless you let the fly swing too fast across or against the current. Fish it down and around, let it swing slowly. Give it some action on every other cast if you feel the need to experiment. But always remember that a natural ant or beetle on the currents is a rather helpless bit of drift, and trout are not used to seeing them swimming with any vigor. Fish your wet flies, as always, so they look alive, but not like they possess superpowers, and you'll fool more than your share of trout.

Conclusion:
A Small Box of Wet Flies

This idea about imitating insects with subsurface patterns is infinitely old, yet relatively new. When fly fishing first got started, at least as recorded in the earliest fly-fishing literature, wet flies were all that were used, though it's speculated that some patterns were tied to float, at least for a short time, and therefore could be considered dry flies. But the materials of the times made it nearly impossible to tie a fly that would float for more than moments. Most of the earliest patterns listed in books such as Dame Juliana Berners's 1496 *A Treatyse of Fysshynge wyth an Angle* were based on foods that trout ate; the books were hatch guides of a sort. Most of the flies they listed were for adult forms of aquatic insects: mayflies, stoneflies, and caddisflies. The aquatic stages were either not noticed or never written about, and were not matched until Skues came along at the turn of the century.

Skues's work on subsurface flies was largely lost when fly fishing crossed the Atlantic to American shores. Brook trout were willing to dash at and take bright wet flies. That pushed wet-fly development away from imitative patterns. At about the same time that more selective brown trout began to replace brookies on our most popular North American trout streams, dry-fly fishing, and later nymph fishing, swept those bright wets aside. Except in the work of James Leisenring and Pete Hidy, wet flies on our waters were attractors, not imitative. Those fancy flies failed, for the most part, on the introduced browns, but were never refined into wet flies that looked like food forms, and that therefore took the more sophisticated trout.

The prescription to match natural trout foods with wet flies has rarely been followed in America. Add to that the vastness of our geography and the diversity of our insect hatches, and you can see that it will be a long time before there is a single battery of wet-fly patterns that works on all of our waters. Of course, that's not a smart goal for an individual to have anyway. To imitate everything, everywhere, even if you stick to wet flies—which I don't recommend that you do—you would have to carry enough fly boxes to require a caddy. What you want is a narrow selection of flies that average the hatches out, everywhere, and work for specific hatches on your own home waters.

Most of the fly patterns that I've mentioned in this book are designed to represent a wide range of insects rather than a single species. When you look at insects, and the fly patterns that match them, at that level, you're looking at dressings that fool fish over wide geographic areas.

I suggest that you set aside a small- to medium-sized fly box specifically for wet flies. Select a few patterns from those I've listed, tie them, carry them, and try them when conditions seem right. Don't force them on trout. If they don't work at first, you'll get the idea that they'll never work. When things are right for wets, they won't be right for much else. You'll do best with wet flies then.

Your small selection of wet flies might include just a few soft-hackles, flymphs, traditional winged wets, and all-fur wets. Select patterns that cover the narrow color spectrum of natural insects. Tie each selected pattern in just two or three sizes. Fill that single fly box with them, but leave expansion gaps, room for new patterns. That's all you need to get started. Since you need no special tackle beyond what you use for dry-fly fishing, with the exception of an intermediate line, we're talking about a small addition to what you already own and carry.

That's what I like most about wet-fly fishing: It lets you catch lots of trout you wouldn't otherwise, but it doesn't require that you buy or carry much more than your current burden.

Once you've built a basic selection of wet flies, start collecting and observing the insect hatches on your home waters. Be sure to notice the stages that trout take beneath the surface as well as on top. Be aware of when trout focus their feeding subsurface rather than on the surface itself. Then start working out wet flies of your own devising that match what you're seeing and what trout are eating.

This will lead you to fill those gaps in the box of wet flies that you've already tied, perhaps even to add another small fly box to your collection. The box that carries your basic wet-fly selection, perhaps plus the small box that contains wet flies you've devised to take trout on your own home waters, will add greatly to your catch, and immensely to your pleasure.

Here's a sample basic wet-fly box:

Soft-Hackles
#10-12 Partridge & Yellow
#12-16 Partridge & Green
#12-14 Grouse & Orange
#12-14 March Brown Spider
#16 Starling & Herl

Flymphs
#12-14 March Brown Flymph
#16-18 Little Olive Flymph
#14-16 Pale Watery Flymph
#14-16 Tups Nymph

Winged Wets
#12-14 Leadwing Coachman
#12-16 Hare's Ear
#12-14 Black Gnat
#12 Alder
#12-14 Light Cahill

All-Fur Wets
#16-18 Dark Mole & Herl
#12-16 Hare's Ear All-Fur Wet
#14-16 Olive All-Fur Wet
#12-14 Rust All-Fur Wet

Others
#8 Muddler Daddy
#6-10 Hare's Ear Anchor Wet

A main wet-fly box, containing most, though never all, of the dressings listed in the sample, plus a few experiments. The upper-left quadrant includes traditional winged wets, the upper central rows all-fur wets, and the last two rows Muddler Daddies and anchor wets. The lower left half of the box contains soft-hackles, the first four rows on the right flymphs, and the last row experiments that might someday find larger places in the box. This box, which I carry in my vest when wet flies are likely to be on the menu, or keep in my boat bag when I want it near but not necessarily on me, has a few expansion gaps, but should have far more. It's as much fun to discover new wets that suddenly catch trout as it is to catch trout on old dependable patterns. You'll want room in your wet-fly boxes for all those discoveries.

This is one side of a smaller and much more portable wet-fly box. I recommend you buy such a box, at a minimum, and tie a small selection of wet flies to fill it, always leaving those critical expansion gaps for favorites you discover on your own. This side of the box has soft-hackles on the left, flymphs on the right, and a few experiments in the center.

This is the flip side of the same small box that contains a minimal selection of wet flies. It's surprising how often even such a narrow supply will provide a solution when trout are interested in wet flies and not much else. This side of the box has traditional winged wets on the left, all-fur wets in the center, and Muddler Daddies and anchor wets on the right. The box fits easily in a small vest pocket, or a shirt pocket when I really want to go light.

Bibliography

Atherton, John. *The Fly and the Fish*. New York: The Macmillan Co., 1951.

de Bergara, Juan. *El Manuscrito de Astorga*. Copenhagen: Flyleaves, 1984 (reprint of 1624 manuscript).

Bergman, Ray. *Trout*. New York: Alfred A. Knopf, 1938.

Borger, Gary. *Nymphing: A Basic Book*. Harrisburg, PA: Stackpole Books, 1979.

Cutcliffe, H. C. *The Art of Trout Fishing on Rapid Streams*. South Molton, England: W. Tucker, 1863.

Fogg, Roger. *Wet-Fly Tying and Fishing*. Ramsbury: The Crowood Press, 2009.

Gordon, Sid W. *How to Fish from Top to Bottom*. Harrisburg, PA: The Stackpole Co., 1955.

Grey, Viscount. *Fly Fishing*. London: André Deutsch Ltd., 1899.

Hafele, Rick. *Nymph-Fishing Rivers & Streams*. Mechanicsburg, PA: Stackpole Books, 2006.

Hidy, Vernon S., and the editors of *Sports Illustrated*. *Book of Wet-Fly Fishing*. New York: J. B. Lippincott Co., 1961.

———. *Fly Fishing*. New York: J. B. Lippincott Co., 1960.

Kingsley, Canon Charles. *Prose Idylls* (including "Chalk-Stream Studies"). London: R. Clay, Sons, & Taylor, 1873.

Koch, Ed. *Fishing the Midge*. Harrisburg, PA: Stackpole Books, 1987.

LaFontaine, Gary. *Caddisflies*. New York: Nick Lyons Books, 1981.

Lawrie, W. H. *All Fur Flies and How to Dress Them*. South Brunswick: A. S. Barnes & Co., 1967.

———. *English Trout Flies*. South Brunswick: A. S. Barnes & Co., 1967.

Leisenring, James E., and Vernon S. Hidy. *The Art of Tying the Wet Fly & Fishing the Flymph*. New York: Crown Publishing Group, 1971.

McGee, Allen. *Tying & Fishing Soft-Hackled Nymphs*. Portland: Frank Amato Publications, 2007.

Nemes, Sylvester. *The Soft-Hackled Fly*. Old Greenwich, CT: Chatham Press, 1975.

———. *The Soft-Hackled Fly Addict*. Chicago: self-published, 1981.

———. *Soft-Hackled Fly Imitations*. Bozeman, MT: slef-published, 1991.

Norris, Thaddeus. *The American Angler's Book*. Philadelphia: E. H. Butler & Co., 1864.

Ovington, Ray. *How to Take Trout on Wet Flies and Nymphs*. Boston: Little, Brown, & Company, 1951.

Pritt, T. E. *North-Country Flies*. London: Sampson Low, Marston, Searle, & Rivington, 1886.

Ronalds, Alfred. *The Fly-Fisher's Entomology*. London: 1836.

Rosborough, E. H. "Polly." *Tying and Fishing the Fuzzy Nymphs*. Harrisburg, PA: Stackpole Books, 1978.

Sawyer, Frank. *Nymphs and the Trout*. London: Stanley Paul, 1958.

Schullery, Paul. *American Fly Fishing*. New York: Nick Lyons Books, 1987.

Schwiebert, Ernest. *Nymphs*. New York: Winchester Press, 1973.

———. *Trout*. New York: E. P. Dutton, 1978.

Scott, Jock. *Greased Line Fishing for Salmon*. London: Seeley, Service & Co. Ltd., 1935.

Shaw, Helen. *Flies for Fish & Fishermen*. Harrisburg, PA: Stackpole Books, 1989.

Skues, G. E. M. *Minor Tactics of the Chalk Stream*. London: Adam & Charles Black, 1910.

———. *Nymph Fishing for Chalk Stream Trout*. London: Adam & Charles Black, 1939.

———. *The Way of a Trout with a Fly*. London: Adam & Charles Black, 1921.

Solomon, Larry, and Eric Leiser. *The Caddis and the Angler*. Harrisburg, PA: Stackpole Books, 1977.

Stalcup, Shane. *Mayflies: Top to Bottom*. Portland: Frank Amato Publications, 2002.

Stetzer, Randall Scott. *Flies: The Best One Thousand*. Portland, OR: Frank Amato Publications, 1993.

Stewart, W. C. *The Practical Angler*. London: Adam and Charles Black, 1857.

Swisher, Doug, and Carl Richards. *Fly Fishing Strategy*. New York: Crown Publishing Group, 1975.

Theakston, Michael. *British Angling Flies*. London: Sampson Low, Marston, Searle, & Rivington, 1853.

Tod, E. M. *Wet-Fly Fishing*. London: Sampson Low, Marston, & Co., 1914.

Tullis, Larry. *Small Fly Techniques*. Birmingham, AL: Odysseus Editions, 1993.

Walton, Izaak, and Charles Cotton. *The Compleat Angler*. New York: Modern Library (first published 1653; Cotton addition first published 1676).

Younger, John. *On River Angling for Salmon & Trout*. New York: Arno Press, 1967 (reprint from 1840 London edition).

Index